Transformation by Integration

TRANSFORMATION BY INTEGRATION

How Inter-faith Encounter Changes Christianity

Perry Schmidt-Leukel

scm press

© Perry Schmidt-Leukel 2009

Published in 2009 by SCM Press
Editorial office
13–17 Long Lane,
London, EC1A 9PN, UK

SCM Press is an imprint of Hymns Ancient and Modern Ltd
(a registered charity)
St Mary's Works, St Mary's Plain,
Norwich, NR3 3BH, UK
www.scm-canterburypress.co.uk

British Library Cataloguing in Publication data

A catalogue record for this book is available
from the British Library

978 0 334 04317 1

Typeset by Regent Typesetting, London
Printed and bound by
CPI Antony Rowe, Chippenham, Wiltshire

CONTENTS

ACKNOWLEDGEMENTS

'The Struggle for Peace: Can Religions Help?' was first published in *Interreligious Insight. A journal of dialogue and engagement* vol. 5, no. 2 (2007). An earlier version of 'Tolerance and Appreciation' appeared in *Current Dialogue* (2006) no. 46. 'Multireligious Identity: Problems and Considerations' is a revised English version of a German text that appeared in R. Berhardt and P. Schmidt-Leukel (eds), *Multiple religiöse Identität*, Zürich: Theologischer Verlag Zürich, 2008. 'In Defence of Syncretism' is based on a hitherto unpublished paper that was read at an interfaith conference in Winchester in 2008. 'Comparative Theology: Limits and Prospects' first appeared in N. Hintersteiner (ed.): *Naming and Thinking God in Europe Today: Theology in Global Dialogue* (Currents of Encounter 32), Amsterdam/New York: Rodopi, 2007. 'Buddhism and Christianity: Antagonistic or Complementary?' was first published in *Studies in World Christianity* 9 (2003). 'Buddha and Christ as Mediators of the Transcendent' was presented during a Buddhist–Christian dialogue in Glasgow and published in P. Schmidt-Leukel (ed.), *Buddhism and Christianity in Dialogue*, The Gerald Weisfeld Lectures 2004, London: SCM Press, 2005. 'Uniqueness: A Pluralistic Reading of John 14:6' is based on my contribution to J. O'Grady and P. Scherle (eds), *Ecumenics from the Rim: Explorations in Honour of John D'Arcy May*, Berlin: LIT Verlag, 2007. 'Chalcedon Defended: A Pluralistic Re-Reading of the Two-Natures Doctrine' appeared first in *The Expository Times* vol. 118 (2006). 'Four Frogs: Studying Religion with a Religious Interest' is another unpublished paper. I'm grateful to all the publishers for their permission to include revised versions of these publications in this book.

I am indebted to a number of my students and colleagues at the University of Glasgow with whom I discussed several earlier versions of the chapters. Through their own views and partly their own research, they have been a crucial source of inspiration. In particular I am grateful to Sr Isabel Smyth, Rose Drew and David Kahan for reading and amending various chapters in that book.

INTRODUCTION

In the early heyday of modern inter-faith dialogue one could often find the affirmation that the purpose of dialogue is not only learning *about* the religious other, that is getting a better and deeper understanding, but also learning *from* and *through* other religious traditions. Leonard Swidler, for example, established as the first of his famous ten 'ground rules for interreligious dialogue':

> The primary purpose of dialogue is to learn – that is, to change and grow in the perception and understanding of reality, and then to act accordingly.[1]

And Paul Knitter, in his modern classic *No Other Name?*, demanded that in inter-religious dialogue

> all partners must be genuinely open to the possibility of accepting insights into the divine truth that they previously either never realized or had rejected. So they must be ready to reform, change, perhaps even abandon, certain beliefs in their own religion.[2]

As these quotations make quite explicit, the idea of learning from others through inter-religious dialogue implied the expectation

---

1 Swidler (1987), p. 14.
2 Knitter (1985), p. 211.

of a significant transformation, of change, growth, or reform. John Cobb, another pioneer among the Christian proponents of inter-faith dialogue, once stated:

> As a Christian I am challenged to learn as much as I can and to appropriate as richly as I can from these other traditions, allowing myself thereby to be transformed.[3]

What Cobb here says about himself as an individual Christian was also meant to apply to Christianity or other religions as larger collectives. However, Cobb saw clearly that this expectation would not easily encompass a religious tradition in all its forms and branches. As the envisaged transformation process would result from dialogical learning, it would not affect those members of a religious tradition opting not to engage in inter-faith dialogue. Or it may affect those who reject dialogue by leading 'to fundamentalist self-isolation in all the traditions'.[4]

Over the last two decades the latter tendency has apparently won considerable impact also on the theological reflection of inter-faith relations in general and Christianity's relation to other religions in particular. There is a trend in academic writing to emphasize a supposedly radical difference between religious traditions, or even an incommensurability,[5] so that any idea of receiving or appropriating something from a different tradition into one's own would seem to be impossible, and any openness to transformation as an act of infidelity or, in a sense, apostasy.[6] Writers like John Milbank proclaimed the 'end of dialogue'[7] and suggested that the only theologically acceptable form of 'conversation' with the religious other would be the one that is 'continuing the work of conversion'.[8]

Particularly after the attacks of September 11 in 2001 two

---

3 Cobb (1999), p. 46. The quotation is from an essay that was first published in 1984.

4 Cobb (1999), p. 67.

5 E.g. Lindbeck (1984), pp. 40, 48f.

6 Cf. Hedges (2008).

7 Thus the title of Milbank (1990).

8 Ibid., p. 190.

divergent trends can be noted: one sees 9/11 and subsequent events as highlighting the need for inter-faith dialogue and thus calls for even more effort and energy to be marshalled. The antipodal position finds in it another prima facie warrant that any expectation of a deeper-going dialogue is futile, illusory or dangerously naive. Rather than seeking inter-religious commonalities and regarding inter-religious differences as an opportunity for mutual learning and transformation, commonalities are dismissed as ostensible and differences highlighted as a chance to sharpen one's own religious profile against the religious other. The latter position came out quite clearly in a document of the Protestant Churches of Germany from 2006,[9] which was heavily criticized by a number of German Protestant theologians who not only felt that it ignored the positive results of Christian–Muslim dialogue but also feared that it might undermine mutual trust as the basis for further fruitful dialogue.[10]

Despite these opposing developments, inter-faith dialogue nevertheless continues and, with it, the kind of transformation that had been anticipated and hoped for. One of the clearest signs of the latter is perhaps the growing number of those declaring allegiance to two or even more religions, among whom are several well-known and highly reflective theologians who have been committed to inter-faith dialogue for many years.[11] Additionally, on the level of popular religiosity it can be observed that religious identities develop increasingly under the influence of several religious traditions resulting in new forms of hybrid religiosity. Although this cannot be interpreted as the outcome of a reflective, informed and methodologically controlled dialogue, it is nevertheless a result of inter-faith encounter and a product of inter-religious exchange. Looking afresh at the process of

---

9 *Klarheit und gute Nachbarschaft*. Christen und Muslime in Deutschland. Eine Handreichung des Rates der EKD. EKD-Texte 86, 2006; available at http://www.ekd.de/download/ekd_texte_86.pdf. The opposite trend can be found in an official document by the Swiss Protestant churches: *Wahrheit und Offenheit. Der christliche Glaube und die Religionen*. SEK Position 8, 2007; available at http://www.sek-feps.ch/shop/media/position/8/position8_de_web.pdf.

10 Cf. Micksch (ed.) (2007).

11 Cf. Chapter 3 of this book.

religious transformation through integration of beliefs and practices from other religions is a challenging task facing theology.

My own work in the field followed closely what Alan Race
so aptly called the 'twin tracks of theology and dialogue'.[12] Initially I investigated Christian interpretations of Buddhism. In
which ways did Buddhist–Christian dialogue change the various Christian clichés of Buddhism that had developed during
the nineteenth and early twentieth centuries?[13] The question of
how a Christian understanding of Buddhism could do justice to
Buddhist particularity on the one hand and nevertheless relate it
fruitfully to a Christian self-understanding on the other hand –
functioning as a maxim of inter-faith hermeneutics – led me into
the wider and more foundational debate about the most appropriate approach in the theology of religions. It appeared rather
obvious to me that neither an exclusivistic approach with its in-
ability to recognize any salvific value – truth, goodness, holiness
– in other religions, nor an inclusivistic model with its tendency
to measure the value of other religions by their conformity with
one's own, thereby interpreting the otherness of the other religion as a sign of its inferiority, was able to fulfil the hermeneutic
maxim that I had arrived at. Only a pluralistic approach, with
its attempt to combine the acknowledgment of differences with
the idea of religiously equal validity, appeared to me as moving
into the right direction.[14] I joined the 'twin tracks' of dialogue
and theology in my book *God Beyond Boundaries* ('Gott ohne
Grenzen')[15] where I argued for a pluralistic approach that can
legitimately claim to be a form of Christian theology and showed
how this approach has the potential to lead beyond the various
impasses in Christianity's dialogue with Judaism, Islam, Hinduism and Buddhism as they result from mutual exclusivistic or
inclusivistic superiority claims.

But this, in a sense, only prepared the ground for a new question: How is the issue of religious transformation as a result of

---

12 So the subtitle of Race (2001).
13 Cf. Schmidt-Leukel (1992).
14 Cf. Schmidt-Leukel (1997) and (2008b).
15 Cf. Schmidt-Leukel (2005). An English translation is in preparation.

inter-religious integration to be addressed from the perspective of a pluralistic theology of religions? From an exclusivistic perspective this question does not really arise and for an inclusivistic approach any possible transformations will remain of a secondary nature leaving the core beliefs, on which the inclusivist superiority claim is based, untouched. But what about the pluralist? Is a defender of a pluralist theology of religions – one who holds that despite being different other religions can nevertheless be equally valid paths of salvation – obliged to follow all of these paths simultaneously? Such a course of action would be impossible; yet, neither is it required. One can, for example, hold the view that life in a Christian marriage and life as a celibate monk or nun, are both different but equally valid forms of living a good Christian life, without being able or obliged to practise both of them at the same time. Equally so, a religious pluralist can accept the equal salvific validity of different religious paths without being obliged to follow all of them. And yet, this is not the end of the story. The question is what has led the pluralist to the acceptance of a different lifestyle, a different commitment, a different religious persuasion as equally valid? If this acceptance is not merely unreflective opinion, it needs to rest on some genuine appreciation of the other. This appreciation will impact on my life in what will influence and shape me, and in some way it will thus be integrated into my life. It is this process of integration resulting from and reflective of genuine appreciation that leads to religious transformation.

The chapters in this book are based on a selection of various papers, most of which were written on various occasions during the last five years. They mirror how the theme of religious transformation by integration has begun increasingly to occupy my own theological reflection. In a sense, they mark the beginning of a new step. Not a step that would leave a pluralistic theology of religions behind, but one that proceeds theologically on the basis of a pluralistic position. The direction in which this theology moves is that of an 'inter-faith theology' or 'world theology', 'global theology', 'universal theology' – as it has been variously called. As such this theology doesn't cease to be Christian. But it is 'Christian' in a transformed way and the transformation comes through the intake of elements/insights from non-Christian traditions. So it is still Christian, but also more than just Christian; it is 'Christian, plus' – as Wilfred Cantwell Smith has termed it,[16] a theology on its way to find forms in which people from other religions could recognize their own input.

The structure of the book invites the reader to follow me (at least 'for the sake of the argument') on a theological journey, which hopefully will make some of the just outlined perspectives more plausible and more concrete. Chapter 1 starts with what is currently in the forefront of public awareness: religions as a factor of conflict. I hold that a genuinely religious potential of inter-religious conflict does indeed exist and is rooted in the religious superiority claims that inevitably cause religions to perceive each other as threats against which they need to defend themselves. Religions can make a positive contribution towards peace if they acknowledge the existence of such a religious potential for conflict and try to tackle it. This can be done in various ways but central are toleration and appreciation. 'Toleration' is understood as the decision to accept and protect the existence of the religious other despite the fact that the beliefs and practices of other religions are not appreciated. 'Appreciation', in contrast, can emerge from the effort to question the negative assessment of other religions and finally results in the abandonment of any supercessionist intentions. 'Toleration', in a sense, means to control the religious potential of conflict, while 'appreciation' would remove the very source of this potential. Toleration, however, can (and needs to) be demanded, appreciation cannot. It can only result from an honest engagement with other religions, an improved understanding and a theological discovery of the truth, the good and the holy that they contain.

This important difference between tolerance and appreciation, as well as the need for both, is further developed in Chapter 2. Inter-religious friendship is highlighted as one way that may lead towards mutual appreciation. And the theme of friendship eluci-

---

16 Smith (1989), p. 125.

dates a further important distinction: the difference between the identity of a religious tradition as such and the unique identity of an individual who lives under the influence of this tradition but should not be mistaken as a religious stereotype, as a representation of the collective identity of the tradition.

This distinction lies at the heart of my dealing with the question of multireligious identity in Chapter 3. The religious identity of individuals is seen as a unique expression of their own personal life-journey which for an increasing number of people nowadays has become entwined with several religious traditions. In this respect the aspect of appreciation plays a significant role. For if an individual identifies something true, something good, something holy in a religious tradition with which he or she comes in contact, the person has no choice. That which is genuinely appreciated cannot be rejected; it needs to be integrated. Not only the fact that there is truth, goodness and holiness in other religions needs to be integrated into one's own faith, but also that which is identified as true, good and holy – particularly if it appears in a way in which it has not or not yet been realized within one's own tradition. Integration, therefore, raises the issue of syncretism on the individual as well as the collective level.

The negative view of syncretism has served as the major theological barrier against the appropriation and integration of insights and practices from other religions into Christianity; although, as a matter of historical fact, Christianity as much as other religious traditions has always been syncretistic. Chapter 4 reviews the major objections against syncretism and offers a differentiated defence against them. Some of the objections against syncretism depend on an exclusivistic theology of religions; they collapse if exclusivism is shown to be untenable. Others are based on issues of compatibility and identity. These demand a detailed examination, for it is by no means a priori clear that elements from different religious traditions are always incompatible or that their combination would always indicate a loss of identity rather than its further development.

'Comparative theology' would be a suitable theological method of carrying out such examinations. But some among its proponents present comparative theology as an alternative to the theology of religions rather than a welcome complement to it. Chapter 5 critically discusses this claim. It arrives at the conclusion that behind the alleged alternative of comparative theology or theology of religions lies a different issue, namely whether theologians engaged in comparative theology are admitting theological conclusions which would require a change of Christian understanding and teachings and hence a change of the respective option in the theology of religions.

The theoretical questions from Part I of the book are taken up in a more concrete perspective in Part II. Here the focus is on the relationship of Buddhism and Christianity and more specifically on changes in our understanding of incarnation. Chapter 6 illustrates how the differences between Buddhism and Christianity can be understood as complementary instead of incommensurable, incompatible or even antagonistic.

Whether this complementarity, however, is ultimately seen as an 'asymmetrical complementarity' in which Christianity is still superior, as Jacques Dupuis suggested, depends on how the Buddha and the Christ are understood in relation to one another. This is the topic of Chapter 7. It not only compares the Buddhist understanding of the Buddha as the incarnation of the *dharmakāya* with the Christian understanding of Christ as the incarnation of the *logos*, but as an inevitable part of comparative theology it raises the question of how Christian theology might respond to Buddhist incarnation claims. It suggests a concept of incarnation which allows us to see both Gautama Buddha and Jesus Christ as human mediators of transcendent reality.

But how does such an understanding of incarnation appertain to the traditional affirmation of Jesus' uniqueness and the Chalcedonian two-natures Christology? In addressing these questions in Chapters 8 and 9, continuity and transformation on the doctrinal level become explicit. The reader may be surprised to learn that, on my view, acceptance of some form of the two-natures doctrine is inevitable but does not contradict the idea of more than one incarnation.

The book concludes with an epilogue that once more refers

back to the transformation of Christianity by the integration of a Buddhist element, in this case Buddhist meditation practice and the corresponding spirituality. The issue of religious transformation, however, is looked at within a broader horizon: On the one hand, transformation is illustrated as the development of religious ideals, or better as the development of religious views on what the ultimate object of human existential quest is. On the other hand, it is held that an adequate study of religion needs to take this existential quest into account. That is, the study of religion should include a theological element in the broad sense of explicating and discussing religious views of human existence as concrete and serious challenges for each one of us. It is in this spirit that the subsequent chapters are written.

Part One

BETWEEN CONFRONTATION
AND INTERPENETRATION

1

THE STRUGGLE FOR PEACE

Can Religions Help?

Religions and Violence: The Indictment and a Common Defence

'So potent was religion in persuading to evil deeds.'[1] This is not a quotation from Richard Dawkins' TV documentary *Root of All Evil?*, but a statement made by Lucretius, a Roman writer and philosopher, in the first century BCE. Lucretius, however, based his judgement just on various narratives of Greek mythology. When in modern times history became a subject of serious academic study, the Scottish philosopher David Hume (1711–76) arrived at an even harsher conclusion: 'If the religious spirit be ever mentioned in any historical narration, we are sure to meet afterwards with a detail of the miseries which attend it', as, for example, 'factions, civil wars, persecutions, subversions of government, oppression, slavery'.[2] '(W)here the interests of religion are concerned,' says Hume, 'no morality can be forcible enough to bind the religious zealot. The sacredness of the cause sanctifies every measure which can be made use of to promote it.'[3] Thus Hume concludes that 'no period of time can be happier or more prosperous than those in which it [the religious spirit; PSL] is never regarded or heard of'.[4]

---

1 'Tantum religio portuit suadere malorum', *De Rerum Natura* I, 101.
2 Hume (1983), p. 82.
3 Ibid., p. 84.
4 Ibid., p. 82.

From such a perspective, the greatest contribution that religions could make to the struggle for peace would be their own complete disappearance – an idea that we also find in John Lennon's famous song 'Imagine'. Here Lennon dreams of a future where 'all the people' are 'living life in peace' because there is 'nothing to kill or die for and no religion too'. Many, I suppose, have cheerfully joined in humming the tune and singing the words.

Almost as common as this indictment of religion is the standard defence advanced by religious people: whenever religions are involved in violent action and violent conflicts, this is explained as or declared to be a 'misuse of religion'. A Google search for the phrase 'misuse of religion' gives more than 32,000 pages![5] This 'misuse of religion' in violent conflicts has frequently been decried by political and religious leaders alike: by Buddhists, Hindus, Muslims, Jews, the World Council of Churches or the Vatican. At an inter-religious gathering in Assisi (4–5 September 2006) the assembled religious leaders issued a statement which says: 'Religions never justify hatred and violence. Those using the name of God to destroy others move away from true religion.'[6] It may be true that religions do not 'justify hatred', but it is historically, simply and bluntly, false to claim that they never justify violence.

I have no doubts that those who speak of a 'misuse of religion' are usually well-meaning people and I share their ecumenical and peace-loving intentions. Nevertheless, I find the explanation that the involvement of religion in violent conflicts is always a form of misuse – running against the true nature of religion – unconvincing, naive and dangerously misleading. This explanation suggests that there can be no genuine religious motivation for the use of violence and that, therefore, all those who have justified the use of violence in the name of whatever religion were motivated by other than truly religious intentions. Hence the presumption that they 'misused' religion for their non-religious interests in these conflicts.

---

5 This was at the time when the first draft of this chapter was written (autumn 2006).

6 http://www.catholicnews.com/data/stories/cns/0605044.htm

I am not denying that there are cases where religions are indeed misused to instigate violence. But I do deny that this is always so. When we look at the people who have justified and even encouraged the use of violence for religious reasons, we will find the most respected and authoritative figures of the world's religious traditions among them – in Christianity, for example, theologians like Augustine, Aquinas, Luther and Calvin. Various names from the Jewish, Muslim, Hindu and Buddhist tradition could be added to this list.[7] Should we really assume that they were all 'misusing' religion for some non-religious and presumably rather sinister interests? Should we really judge with the just quoted Assisi declaration that they were all moving away from true religion? When, for example, Dietrich Bonhoeffer made the decision to support the preparations for the assault on Hitler, or when Paul Tillich, through his radio talks for the 'Voice of America', actively supported the war against Nazi Germany, should we really judge that their endorsement of violent action against the Nazis was not properly motivated by their Christian faith? Karl Barth, for example, saw the war against Nazi Germany not only as 'inevitable', but as a 'just war, not merely admitted but positively commanded by God'.[8] It might be replied that one should confine the idea of 'misuse' to cases of inter-religious conflicts and not to a situation like fighting against such a dangerous and evil ideology as Nazism. But as I will try to show, the problem is that, in the eyes of those who justified violent means against other religious groups, these religious groups and their beliefs were often regarded as being as dangerous and threatening as Nazism, or even more so. They were perceived as a threat to the eternal salvation and well-being of the people, as a threat to whatever is good and true and holy.

Moreover, if religions were indeed as peaceful as the 'misuse'-thesis presupposes, it would become rather incomprehensible how in the world they could ever be misused. I think religions can be misused to instigate conflicts precisely because religions harbour a genuine potential for conflict. If someone wants to

---

7 Cf. the respective contributions to Schmidt-Leukel (ed.) (2004).
8 Cf. Barth (1945), pp. 181ff.

burn down a house, he or she will use petrol, not water. There is something within religions that makes them open to misuse. If we want to address honestly and seriously the connection between violence and religion, we need to identify what the genuine religious roots of violent conflicts are and not deny that such roots exist. This is the reason why I find the 'misuse'-theory dangerously misleading. It is a hasty explanation which holds us back from an uncomfortable enquiry into the religious motives behind violent religious conflicts. But it is only by identifying these motives that we can explore ways in which they might be overcome or, at least, how they can be efficiently controlled.

Religious Roots of Religious Violence

When we look into the writings of those who take religion to be the root of so many evils, we find that the critics of religion are not entirely unanimous in their explanation of why the religious mind should bring about these evils. Richard Dawkins, for example, sees religion simply as a form of 'collective delusion', as 'irrational superstition'. It makes people ready to fight for God or for whatever religious ideal just because it is *irrational*.[9] But this explanation is far too simplistic. First of all, it can and must be disputed whether religion is indeed as irrational as Dawkins claims. There are certainly religious people who behave irrationally, but there are non-religious people who do so as well. And I would strongly dispute that religions are essentially at variance with reason. But even if religion were essentially irrational, as Dawkins claims, would this be a sufficient and comprehensive explanation of the connection between religion and violence? This would entail that non-religious people, or at least rational non-religious people, could never endorse the use of violence. But is this true? One might respond that the right question is whether the reasons which are produced to justify the use of violence are rational reasons or not, and that religious reasons

---

9 This is basically the argument in *Root of All Evil?* See also Dawkins (2007), pp. 341–8.

justifying violence are by definition always non-rational reasons which therefore can never provide an acceptable justification for violence. But this would be a circular argument, that is: a religious justification of violence is not acceptable because it is irrational; and it is irrational because it is religious. Circular arguments, however, are – as every rational person would admit – not very persuasive.

In David Hume's *Dialogues Concerning Natural Religion* we find the idea that religion, at least in its usual, popular form, is essentially at variance with morality. According to Hume, the primary goal of the religious people is to ensure divine favour for themselves. Hence religion basically fosters self-centredness:

> The steady attention alone to so important an interest as that of eternal salvation is apt to extinguish the benevolent affections, and beget a narrow, contracted selfishness. And when such a temper is encouraged, it easily eludes all the general precepts of charity and benevolence.[10]

David Hume has a point when he says that there is – or can be – a conflict between self-interest and the precepts of morality. But this is not a specific conflict between a religious self-interest and morality. It is rather one between self-interest as such and the moral demands which sometimes go against our selfish desires. Self-interest can certainly assume a religious form in the way that Hume describes, but in fact the various religions often show an awareness of this problem and therefore suggest, somewhat paradoxically, that the highest fulfilment of self-interest is bound to moral acts of self-denial. It was Immanuel Kant (1724–1804) who succinctly argued that if we could ever hope for some sort of ultimate resolution of the conflict between practical self-interest and the moral demand to act in a non-selfish way, such a hope could only be based on a religious assumption – that is, on the assumption that, in the end, moral selflessness will meet with a lasting satisfaction of our deepest and, in a sense, 'selfish' longing for

---

10 Hume (1983), p. 84.

happiness. This, however, could only be guaranteed by some sort of good divine reality. So Hume's argument was turned by Kant into an argument in favour of religion rather than against it.

It was another critic of religion, Ludwig Feuerbach (1804–72), who gave Hume's thought a more powerful twist. 'In faith there lies a pernicious principle' says Feuerbach.[11] For two reasons: First, religious faith is pernicious because it inevitably creates a judgemental chasm between believers and non-believers. If faith is seen as the right attitude towards life, towards God or to-wards whatever religion sees as ultimate, then – by implication – not having faith must be wrong, or bad, or missing the true purpose of life. Therefore faith, says Feuerbach, is only good to the believer, but inevitably pernicious towards the non-believer. According to Feuerbach, this judgemental chasm between the good status of being a believer and the bad status of being a non-believer need not necessarily lead to the open use of violence against the purported non-believer, but it creates the hostile at-titude towards the other from which violent actions against the other can easily emerge.[12] The reason behind this hostile attitude against the non-believer is the conviction that the case of faith is always the case of God. A believer, according to Feuerbach, can never accept a non-believer as being good or right, because all goodness and rightness pertains to God alone. Whoever is not on God's side must be necessarily against God, and thus against all the good that God stands for.[13]

This argument leads to the second and deeper reason why Feuerbach views faith as pernicious. It is the subordination of humans – and of every human value – to God. If the authority, power, or rank of God is seen as something superior to everything else then, in the end, human beings can and will be sacrificed to God. If morality is subordinate to God and hence understood as being based on divine decree then every divine command-ment will have to count – by definition – as morally right, even if God commands the most appalling misdeeds. This can only be

---

11 Feuerbach (1988), p. 376.
12 Ibid., p. 377.
13 Ibid., p. 380.

avoided, says Feuerbach, if not God but the human being is seen as the highest good, if – as Feuerbach says – only the human is the human's God (*homo homini Deus est*).[14]

Feuerbach wrote in the nineteenth century. But the twentieth century has taught us in numerous horrible ways that explicitly non-religious ideologies whose sole 'God' were humans – the liberation, emancipation or evolutionary cultivation of humans – are not less powerful in sacrificing human beings to their ideals than the religions but perhaps even more potent or scrupulous in that regard. What Feuerbach says is in a sense analytically true: Humans will always be prepared to sacrifice other human lives, or their own ones, for something that they regard as higher, as more important, as being worth the price. But this 'something' need not necessarily be of a religious nature. It can be God, but it can also easily be the ideal of a just and classless society, or Nietzsche's ideal of the *Übermensch*, or simply something like one's own people or country. Whenever you agree with Aristotle's principle that the whole is more than the sum of its parts ('more' in some qualitative or ontological sense) it might be seen as justified, under certain circumstances, to sacrifice some of the 'parts' for the sake of the 'whole'. The mechanism that Feuerbach analysed is not a specifically religious phenomenon. He only described the religious version of a far more general principle. For example, most people would agree that the common good of public order and safety justifies the use of violence in order to protect it – hence we need an armed police. Or that the safety of a country justifies the existence of an armed army, or that the inhumane rule of a barbarian tyrant justifies the use of violence in an attempt to remove him. But if we agree that violence, the use of physical force, is not always and generally wrong, if we agree that there are or may be certain reasons which do in fact justify the use of violence, then we need to get clearer on what the specific problem with religious violence is, that is, with religious justifications or motivations for the use of force.

Over recent years an impressive number of books have been

14 Ibid., p. 401.

published dealing with the phenomenon of religious terrorism. One of the more commendable works among these is Mark Juergensmeyer's *Terror in the Mind of God*. On the basis of detailed case studies, Juergensmeyer shows that religious militants are not setting religious motivations over against moral reasons. The point is rather that 'one of their motivations might be a spiritual conviction so strong that they are willing to kill and to be killed for moral reasons'.[15] One could almost establish as a kind of principle that genuine religious forms of violence are motivated by what those who perform or justify violence regard as *moral reasons*. At least subjectively, genuine religious violence is not committed against moral principles, but in accordance with them. As Juergensmeyer states, a characteristic feature of religious terrorism is 'the transcendent moralism with which such acts are justified'.[16] And he rightly observes that this moralism is usually drawn from traditional doctrinal or theological justifications of religious violence – justifications that 'have appeared in virtually every religious tradition'.[17] I would like to illustrate this by two brief examples:

One of the most influential Christian theologians is Thomas Aquinas (1225–74). In his *Summa Theologiae* Aquinas discusses at length the appropriate treatment of heretics (STh II/II 11:3–4). Facing the question of whether heretics should be killed, Aquinas' central argument in favour of killing them is based on the biblical commandment to love one's neighbour. Love, says Aquinas, entails that we do everything for the well-being of our neighbour. But eternal well-being is far more important than any earthly goods. Hence our primary concern must be the eternal well-being and final salvation of human beings. This obliges us to protect our neighbour against the evil influence of heresy, for heresy is a major threat to the true doctrine and thus to its salvific potential. Due to the negative influence of heresy, people might lose the true saving faith and thereby lose their eternal life. If we were not obliged to care for our neighbours and their eternal

---

15 Juergensmeyer (2003), p. xiv.
16 Ibid., p. 10.
17 Ibid., p. 221.

well-being, then we could simply tolerate the heretics and let them continue spreading their false ideas. But the commandment to love our neighbour forces us to put an end to the dangerous activities of heretics, if necessary even by the use of violence. Aquinas quotes the Church father Jerome (Hieronymus):

> Cut off the decayed flesh, expel the mangy sheep from the fold, lest the whole house, the whole paste, the whole body, the whole flock burn, perish, rot, die. (*Summa theologiae* II/II 11, 3)

It should be noted that this argument is in and of itself consistent and moral. If someone were about to poison the water supplies of a modern large city by deadly bacteria, which would cause the death of hundreds of thousands of people, would we not feel the moral obligation to prevent that person from doing so, if necessary even by killing him? This, however, is exactly how the medieval Church felt. Throughout the Middle Ages and until modernity, heresy was compared to a dangerous virus, a pestilence threatening not the earthly life but the far more important eternal life of the people.[18]

My second illustration also refers to the killing of heretics. This time the issue is addressed in two closely related Mahāyāna Buddhist texts: the *Aṅgulimālīya Sūtra* and the *Mahāparinirvāṇa Sūtra*.[19] Both texts deal primarily with the so-called *tathāgatagarbha* teaching, the doctrine that all sentient beings share the Buddha-Nature. According to the two texts, this doctrine has the ethical implication that one should approach and treat all sentient beings like one's close and beloved relatives or even like one's own self. Taking the life of others is therefore ultimately 'like killing oneself, for it destroys one's dhātu', that is, one's inner unity with the others in the same Buddha-Nature.[20] But

---

18 Cf. Moore (1983).

19 What follows is based on the careful analysis and part translations of the respective text passages in Schmithausen (2003), here pp. 22–34.

20 *Aṅgulimālīya Sūtra.* Stephen Hodge has translated some sections of the *Aṅgulimālīya Sūtra* (see: http://www.webspawner.com/users/tathagatagarbha16/index.html). My translations are either taken from Hodge or from the German translations in Schmithausen (2003).

if this is so, why then has the Buddha taught the 'severing and killing' of the heretics? This is the problem addressed in several places in these two texts. The basic answer is that the harsh treatment of those who slander the true Dharma, the Buddhist teaching, must evolve from a good, compassionate and loving mind. This entails at least three aspects: First, the goal must be the 'protection of the Dharma', the implication being that protecting the Dharma is in the best interests of all. It can be compared to the eradication of weeds in order to protect the good seeds, or to a painful medical treatment, or to the behaviour of good parents. If their young child has picked up something dangerous and has put it into his mouth, the parents will use some force to take the dangerous object out.[21] In a similar way a Bodhisattva extracts or removes whatever is harmful. Second, even the killing of the heretics does not necessarily violate the principle to treat them like one's own self, for there can be cases in which it is also justified to commit suicide for good spiritual reasons. For example, if someone has very strong and evil inclinations which cannot be controlled otherwise, it may be justified and even spiritually meritorious if such a person takes his own life. Killing the heretics who threaten the true Dharma is therefore similar to an act of spiritually wholesome suicide. Hence it does not do any harm to the unity in the common Buddha-Nature; on the contrary, it honours our true nature.[22] Third, such a killing is or can be advantageous for the victim. In the *Mahāparinirvāṇa Sūtra* (chapter 22) the Buddha explains how he himself in a previous life had killed a Brahmin who was a slanderer of the Mahāyāna Sūtras. 'Out of love, I took his life. It was not done with an evil mind.'[23] For after his death the Brahmin was reborn in the worst hell where he realized that the true cause for this horrible rebirth was his slandering of the Dharma. From this insight he developed respect towards the Mahāyāna, so that later on he was

---

21 This parable goes back to *Majjhimanikāya* 58 where it justifies that the Buddha, at times, teaches truths which are unwelcome but nevertheless beneficial.

22 See Schmithausen (2003), p. 31, fn. 35.

23 Translation from Kosho Yamamoto, Tony Page, published on the web: http://www.nirvanasutra.org.uk/nirvanasutrap.htm.

reborn into the realm of another Buddha where he lived a very long and presumably spiritually far better life.[24]

These examples from the Christian and the Buddhist tradition can provide us with two important insights for our topic:

First, in both cases a *hierarchy of values* is presupposed. But the hierarchy is not one of ranking religion above morality, as so many critics of religion have alleged. It ranks the value of ultimate salvation over the value of an individual biological life.[25] Within that hierarchy the use of violence is then justified on *moral grounds*. The assumption that such a hierarchy is valid is of a religious nature. However, the hierarchy of values does not rank salvation above biological, or more specifically human, life in general.[26] Life is always the subject or object of salvation, and hence its indispensable basis. It is precisely because of this fundamental pro-life attitude that religions felt and feel the need to produce special justifications for those limited and exceptional cases in which the use of violence is legitimate.

The second important point is that the use of violence is connected to a *perceived threat* coming from people with different religious beliefs, in our two cases the Christian heretics or the Buddhist heretics (the 'slanderers' of the true Dharma), so that the employed violence is seen as *defensive* or *protective*, and not as aggressive. It is employed in order to defend and protect the saving truth and thus the ultimate well-being of the people against the perceived threat coming from the religious other.

I suppose that one can find similar texts in other religious traditions which would exhibit an analogous structure. However, rather than doing this, I would like to jump from here to a fairly general conclusion.

The major religious root of religious conflicts, I suspect, is the combination of two convictions: on the one hand, the conviction that we *know* – through revelation or otherwise – the highest

24 For the role that such arguments have actually played within violent inner-Buddhist conflicts cf. Kleine (2006).

25 See also Schmithausen (2003), p. 31.

26 This was the basic point of criticism levelled by Friedrich Nietzsche against Christianity.

truth, the truth that is on top of our hierarchy of values (because it is essential to right human living, to ultimate well-being, salvation or liberation). And on the other hand, the conviction that we know this truth either *exclusively*, so that all other religions are basically wrong, or that we know it at least in a *uniquely superior* way, so that all other religions are inferior and their members 'objectively . . . in a gravely deficient situation in comparison with those who, in' one's own religion, 'have the fullness of the means of salvation'.[27] If these two convictions are held together, then – quite naturally and with genuine religious integrity – one would ideally wish that all human beings should become partakers of the highest and most important truth as it is manifested in one's own religion. But this, of course, implies that ideally all other religions should disappear for the sake of one's own. This is the reason why religions perceive each other as a mutual threat. Here, I suggest, we have arrived at the religious root of the potential for inter-religious conflict. It lies in the explicit or implicit intention to supersede all other religions and in the resulting readiness to defend one's own religion against analogous ambitions on the part of the others. And as we saw from the previous examples, potential acts of violence could then easily qualify as basically defensive and as morally justified.

Can Religions Help?

If my analysis is correct, what contribution can religions then make to the struggle for peace? First of all, I think that in the global struggle for peace, religions – or better, religious people – should not expect or be expected to extinguish all 'fires', but they could and should make a contribution to the resolution or reduction of those conflicts for which religions themselves bear some responsibility. Acknowledging that such a responsibility does in fact exist (and not denying it by means of the 'misuse'-cliché) might very well be a first significant step. However, if

---

27 The wording is borrowed from the Roman Catholic document *Dominus Iesus* (2001) no. 22.

the religions' contribution to the struggle for peace can mean something other than their own dissolution, as the radical critics would hold, then it must relate to the religious roots of religiously motivated violence. The point, I think, is not the removal of the typical religious hierarchy of values which ranks ultimate salvation on top – for this would be equivalent to the atheist suggestion of removing religions completely; but what can and should be tackled are the claims to infallible knowledge and the perceived threat resulting from religious superiority claims.

For the remainder of this chapter I would like to flesh this out briefly under four headings: toleration, co-operation, appreciation and education.

Toleration

I understand the term 'toleration' in its classical meaning of 'endurance', that is, the endurance of what we cannot accept or appreciate. Hence, tolerance should not be confused with appreciation. Tolerance means to forbear or endure what we deem to be wrong. This is the only sense in which tolerance is really important. Living together in pluralistic societies and in a pluralistic world must be based primarily on toleration and not on appreciation. Appreciation is desirable, but toleration is indispensable.[28]

The justification of tolerance in this sense has very much to do with the claim to infallible knowledge, or more precisely, with the rejection of such a claim. Usually religious tolerance is justified on three grounds: First, tolerating the other is a minor evil compared to the disruption of social peace arising from the attempt to eliminate the other. Second, toleration results from the respect for the individual's personal freedom in matters of faith, even if the individual makes a choice which we deem to be wrong. But perhaps the most important reason for religious toleration is of an epistemological nature, that is, intolerant restrictions cannot be based on presuppositions which are – epistemologically

---

28 On this important distinction between tolerance and appreciation, see also the following chapter.

– uncertain. Religious faith is not indubitable knowledge. As humans we can never be sure that our knowledge is absolutely infallible. We might assume that if there is a God then God's knowledge will be infallible. And in a range of religions we find the argument that their knowledge is infallible, not because it is 'theirs' but because it comes from God. However, the problem is that we do not have infallible knowledge about the issue of whether that which is claimed to come from God is really divine. We may be entitled to believe this, but this is not the same as knowing this beyond any rational doubt. In matters of faith we may thus have enough light to risk our own lives, but not enough light to justify the destruction of our neighbours' lives. If we have clear and highly probable evidence that the religious or ideological views of some group create a serious threat for the well-being of the people in the here and now, this might be a good reason to limit toleration and use the appropriate forms of force to control or combat this threat. But the idea that the religious beliefs of others form a threat to the eternal or ultimate well-being is simply not certain enough to serve as a good justification for the use of force or violence against that sort of supposed 'threat'. Hence, such beliefs are to be tolerated.[29]

Co-operation

Once religions are committed to tolerating each other, they are free to explore whether they do have some common interests and common values which would enable them to co-operate in pursuit of common welfare. This is by and large the idea on which a multi-religious co-operation for peace is possible. The best example is probably the work of the 'World Conference of Religions for Peace' (WCRP). Issues of religious truth, doctrinal disagreement, claims to absoluteness, etc. are simply excluded from the agenda of the WCRP deliberately confining itself to the one goal of fostering world peace.[30]

29 I have elaborated on this more fully in Schmidt-Leukel (2000) and (2002).
30 Cf. Klaes (2004).

But while toleration and social co-operation certainly form a basis on which religions can positively contribute to the struggle for peace, they do not address the issue of the reciprocal threat which emerges from religious superiority claims. This unresolved problem may very well hang as a Damoclean sword over the attempts to develop endurable forms of inter-religious co-operation. Can one really build up mutual trust, if there is subconsciously the fear that all readiness and willingness to co-operate might in the end be a strategy within a hidden, but dominant missionary agenda? And that the inner logic of this agenda is to replace, to supersede all other religion, including one's own?

Appreciation

Religions should therefore move beyond the goal of social co-operation and explore how justified their own superiority claims really are. This means to critically review traditional prejudices against, and clichés of, the religious other. It means the effort to arrive at an understanding of the other's faith which is as far as possible an understanding from within the other's own perspective. Once we discover that the other's religion is far better, far more true and far more beautiful than we originally thought, we can overcome our supersessionist intentions and arrive at a genuine religious appreciation of the other – an appreciation which no longer wants to overcome the religion of the other, which no longer harbours the belief that all people should ideally become members of one's own religion, but which rejoices in the ideal of an ongoing process of cross-fertilization and mutual enrichment.

The serious theological efforts over the last fifty years to identify the religious roots of Christian anti-Judaism have clearly pointed out that these are all connected, in one way or another, to Christian supersessionism regarding the Jewish religion.[31] The idea that Christianity is the fulfilment of Judaism implies that the Church – as the 'New Israel' – replaces the synagogue, in

---

31 I think, in this respect, Rosemary Ruether's *Faith and Fratricide* (Ruether 1974) is still the unsurpassed theological work.

other words, the Jewish religion. Today many Christian theologians are ready to abandon this idea completely. But a similar supersessionism is also operative in the relation of Christianity to all other religions;[32] and it is also found, in various versions, in other religions and in their approaches to religious diversity.[33] To the extent that religions transform their supersessionist impulses into active forms of mutual appreciation, they make a tremendous contribution to the struggle for peace.[34]

Education

This transformation will take much time. Therefore, the religious education of the future generations is of crucial importance. It is important to teach our children respect for the religious other, so that they learn to tolerate. But this is not enough. Wherever possible, we need to teach them also about the truth, the good and the holy as reflected in other religions, so that they will learn to appreciate them. But again, this is not enough, for denigrating, negative images of the religious other are often deeply embedded in religious narratives and rituals. This is a very serious problem, and one that is extremely difficult to tackle; but it needs to be done. Let me give a very personal example. One day one of my two sons came home from primary school and told me how he had learned in school about Judaism and about Pesach. Oh, how good, I thought. Then he went on to tell me how the teacher had explained to them that Pesach was celebrated in remembrance of that night when God had liberated his people from the slavery in Egypt by killing all the first-born children of the Egyptians. I was shocked, for my son drew from this the conclusion (or had it been his teacher?) that God loved the Israelites but not the Egyptians, not even their little children. So I had to assure him –

---

32 For the need to draw from the abandonment of supersessionism towards Judaism the due consequences for Christianity's relationship to other religions, see Race (2001), pp. 43–64, and Schmidt-Leukel (2005), pp. 307–48.

33 Cf. Coward (2000); Gort, Jansen and Vroom (eds) (2006); Schmidt-Leukel and Ridgeon (eds) (2007); Schmidt-Leukel (ed.) (2008).

34 For the potential within the religious traditions to overcome their supersessionist inclinations, see Knitter (ed.) (2005).

against the obvious implication of this story and against what he had learned in school – that God loves all children, whether they are from Israel, from Egypt, from India (as my son is), from Germany (as his parents are) or from Scotland (as his friends are). I had to get this message to him against the contrary message in one of the central Jewish and Christian narratives. This is by no means a specific problem of Judaism and Christianity. May I suggest that all of us, from whatever religious background, start looking self-critically at our own religious tradition and discover those negative, denigrating images of the religious others which are built into its religious narratives, rituals, liturgical texts, etc. Is it not the case that, for example, the bad people in the nice Buddhist stories of the Jātakas, frequently used in Buddhist religious education, are usually Brahmins, that is Hindus? Even traditional Buddhist paintings are often replete with extremely denigrating caricatures of the Brahmins, the 'bad guys'. And is it not the case that this applies analogically to each of our religious traditions? Let us investigate them honestly and find ways to stop the further transmission of such deep-seated prejudices against the religious others. Then there is a chance that religions can help in extinguishing at least those fires for which they bear responsibility.

2

TOLERANCE AND APPRECIATION

Celebrating Diversity?

In the world of multicultural, multiethnic or multifaith work we often hear the slogan, 'celebrating diversity'. Although I really like the phrase, I think it is not free from a serious problem: It seems clear to me that diversity as such is not of any value. There can be no reason to celebrate diversity simply for the sake of diversity. The fact that there is a diversity of deadly diseases, for example, does not make fatal illnesses any better. Or the fact that humanity has invented a vast diversity of torturing methods rather than just one does not make this a pleasant and praiseworthy cultural achievement. However, the fact that there is not only one beautiful flower but a whole range of different ones makes natural beauty even more stunning. Or the fact that there is a vast variety of ways in which lovers can show their affection to one another is indeed wonderfully enriching.

So it appears to me that diversity is not good or valuable in itself. It rather seems to be a kind of accelerator or intensifier: a diversity of evils makes evil even more evil, and a diversity of goods makes good even better. The problem with religious diversity is that religions are usually not sure whether they should regard other religions as good or bad. And, consequently, whether they should look upon religious diversity as a diversity of evils or a diversity of goods, whether religious diversity is something to welcome or to overcome.

At times I suggest a kind of little self-test: Imagine for a moment that all the religious people in the world were to give up their present faith and become members of your own religious community or church. This would mean that all other religions or churches would disappear. Your own religion would be the only one left, the one and only existent religion in the world. How would you feel about such a situation? Would you feel that this is too good to be true? That this would indeed be the ideal state – the whole world being Christian, or Muslim, or Buddhist, etc.? Or would you feel the opposite – that this would be a tremendous, deplorable loss? If your feelings tend towards the first response, if you think a conversion of the whole world to your own form of religion would be great, then you do not really or deeply appreciate religious diversity. Religious diversity, therefore, will be something that you have to tolerate, something that you have to endure as a kind of evil. But if you feel that the disappearance of all religions other than your own would be a great loss, then there is something in you that does indeed appreciate religious diversity and sees in it a genuine value.

Perhaps, and presumably, your feelings are a bit more complicated than my little self-test would indicate. One possible complication, for example, is that even if one genuinely appreciates religious diversity, no one is likely to appreciate everything in the world of religions. Thus even if we feel there is a range of diverse religious phenomena which we assess to be good and valuable, there will also be a range of other phenomena which we do not and can not appreciate – things which we feel should perish or not exist at all.

This brings me to my basic point: Whenever there is something in the world of religions, either in our own religion or in the religious traditions and communities of our fellow human beings, that we do not like, something that we cannot regard as good or true or holy, then *toleration* is needed. But for those things which we *do* like, either in our own religion or in our neighbour's faith, we don't need tolerance but ways – theological and practical ways – of showing our *appreciation*. These two, tolerance and appreciation, should be clearly distinguished and not confused. Both are necessary, but they are very different. That is, we should not speak of 'tolerance' when we mean 'appreciation'; for then we would lose the whole point of what 'tolerance' is all about, namely to live with what we disapprove of. And we should not impute the meaning of 'appreciation' when we speak of 'tolerance'. There are cases in which it makes very good sense to ask for tolerance and even speak of a certain obligation to be tolerant. But this should not and must not imply any need or obligation to 'appreciate'. For the rest of this chapter I will try to elucidate the two concepts a bit further.[1] That is, I will first speak in more detail about tolerance and the reasons why tolerance is a necessary and indispensable virtue. Subsequently I will look more closely at the implications of inter-religious appreciation.

Why Tolerance is Necessary

The original meaning of the word 'tolerance' is 'endurance'. The point is, to bear something that is not that easy to bear. The meaning of tolerance here is similar to the question of how much of a poisonous substance an organism can *tolerate* without suffering serious damage. Tolerance is not approval, just the opposite. To tolerate something presupposes that we do not approve of it, and this is precisely why we are called to bear or tolerate it. To tolerate a different opinion does not mean that we share this opinion but that we are prepared to accept and allow for the fact that there are people who have views which we think are wrong. Or to tolerate a different lifestyle does not mean we approve of this lifestyle. Quite the contrary, to tolerate it means that we accept and allow that people choose lifestyles which we deem to be false.

It is therefore nonsensical to accuse people who are critical of certain views or lifestyles as being intolerant. To tolerate something *implies* that you are very critical of it. This is precisely what makes tolerance important. Tolerance is an attitude that

---

1 In so doing, I take up and develop further some of the ideas published in Schmidt-Leukel (2000) and (2002).

we need in the face of those views or practices of which we are highly critical. If we were to lose this original meaning of tolerance, we would lose a crucial achievement of the Enlightenment. For what would be the alternative? If we equate tolerance with approval, what then would be our attitude towards those people who hold views and who pursue lifestyles which we cannot approve of? If we don't tolerate, we will repress or even eliminate them. This is what intolerance means. Intolerance is: not to bear or endure the fact that people have views and follow lifestyles that we reject, and it is to deny these people the freedom to do so. Therefore tolerance is needed, in the first instance, to guarantee as much freedom and peace as possible within a society of diverse views and lifestyles. To quote the Harvard philosopher T. M. Scanlon: 'tolerance requires us to accept people and permit their practices even when we strongly disapprove of them'.[2] This makes tolerance a rather difficult thing. It has even been called an 'impossible virtue', for – as Bernard Williams from Oxford rightly remarked – 'Toleration, we may say, is required only for the intolerable. That is the basic problem.'[3]

Let me now introduce a distinction which may be of some help at this stage: the distinction between tolerance as a guideline for political action primarily related to the state, and tolerance as a moral demand primarily relevant to individuals or individual groups within the state.

When it comes to religious tolerance, the demand on the state is to grant equal rights and freedom of religious practice indiscriminately to all religious communities and churches. The state itself must not persecute any religious group and, in addition, the state must protect them against unfair treatment by any other powerful or influential group or institution within society. For the religious individual and for the individual religious community the quest for tolerance requires that they accept and support the ideal of a tolerant state. And the crucial question is whether their own religious beliefs and convictions permit them to do precisely this.

---

2 Scanlon (1996), p. 227.
3 B. Williams (1996), p. 18.

Clearly, it is here where the problems begin. For how can I or how could any religious community accept the idea that the state should tolerate and, even to some extent, support religious groups whose beliefs and practices my religious community or I do not and cannot approve of? If tolerance necessarily includes the element of disapproval, and if tolerance is primarily about equal rights and support, it seems to be self-contradictory to accept the idea of tolerance and to demand freedom and support for something that my religious community or I do not appreciate at all. Nevertheless, there are, I think, at least three arguments which do provide a strong support for religious tolerance in this sense.

The first one is the pragmatic argument of the *lesser evil*. This is to say, tolerance can and should be recommended as the lesser evil compared to violent conflict, especially when related to tensions between religious groups. These groups themselves might come to accept that it is a lesser evil to tolerate the other than to face a complete disruption of peace within or between societies. The strength of this argument was convincingly illustrated by the confessional wars in Europe which are rightly regarded as the main historical force behind the rise of the Enlightenment ideal of religious toleration. But on the other hand, the evident weakness of the pragmatic argument is that it does not work very well in a situation in which one of the parties is incomparably stronger than the others. Thus it does not work when it comes to the rights and protection of small minorities, or even individuals, whose beliefs and practices are disapproved of by the majority and who could be easily silenced by the majority without any risk to the peace of society. I am sure that most, perhaps even all religious communities could tell stories and have historical memories of situations in which they were, or are, a minority threatened with elimination by a religiously or ideologically different majority.

This apparent weakness in the pragmatic argument can be redeemed by a second argument, which understands tolerance as something intrinsically connected with the value of *individual autonomy*. One can disapprove of certain beliefs and practices but still support the view that the subject of these beliefs and practices should nevertheless be respected and protected in his or her individual freedom to hold or pursue them, even when those subjects form a small minority.

The concept of individual autonomy and its great value is rightly associated with the central ideas of the European Enlightenment. But it does not exclusively depend on the Enlightenment. There can be various reasons and justifications for the endorsement of individual autonomy, and surely one among them is the widespread religious conviction that individual faith, saving faith, must be free. To mention just a few random examples: There is the famous statement in the Qur'an that 'there should be no compulsion in religion' (Sura 2.256). Or the Buddha admonishes his disciples that their conduct is spiritually wholesome only when it emerges from their own genuine insight (*Aṅguttara Nikāya* 3:65). According to the great Vedānta philosopher Rāmānuja, God has provided human beings with the freedom and power to do either what is good or what is evil, so that through their own actions they may find the way to ultimate goodness and bliss (cf. *Commentary on Brahma Sūtra* 2:2:3).[4] Among the Jewish narrations of the Chassidim the idea of human self-governance and authenticity is marvellously expressed in the following little story: Before his death, Rabbi Zusya said 'In the coming world they will not ask me: "Why were you not Moses?" They will ask me: "Why were you not Zusya?"'[5]

In early Christianity it was Tertullian who vehemently expressed the idea that faith must be free[6] and subsequently this has been affirmed by a number of Church fathers. But the fact that freedom of faith was – not always, but nevertheless frequently – reaffirmed by Christian theologians demonstrates that this affirmation alone was obviously not strong enough to establish the ideal of religious tolerance. One can even observe that sometimes the same theologians who defended the freedom of faith also argued in favour of religious intolerance, as, for example, in

---

4 Cf. Radhakrishnan and Moore (eds) (1989), p. 553.
5 Buber (1991), p. 251.
6 *Patrologia Latina* (PL), ed. J. P. Migne (Paris 1844–55), vol. 1, col. 777.

the case of Thomas Aquinas.[7] According to Aquinas, faith must be free and cannot be enforced. But at the same time, says Aquinas, it must be protected from the evil influence of heretics. Thus Aquinas was on the one hand opposing any converting of non-Christians by violent means, but on the other hand defending violence against Christians with deviant theological convictions. His main argument was that, by distorting the true faith, heretics threaten the eternal salvation of the ordinary believer and thus constitute one of the worst evils. For if the use of violence is justified in fighting lesser evils, for example in order to safeguard one's earthly well-being or to protect one's earthly goods, it must be even more justified when it is necessary to protect the eternal well-being of people.

This type of argument is in no way an exclusively Thomistic one, but it was often used in theological debates on religious tolerance. Thus a standard position from the early Church onwards was to compare the activity of so-called heretics with the spread of a dangerous pestilence.[8] It therefore seemed not only justified, but even ethically required, to employ all means to eliminate the dangerous virus and protect people from becoming victims of the plague. It would be interesting to see whether similar pictures were used in other religions to justify religious intolerance, that is the comparison with a physician who has to employ some painful and nasty remedy to protect the higher good of health.[9]

Within Christianity, defenders of religious tolerance, few as they in fact were, put forward a counter-argument which I regard as the third important point in favour of religious tolerance. It can properly be called a *sceptical* argument despite the fact that it began as a theological one. It refers to the biblical parable of the tares among the wheat (Matt. 12.24ff). If someone has sown tares among wheat, it would not be wise to try to gather up the tares, since one might very well root up the wheat with them. Thus, Jesus finishes the parable: 'Allow both to grow

7 Cf. Aquinas' discussions in *Summa Theologica* II/II qq. 10 and 11.
8 Cf. Moore (1983).
9 Some examples for a Buddhist employment of this comparison in order to justify the use of violence are mentioned in Schmidt-Leukel (2004b), p. 47f.

together until the harvest.' Christian defenders of religious tolerance made use of this parable and argued that in religious affairs it is frequently quite uncertain, what and who are tares and what and who are the wheat. In persecuting so-called heretics, we run the risk of killing those who are in fact justified in the eyes of God. This argument can and needs to be stretched so far as to rule out any religious intolerance that is based on the reason of protecting people from eternal damnation: It is simply not certain enough whether there really is eternal damnation, and if so what would lead to it. At least it is not certain enough to be used as grounds for justifying intolerant means. For some people, belief in hell might be an integral part of their religious world-view, but even they should concede that belief is not the same as indubitable knowledge. In matters of eternal things there might be enough light and enough darkness to take one's own personal risk of faith, but there is not enough light to risk the life of our neighbour.

Let me summarize. If we keep the original meaning of tolerance and understand it as toleration of the disapproved, the three arguments I just described seem to me to be still valid and important in justifying tolerance. That is, religious people can and should support the idea of religious tolerance, because first toleration is the lesser evil compared to violent conflict or suppression. Second, because religious faith or conviction needs to be free in order to be genuine. And third, because it is not certain enough whether what we consider to be a false religion leads to any negative results in the afterlife, at least not certain enough to justify public and legal forms of intolerance, of restriction and repression.

But – and this is an important clause – such an understanding of tolerance implies that there are also limits to tolerance. Not everything that we disapprove of can or should be tolerated. The views and behaviour of people, individually and collectively, can become so evil – undoubtedly evil – that they are no longer tolerable. For example, tolerance cannot be regarded as the lesser evil when it comes to the question of whether one should tolerate something like Hitler's Nazism. Or consider the cases where tolerance cannot be justified by individual autonomy: for instance, when an individual commits a crime, or when that which is to be tolerated is itself an attack on individual freedom. The evil consequences of some religious beliefs and practices – evil consequences not in any uncertain afterlife but in the here and now – can sometimes be so evident that there is no more room for any reasonable doubt as to whether this would cause serious harm or not. Cases like these are clearly setting limits to tolerance. However, the inner drive behind the ideal of tolerance is to keep these limits as wide as possible.

Let me come back now to the religious attitude towards religious diversity. Can religious people see religious diversity only as a diversity of evils? As a diversity which they need to tolerate, but which ideally should be overcome, for example through peaceful missionary efforts? Or is there also the possibility of understanding religious diversity as a diversity of what is good, true and holy? As something that we – from the bottom of our heart and faith – can really rejoice in and celebrate?

The Move Towards Appreciation

What would such a genuine appreciation of religious diversity entail? Let me retell a little anecdote. Towards the end of the seventeenth century Louis XIV, the so-called 'Sun King' of France, exchanged a number of embassies with Narai, the king of Siam, or – as it is called today – Thailand. One of the French embassies brought a letter from Louis XIV, in which he suggested that King Narai might convert to Christianity because, as the Sun King wrote, 'Knowledge and Worship of the true God . . . is only to be found in the Christian Religion.'[10] In his polite but firm response, King Narai declined and explained his stance by the following words:

> For would not the true God that made Heaven and Earth, and all things that are therein, and hath given them so different

10 Tachard (1985), p. 221.

natures and inclinations, when he gave to Men like Bodies and Souls, if he had pleased have also inspired into them the same sentiments for the Religion they ought to follow, and for the Worship that was most acceptable to him, and make all Nations live and die in the same Laws?

. . . ought not one to think that the true God takes as great pleasure to be honoured by different Worships and Ceremonies, as to be Glorified by a prodigious number of Creatures that Praise him every one in their own way? Would that Beauty and Variety which we admire in the order of Nature, be less admirable in the Supernatural Order, or less beseeming the Wisdom of God?[11]

I think that King Narai's response points us in the right direction. Religious diversity is admirable to the extent that we can understand it as a reflection of the diversity of humanity itself. Narai is by no means a postmodern relativist. He affirms that all humans were given 'like bodies and souls'. Thus there is a basic equality and common dignity among human beings. But this goes together with a vast cultural, ethnic and individual diversity and variety. Most importantly, King Narai suggests that the diversity in religion too reflects this natural diversity of humanity and is therefore welcome to Godself. God enjoys the diversity of 'Worships and Ceremonies' as much as God enjoys the vast variety of natural beauty.

So why do I think that this points in the right direction? Because we can arrive at a genuine appreciation of the religious other to the extent to which we understand that there is a legitimate diversity of ways in which human beings relate themselves to the ultimate divine reality. And it is part of the legitimate diversity that this ultimate reality is designated by a number of different names and approached under a variety of different images and metaphors. For in itself, it is – as the great medieval theologian Anselm of Canterbury affirmed – necessarily greater than everything that we humans can conceive.[12] Similar affirmations

---

11 Ibid., p. 224.
12 Anselm, *Proslogion* 15.

can be found in all the major religious traditions. If there is this common awareness of the trans-conceptual, ineffable nature of the ultimate across the different religions, what is then the point of all their various images, metaphors and concepts under which humans relate themselves to ultimate divine reality? I think these are deeply interwoven with a corresponding diversity of religious practices and a wealth of age-old experiences, gathered and transmitted by countless generations. It would be misleading to say that all these different concepts refer to the same reality; they refer to different experiences with the same reality and to different ways of arriving at these experiences, and therefore there is room for mutual learning and benefiting. Out of their spiritual treasuries religions can still teach us how whatever is good and true and holy might flourish among us.

Inter-faith encounter, as I see it, is a process – the process of moving from toleration towards genuine appreciation. Both aspects are important. Initiatives like public inter-faith councils or larger inter-faith organizations should be primarily based on toleration and on the awareness of some common interest. It cannot and should not be expected that all members of inter-religious bodies are motivated by a full appreciation and acceptance of the others. But it is sufficient if there is mutual toleration and the recognition of certain fields where different faith communities can meaningfully co-operate in their own interest and in the interest of the wider society. While this is entirely sufficient as the basis and starting-point of inter-religious encounter, it is also desirable that every participating individual and community is open to make some new discoveries. To encounter the other is to move beyond our preconceived image of the other. It means to keep oneself prepared for a genuine learning process, for uncovering something new about the other and thereby, in the long run, also about oneself and one's own religion. Appreciation of the religious other is not a prerequisite of inter-faith encounter, but something that may very well happen through this encounter and for which the participants should keep themselves open.

On a theological level – and here I am not only speaking about Christian theology but about its analogous reflective traditions in other religions as well – the move from tolerance to appreciation corresponds to and is expressed in the move from an exclusivistic over an inclusivistic towards a pluralistic understanding of other religions.[13] Exclusivism entails the view that another religion is lacking any kind of saving or redeeming force, while inclusivism recognizes certain elements of truth or rays of the light in another religion. It is seen as being of some limited redemptive value, but is nevertheless understood as inferior compared to the fullness of truth within one's own tradition. Pluralism takes a further step and acknowledges that another religious tradition, despite being different from one's own, is nevertheless equally valid, equally redemptive or liberative. It is related to the same ultimate reality which is the final source of truth and salvation, but in a different, though not inferior, way.[14]

At times one finds the argument that tolerance requires pluralism. This can be misleading if 'pluralism' is identified with one of the three options in a theology of religions as I just sketched them. Tolerance requires 'pluralism' in the sense of a pluralistic society, that is, in the sense of a state that guarantees human rights, the freedom of self-determination, and hence the freedom of choosing one's religion (or no religion). This is a pluralism which necessarily involves incompatible, opposed views and the fact that the adherents of one particular world-view or religion will not appreciate the positions of all others. They are only asked to tolerate them. It is in this sense that tolerance and a pluralistic society condition and require each other. But this is something totally different from pluralism as an option within the theology of religions. In the latter sense pluralism is not an expression of tolerance but of genuine appreciation.

Let me be very precise on this important point. Tolerance as the toleration of something that we don't approve nor appreciate corresponds to an exclusivistic theology of religions. In that

---

13 For my interpretation of this tripolar classification (and a response to its critics), see Schmidt-Leukel (2005c).

14 For moves towards a pluralistic theology of religions within the non-Christian religions, see, for example, Hick and Askari (eds) (1985); Knitter (ed.) (2005); Coward (2000); Schmidt Leukel and Ridgeon (eds) (2007); Schmidt-Leukel (ed.) (2008).

sense tolerance does not require pluralism but presupposes exclusivism. As I said before, it would be nonsensical to require
tolerance for something that we genuinely appreciate. Therefore
exclusivism should not be blamed as being 'intolerant' (but an
exclusivist should be blamed if he/she is not prepared to combine
exclusivism with as much tolerance as possible). Inclusivism, although it does entail appreciation of other religions to a certain
extent, will also have to exercise tolerance, that is, it will have to
refrain from the temptation of using any sort of force in order to
convert those who live with a supposedly inferior knowledge of
truth to what is seen as the superior religion. The tolerance that
a number of Islamic societies in the past have shown towards
Christians and Jews among them would be a good example for
this (although it was not a full tolerance in that Jews and Christians were denied the same rights as Muslims). Pluralism as the
acceptance of another religion as different but equal is not an
expression of tolerance but of a genuine theological appreciation. Nor is it an expression of relativism. Pluralism involves
a theological assessment that claims universal validity and has
nothing in common with the relativistic denial of any universally
valid norms or standards. But a religious pluralist in that sense
will never appreciate everything in religion. There will always
be certain ideas, practices, values among religions and religious
communities that a pluralist cannot assess as being equally valid.
Some may be seen as inferior (in an inclusivistic manner), others
as completely false, so that an exclusivistic approach will be
taken in relation to this particular group or phenomenon. And
here a pluralist is as much as an inclusivist or an exclusivist con-
fronted with the question of whether he/she might be willing to
display tolerance towards that which he/she cannot approve. A
pluralist, for example, is certainly called to practise tolerance towards the exclusivistic and inclusivistic positions within his/her
own religious tradition, which are by definition positions that
he/she does not approve. In that sense, it is not acceptable when
certain ideologists of the Hindutva movement justify intolerant
means against Christians and Muslims with the argument that
Hinduism, as the allegedly most pluralistic of all religions, needs

to be protected against the absolutist and superioristic claims of Christianity and Islam. Thus, although there can be a development from tolerance to appreciation in and through inter-faith encounter, there will always be the necessity to emphasize the importance and value of tolerance.

Inter-religious Appreciation and Friendship

A major inter-faith gathering, which took place in Lyon (11–13 September 2005) and which brought together 360 leaders from 10 different faith communities, expressed the transformation that may happen through inter-faith encounter with the appropriate words: 'Dialogue transforms strangers into friends'.[15] This suggests that partners in dialogue progressively acquire a better mutual understanding. We need to learn what those religious traditions that are different from our own, mean to those who live in and by them. If we do not understand what a certain belief, a symbol, a ritual, a practice, etc. means to those who live with it, we have not understood it properly. In order to acquire this kind of understanding we need to learn seeing the world through the others' eyes. As Wilfred Cantwell Smith, one of the outstanding scholars of religion in the twentieth century, repeatedly said: 'In order to understand the faith of Buddhists, one must not look at something called "Buddhism". Rather, one must look at the world – so far as possible, through Buddhist eyes . . .'[16] And this applies, of course, to all religions.

Among the things that we will see when we begin looking through the eyes of our friends from other faiths is our own religious tradition. I think it is a crucial step in the process of inter-faith encounter and a real sign of maturing, when we are able to see our own religion through the eyes of our religious neighbours. This can, at times, be a sobering and perhaps even painful experience. But it is an important and truly enriching one, because it will lead to a more realistic perception and understanding.

---

15 www.santegidio.org/en/ecumenismo/uer/2005/form_appel.htm
16 E.g. Smith (1997), p.137.

In developing a better understanding of what our religious traditions mean to us we should remain aware of the difference between a religious tradition and the individual human being who lives under the influence and by the inspiration of this tradition. There is a clear danger in inter-religious perception that we do not perceive each other as the unmistakably individual persons that we are, but as representatives of a collective religious identity. This may be a particularly strong danger in inter-religious organizations which, in a sense, can easily tempt us to see our neighbour not as the particular individual person that he or she is, but as *the* Buddhist, *the* Hindu, *the* Muslim, *the* Sikh, *the* Catholic, *the* Presbyterian, *the* Jew, etc. I call this a danger, because it implies once again a distorted view. Our personal identities are far too complex to be easily equated with a kind of collective pattern or stereotype.[17] And so are the religious traditions themselves. It is an illusion to assume that there is something like *the* Islam, or *the* Buddhism or *the* Christian religion. None of these traditions is monolithic but they are internally diverse and varied. When strangers are transformed into genuine friends – across the borders of religious communities – it is quite evident that we cannot be friends with a religious stereotype: we cannot be friends with a Muslim as a Muslim as such, or a Catholic as a Catholic as such, etc. We can only be friends with a concrete person and then – perhaps, hopefully – learn how our friend in his or her life is nourished, sustained, guided and comforted by certain features of a complex religious tradition. Then we may begin to appreciate how good it is that there is such a broad diversity of ways in which the many different individual human beings are related to the ultimate and in which the ultimate is related to each one of us. And so we will begin to celebrate religious diversity as something really precious. The more, however, we understand how other religious traditions are capable of spiritually sustaining the lives of their adherents the more they might also begin to exert their influence on us. This

---

17 Hasan Askari, one of the great Muslim pioneers of modern inter-faith dialogue, has rightly warned against this danger. See in particular his 'Towards a Trans-Religious Dimension', in Askari (1991), pp. 120–39.

throws up the questions of a multireligious identity to which I will turn in the next chapter.

One final word: The sort of inter-religious appreciation that I just described does not mean that we become uncritical or naive in relation to religions, not even in relation to those religions which we appreciate as being, in principle, on a par with our own tradition. Not everything in religion is good and far too much is rather dreadful. We all know this from our own religion, and the more we know about its history, the more we will be aware of its own ambiguities, of its light and its dark sides. When it comes to the issue of inter-religious criticism, we need to admit that in the past the perception of other religions has far too often been extremely biased and was focused on whatever appeared to be negative in the religion of the other. It is a quite human feature to idealize one's own faith and demonize the faith of others. But through genuine inter-religious learning and friendship, we may come to understand that these sorts of negative judgements were often based on misunderstanding and mischief. What we need to do is learn how to articulate inter-religious criticism as friends do – being slow and not fast to do it; but also remaining honest and not being hypocritical. And always to do so in the knowledge that it is much easier to see the speck in the eye of the other than the log in our own (cf. Matt. 7.5). But this is just another good reason to listen to every honest criticism that comes from our friends in the other traditions.

3

MULTIRELIGIOUS IDENTITY

Problems and Considerations

Identities

Each one of us has several identities resulting from different relational systems. I, for example, am a German, at the same time a citizen of Glasgow, husband, father, university professor, Anglican Christian, etc. Combining such different identities in one person is, in principle, not a problem, because these identities are located on something like different planes (although occasionally there can be conflicts, as for example the typical tension between the demands of family and profession). However, things are different if different identities appear on the same plane. In this case tensions can increase significantly, possibly even to the point that a decision for *one* identity becomes inevitable. The question of double citizenship, for instance, can cause such problems, as the political authorities of some countries won't tolerate a second citizenship and thus demand a decision. Other examples would be cases where someone has two incompatible jobs, or belongs to two rival political parties, or is married with two different partners. Apparently, the question of multiple religious belonging or multiple religious identity seems to fall under this category, that is, it raises the question of the compatibility of different identities on the same plane.

But is this really the right way to pose the problem? In his best-selling book *On Identity* the Lebanese author Amin Maalouf, who lives in France, reports that he is often asked whether he feels 'more French' or 'more Lebanese'. 'And', says Maalouf, 'I always give the same answer: "Both!"':

So am I half French and half Lebanese? Of course not. Identity can't be compartmentalised. You can't divide it up into halves or thirds or any other separate segments. I haven't got several identities: I've got just one, made up of many components combined together in a mixture that is unique to every individual.[1]

This unique individual mixture reflects, according to Maalouf,

a person's whole journey through time as a free agent; the beliefs he acquires in the course of that journey; his own individual tastes, sensibilities and affinities; in short his life itself.[2]

A Transformed Theological Starting Point

Can a similar understanding of identity be applied to the *religious* identity of a person? In this case, any talk about multiple religious identity would be misleading and would need to be discarded as much as Maalouf rejects the idea of being half French and half Lebanese. It would be more adequate to speak of people having a 'multireligious identity', that is, having a unique identity, but one that is formed and developed under the influence of several religious traditions. It cannot be denied that this kind of identity-formation is something that one would expect under the conditions of religiously plural societies – and it is indeed a widespread phenomenon in the East and now also increasingly in the West.[3]

---

1 Maalouf (2000), p. 3.
2 Ibid., p. 4.
3 See, for example, the study of Paul Heelas and Linda Woodhead (2005), which is based on empirical research in the British town of Kendal. A report on a similar study in Enköping, Sweden is found in Kajsa Ahlstrand (2007). A study on 'Spirituality in Germany', based on a representative selection, was done in 2006 by the Identity Foundation in co-operation with the University of

A different question, of course, is how, from a theological point of view, this phenomenon is to be assessed.[4]

Only someone who assumes that the decisive salvific truth is to be found exclusively in one particular religious tradition – or even within a specific sub-tradition – will see it a priori as negative or dangerous if people expose themselves to the spiritual influence of other religious traditions.[5] The widespread Christian rejection of syncretism is to a considerable extent based on a view that understands syncretism as the mixing of light and darkness, of truth and lie, of the divine and the demonic.[6] But what if such a theologically exclusivistic position can no longer be taken for granted? If one can assume, for good theological reasons,[7] that the good, true and holy is not confined to one's own religious tradition but can also be found within others, then the idea of a spiritual formation by various traditions can no longer be seen as a priori devious or dangerous. So what is really new about the

---

Hohenheim. According to this study about 10–15% of the German population are 'spiritual seekers', who construct meaning by drawing on 'fragments from Humanism, Anthroposophy, Mysticism and Esoteric'. An additional 35% of the population is seen as being 'religiously creative'. Although belonging to the religious mainstream communities, they integrate into their spirituality 'inspiration from various world religions in a rather carefree manner'. Cf. the press report: www.identityfoundation.de/fileadmin/templates_identityfoundation/downloads/presse/frauen_spiritualitaet/PM_Lang_Studie_Spiritualitaet.pdf.
See also the empirical research related by C. Bochinger (2008).

4 For the emerging theological discussion of multireligious identity, see Sharma and Dugan (eds) (1999); Cornille (ed.) (2002); Kasimow, Keenan and Klepinger-Keenan (eds) (2003); *Buddhist-Christian Studies* 23 (2003); Phan (2004); May (ed.) (2007); Bernhardt and Schmidt-Leukel (eds) (2008).

5 Peter Phan is therefore right in stating that, theologically, the possibility of a multiple religious identity at least requires the acknowledgement that non-Christian religions 'contain "elements of truth and grace"'. Cf. Phan (2004), p. 64.

6 Cf. Michael Pye's statement that Christianity has fostered an understanding of 'syncretism as an illicit contamination, as a threat or danger, as taboo, or as a sign of religious decadence' (2004, p. 59). On the more recent theological discussion of syncretism (within the context of an enhanced awareness of religious diversity), see Gort, Vroom, Fernhout and Wessels (eds) (1989); Greive and Niemann (eds) (1990); Siller (ed.) (1991).

7 A concise overview on the theological discussions about exclusivistic, inclusivistic and pluralistic positions within the theological assessment of other religions is given in Schmidt-Leukel (2005), pp. 96–192 (English translation forthcoming).

problem of multireligious identity is not so much the fact that people in the past, at least in Western societies, were less exposed to the influence of several religions. The really new point is that today we need to reflect this influence on the basis of a theologically transformed, that is, far more positive, view of the other religions.[8] For someone who does not endorse this more positive view, the front line remains largely unchanged and the problem that I am discussing here will not even be perceived as a serious theological issue.

If a member of a particular religion gets, in more than just a superficial way, in contact with the manifestations, the teachings, the life of another religion, and finds in it something good, true and holy, that is, in Christian terms, a reflection of revelation, then, from a spiritual point of view, he or she has no choice. It is simply no option to close one's mind and heart to it. The Catholic theologian Karl Rahner held that if a non-Christian, who is subjectively upright, encounters the Christian gospel but still rejects it, then he or she had apparently not yet heard the gospel in such a way that it hit him or her existentially, that is, that he or she recognized the voice of God in it. For if he or she would hear the gospel in this way, it would be impossible to reject it and remain a person of integrity.[9] However, this must also apply the other way round – and that is something that Rahner had not considered. I think that, for example, a Christian who encounters the Buddha in such a way that thereby a deep and existentially relevant truth is revealed to him or her, has simply not the option to reject the Buddha.

Commitment versus Openness?

In former times one would have said that people finding themselves in such a situation have an obligation to convert to the

---

8 Perhaps this judgement too needs to be relativized. For already in the early Church the question of how much Greek influence the Church can bear was discussed in dependence on how much truth the various theologians were able to see in Greek, that is 'pagan', philosophy.

9 Cf. Rahner (1967), p. 327.

other religion. Or, one would have concluded that such people have already converted internally, even if this step has not been – or not yet been – manifested in an institutional change of religious belonging. This view is, of course, still existent. Thomas Merton's Polunnaruwa experience, for example, which Merton had shortly before his death and which he describes in his diary entirely in terms of a Buddhist enlightenment experience,[10] has been interpreted by some as a conversion from Christianity to Buddhism.[11] Such an understanding of conversion, however, still presupposes that the acceptance of what is good, true and holy in another tradition is inevitably connected with a break with one's own present religion. But what if this is not the case? Then what is needed is not conversion but integration. But how far may such integration go? From a theological point of view, can and may it go so far that it will be no longer clear from which source the resulting religious identity is now primarily nourished?

According to Catherine Cornille inter-religious encounter seems to require both, 'complete openness' to the other and the possible truth in his or her religion, and at the same time 'total commitment' to one's own religious tradition. But between these two requirements exists, according to Cornille, a significant tension:

> total commitment to a particular tradition seems by definition to involve a high degree of exclusivity and thus lack of openness to the other. Complete openness, on the other hand, implies the possibility of abstracting completely from any particular commitment to truth . . . Whereas an attitude of total commitment risks losing any sense of the otherness of the other, complete openness contradicts one's own religious identity and takes away the possibility of having anything worthwhile to say for oneself. A fruitful interreligious dialogue must therefore move between complete openness and total commitment.[12]

---

10 Cf. Merton (1973), pp. 234ff.

11 Cf. the information in Ott (1977), pp. 20, 33f, 173ff and *passim*. In a sense Ott's whole book deals with the issue that, given Merton's Buddhistically shaped religious experiences, his religious identity is no longer clearly definable.

12 Cornille (2005), p. 8f.

To me this 'between' sounds very much like a hardly convincing compromise. Why should 'complete commitment' constitute an obstacle to 'complete openness'? Because, according to Cornille, 'complete openness' would involve the openness to a possible conversion and thereby, as she says, 'the possibility of abstracting completely from any particular commitment to truth'. Belonging to a particular religion involves, according to Cornille,

> the abandonment to a transcendent reality mediated through the concrete symbols and rituals of a particular religion. Surrender is thus not to the ultimate as such, but through – and in the end – to the teachings and practices embedded in a concrete religious tradition.[13]

On this view the possibility of spiritual openness to other religions is indeed significantly limited. If 'complete commitment' to the divine reality can only be realized in committing oneself completely to one particular religious tradition, so that both in the end coincide, then any serious openness to a different religious tradition will inevitably appear as jeopardizing the commitment to one's own tradition and thereby one's commitment to God. Cornille compares the commitment to a particular religion with the 'life commitment to another person'.[14] In other words, if the openness to another religious tradition goes too far, it would easily acquire the smack of 'adultery'.[15] This would even be true if one assumes, as the pluralistic theology of religions does, that

13 Cornille (2003), p. 44. Similarly in her 'Introduction' to Cornille (ed.) (2002), where she also emphasizes that the 'total commitment' is to an 'ultimate reality' that may 'itself transcend all historical forms and religious boundaries', but that 'it is nevertheless only through and ultimately to a particular person, symbolic system, and ritual tradition that this total surrender can take place' (p. 3).

14 Cornille (2003), p. 48.

15 It is instructive that, in view of his perception of the spiritual force of Hinduism, Henri Le Saux/Swami Abhishiktananda too had the feeling of being 'unfaithful' to his Christian vocation. In this context his diary note of 26 December 1954 refers to the word of the Sermon on the Mount that one who looks at a woman with lust has already committed adultery within his heart (Le Saux 1998, p. 97).

other religions mediate awareness of the divine in different but nevertheless equally genuine and salvific ways. Cornille's argument implies that even in this case one would have to remain strictly faithful to one's own tradition – as the faithful spouse may very well acknowledge the attraction of other men or women, but must not be overcome by this, and leave that to others. On this view, religious identity is rooted not only psychologically but also theologically in a stable, reliable and exclusive relationship. Indeed, one of the leading representatives of a pluralistic theology of religions, John Hick, has also concluded that, in relation to the different formative sources of the major religions,

> one can only centre one's religious life wholeheartedly and unambiguously upon any one of them – upon the Vedic revelation, or upon the Buddha's enlightenment, or upon the Torah, or upon the person of Christ, or upon the words of the Qur'an; but not upon more than one at once.[16]

Although I hold this objection to be exceptionally strong, I need to confess that I am not entirely convinced.

I doubt that it really makes sense to compare one's belonging to a particular religious tradition with the life commitment to another person. Religions, I think, are not ends in themselves. As Cornille rightly says, they mediate the abandonment to a reality that transcends the concrete religions. I feel that identifying this abandonment to transcendent reality with the commitment to a particular religion might even be dangerous. Here looms the danger of idolatry! However, I presume that Cornille's argument is based on an incarnational logic, and, in consequence, on a sacramental line of thought. From this perspective, it is entirely correct to hold that we cannot relate to God in bypassing the earthly realities. One cannot love God if one does not love one's neighbour. But even for the incarnation it is true that God's presence in a human being is such that this particular human being points beyond himself to the transcendent God: 'The father is

---

16 Hick (1989), p. 373.

greater than I' (John 14.28) says the Johannine Christ. And each sacrament accomplishes its sacramental efficacy only by being a sign and instrument for something else, namely, for the divine grace. I am personally inclined to understand religions as something like sacraments. But precisely as that they are not and must not be final points or ends in themselves.

One could cite various examples from other religious traditions that testify to such a self-transcending view of religions. They are, in Zen Buddhist terms, just 'fingers pointing to the moon', or to the One, as the Qur'an says, 'unto Him no one is like' (Sura 112), and who is therefore by essence always 'greater' (*akbar*) than everything else.

But, as one could object, even if religions always point beyond themselves, that is, even if the end to which they lead is not identical with them, have they not still the concreteness of a particular route or way? Even if there might be different ways leading to the same summit, one would nevertheless have to decide for a specific way or one won't reach the summit at all.

The image is tempting and its message can be well corroborated. The Eastern traditions in particular often hold that following a spiritual path will usually imply surrendering oneself to the spiritual guidance of a specific guru or master, to the guidance of *one* master! It is frequently and rigorously asserted that one cannot belong at the same time to the schools of two different masters. Ordinary experience too teaches us, for example, that it can be disastrous if in the education of children two parents don't pull together. Or even worse, if two sides constantly interfere in educational matters.

I think these examples are correct. However, is it not the aim of every education, whether spiritual or ordinary, that the disciple shall eventually become a master and that the child shall not remain a child but reach its own maturity with the capacity of making its own decisions and choices and of listening, in the course of that process, quite deliberately and increasingly so to more than just one voice? As much as it is right and helpful to compare religions to ways, it may be even more adequate to compare them to signposts or better to travel guides. And

on some routes it might be advisable to consult more than one
guidebook, for certain parts of the way may be better explained
in one guide while another gives better advice for some other
sections of the route. In that sense, it is not the religion that is
the way but the actual life itself, and religions should be instru-
mental in helping us to live it.

I don't want to overstretch the images and metaphors. In his
sketch of 'A Theology of Multiple Religious Identity', Michael
von Brück has rightly, because realistically, emphasized the
formative role of religious socialization early in one's life. Like
one's mother tongue, which will always be much closer to one's
whole personality than any other language acquired later, one's
'mother-religion' will make a similar difference, at least emotionally, to one's religious identity formation.[17] Von Brück, however, is not denying that a religion acquired later in life may
perhaps be felt to articulate one's religious experiences better
than one's first or former religion.[18] And he also admits that
the whole situation may be different, including emotionally, if
several religious identities are already combined at an early stage
in childhood.[19] This, of course, is a situation which increasingly
occurs to the extent to which the phenomenon of inter-religious
marriages is growing. Moreover, one should not ignore that in
the future presumably a rapidly growing number of people in
the West will grow up without a clear, or even without any, religious socialization. Do those among them who embark on a
religious search at some later stage in their lives have to make
good for this by first undergoing a socialization within a nar-
rowly confined and clearly defined religious community? Or is
it justified and making sense if these people will right from the
start quench their spiritual thirst by drinking eclectically from
several religious sources?

---

17 Brück (2007), pp. 199, 204f.
18 Ibid., p. 205.
19 Ibid., p. 199.

Religious Individualism

Understanding religions as signposts or travel guides and emphasizing the personal responsibility of each individual, as I have now done, amounts of course to religious individualism. There exists, however, within religions themselves a clear awareness of the fundamental significance and legitimacy of at least some religious individualism. I would like to highlight and illustrate this with a few brief samples by referring to some modern representatives of various religious traditions.

The Theravāda Buddhist monk and scholar Walpola Rahula (1907–97) begins his book *What the Buddha Taught*, a widespread introduction to Buddhism, with a chapter on the 'Buddhist Attitude of Mind'. This attitude consists, according to Rahula, in 'the principle of personal responsibility':[20]

> The freedom of thought allowed by the Buddha . . . is necessary because, according to the Buddha, man's emancipation depends on his own realization of Truth . . .[21]

Subsequently Rahula quotes the famous Kālāma Sutta (*Anguttara Nikāya* III 188ff) where the Buddha encourages his listeners to assess the word of the wise by the criterion of their own personal and experience-based insight.

In his programmatic speech on *The Common Bases of Hinduism*, the influential Neo-Hindu Swami Vivekananda (1863–1902) exhorts his audience with the words:

> And do not imitate, do not imitate! If you are working, even in spiritual things, at the dictation of others, slowly you lose all faculty, even of thought. Bring out through your own exertions what you have, but do not imitate, yet take what is good from others . . . Learn everything that is good from others, but bring it in, and in your own way absorb it; do not become others.[22]

---

20 Rahula (1994), p. 2.
21 Ibid.
22 Vivekananda (1994), p. 381f.

The famous Jewish philosopher Martin Buber (1878–1965) writes in the introduction to his work *Tales of the Hasidim* the following words about the role of a Hasidic master (*Zaddik*):

> And over and over he takes you by the hand and guides you until you are able to venture on alone. He does not relieve you of doing what you have grown strong enough to do for yourself . . . The zaddik must make communication with God easier for his hasidim, but he cannot take their place . . . he never permits the soul of the hasid to rely so wholly on his own that it relinquishes independent concentration and tension, in other words, that striving-to-God of the soul without which life on this earth is bound to be unfulfilled.[23]

Even more pointed is the Jewish individualism or personalism expressed in one of the stories that Buber relates:

> Before his death, Rabbi Zusya said 'In the coming world they will not ask me: "Why were you not Moses?" They will ask me: "Why were you not Zusya?"'[24]

Muhammad Kalisch, a professor of Islam and himself a Shi'ite Muslim who teaches at the University of Münster, refers to the spiritual significance of the traditional Islamic prohibition to imitate. He says:

> What is important is to struggle for the truth, but no human being can ever reach all truth and can ever be free from subjective ideas . . . Wherever is real freedom of thought, there will inevitably be a diversity of opinions. Everyone can only be responsible for what he can understand . . . The vast majority of traditional Muslim theologians hold the view that *taqlīd* (blind imitation without personal verification) in matters of *uṣūl* (principle of religion) is forbidden. If one takes this view seriously it means nothing else than that no

23 Buber (1991), p. 5f.
24 Ibid., p. 251.

one is allowed to believe in anything except what s/he can personally verify.[25]

As a final example I would like to quote a contemporary representative of Christianity of whom one would not necessarily expect such a statement. Josef Ratzinger, now Pope Benedict XVI, was once asked 'How many ways to God are there?' And he replied:

> As many as there are human beings. For even within the same faith tradition the way of each human being is a wholly personal one. We have the word of Christ: I am the Way. In so far there is ultimately one way and everybody who is on the way to God is thereby somehow also on the way of Jesus Christ. But this does not mean that on the level of consciousness and volition all ways are identical – quite the contrary, the one way is so large that it becomes in each human being his or her very personal way.[26]

The conviction, widespread among religions, that the religious way is in its essence the very personal way of each individual towards the ultimate Reality supports, I think, my understanding of religions more as signposts or travel guides than as ways. Moreover, the religious individualism makes it plain that 'religion' in the sense of formal, institutionalized 'religions' is ultimately an abstraction. If what is important for each human being is treading a way that is unmistakably one's own way to God, and if 'religion' in its most genuine sense refers to this ever individual and specific way, then there are in the end as many religions, as many 'ways to God', 'as there are human beings'. On this view, the formal 'religions' will appear within the 'religion' of each individual only through the refraction of a deeply personal and

---

25 Kalisch (2007), p. 82f.

26 Ratzinger (1996), p. 35 (my translation). It is worth mentioning that there exists a close Muslim parallel to Ratzinger's startling statement, the traditional Islamic saying: 'There are as many paths to God as there are human souls.' Cf. Chittick (1994), p. 4.

individually unique appropriation. It was Mahātma Gandhi who once said: 'no two persons I have known have had the same and identical conception of God'.[27]

Multireligious Identity and Patchwork Religiosity

So if religion is, in the end, always something unmistakably in-dividual and personal (descriptively) and has to be so (norma-tively), then it seems to be the case that we can indeed assume for religious identity the same as what Maalouf has said on identity in general, namely that it assembles in a 'unique mixture' 'a per-son's whole journey through time as a free agent'. Patchwork-religiosity, so often decried, would then be something that on the personal level is absolutely inevitable. The individual religion of each person is always 'patchwork-religion'. Nobody internal-izes and represents a complete religious tradition. The individual religiosity of each human being is rather nourished by those ex-tracts or 'patches' of a religious tradition which have become significant to his/her very personal spirituality in the course of one's life and were digested in the very same personal manner. Thus, we would neither do justice to the descriptive facts nor to the normative matter if we were to understand our individual religious identity in terms of religious stereotypes: that is, I *as* a Christian, I *as* a Buddhist, I *as* a Hindu, I *as* a Muslim, etc. We deceive ourselves if we see ourselves – or others who live under the influence of a different religious tradition – as representa-tions of a religious stereotype. Stereotypes do not correspond to unique individual persons. Imitating a stereotype becomes a spiritual danger. The question of religious identity needs to be transformed into the question of *personal religious authenticity*. For personal authenticity, as Hasan Askari has so impressively shown, can not and must not be misunderstood as 'the equation of personal piety with one's collective identity . . .'[28]

---

27 Harijan, 2.2.1934. *Collected Works of Mahatma Gandhi Online*, Vol. 63, S. 85. Available at http://www.gandhiserve.org/cwmg/VOL063.PDF.
28 Askari (1991), p. 128.

So why should the personal patchwork-religion of each individual be composed only of 'patches' stemming from within
the circuit of just one religious tradition? This would be particularly unrealistic if the individual mixture of patches reflects,
in the words of Maalouf, the actual life journey of a person and
if this journey happens, as a matter of fact, under the influence
of several religious traditions.[29] The already cited argument that
truths, once they have been recognized and experienced as truths,
simply cannot be rejected, regardless of the religious tradition
from which they come, speaks against any a priori confinement
of legitimate patchworks to just one religious tradition.

It is often cited as a danger of patchwork-religiosity that it
emerges from and results in an essentially *non-religious consumerist* attitude. The Polish theologian Józef Niewiadomski, for example, says: 'The logic of the subjective choice of faith follows
the laws of mercantile reason. One looks for "special offers", or
"brand names" or "novelties". And once the images or ideas are
no longer in line with people's expectations, or if tensions arise,
one looks for alternatives.'[30] No doubt, a situation as characterized by Niewiadomski does constitute a danger: the danger
of escaping a religious claim once it begins to become serious,
that is, once the message is no longer providing just consola-
tion, edification or spiritual thrill, that is, once it is – to stay
with Niewiadomski – no longer cheap or exclusive or trendy, but
turning into a genuine existential challenge.

However, is this really a specific problem of modern pluralism
or of the free market? Is it not rather a danger that everybody
has to face regardless of whether his or her religiosity is nourished by several or by just one religious tradition? Is it really
only the people of capitalist societies, or only the people with a
multireligious identity, who know how to escape the challenging

---

29 In the past, the individual religiosity of numerous Christians presumably
also included various 'patches' from other religious traditions. Parts of classical
Greek religiosity, for example, were taught to children as part of a humanist
education. Should we then really assume that Homer's poems were without any
influence on the religiosity of their frequently rather young consumers to whom
they were taught over centuries in Christian Europe?

30 Niewiadomski (1996), p. 89f.

character of religious insights? Are such evasive manoeuvres not also found among those who live the whole of their lives under the influence of just one religious tradition? Is a primarily consumerist attitude to religion not also to be found among highly traditional Christians, Muslims, Hindus or Buddhists? And conversely, do we not find examples of radical determination and utmost seriousness also among people with a multireligious identity, as for example in the lives of Swami Abhishiktananda,[31] Thich Nhat Hanh or Thomas Merton? I am not denying that today religious patches are also made into market commodities and thereby deprived of those challenging dimensions which they possess within the religious traditions themselves.[32] Yet the danger of religious consumerism does not depend on the diversity of the religious offer. It is rather inevitably linked to what Niewiadomski calls the 'logic of the subjective choice of faith'. The real danger is that this choice of faith is made out of primarily consumerist motives. But the subjective choice of faith in itself is an indispensable part of the subjective appropriation of faith, is part of 'a person's whole journey through time as a free agent'. Hence it is precisely for religious reasons that no one can be spared or relieved of this choice.

31 Cf. the contribution of Hackbarth-Johnson (2008).

32 A detailed analysis of this process is offered by Carrette and King (2005). The accusation that in the present era the nature of religion has been converted according to neo-liberal economic principles is here presented in a most radical form. And even Carrette and King discover among the various offers on the market of spiritual possibilities still some spiritualities which find their approval (cf. pp. 17–25, 169–82). However, the main informants in their analysis and discernment of the various spiritual spirits are Marx and Nietzsche (cf. p. 23). Hence it is not surprising that, according to them, the good spiritualities are 'Revolutionary or Anti-Capitalist Spiritualities'. What does come as a surprise is the selection of Marx and Nietzsche as authorities in a study that claims to assess spirituality in order to defend religion against its capitalist 'takeover' and reinterpretation (for what about the reinterpretation that functionalizes religion in a sociocultural fashion?). In view of Carrette and King's main objection against a market-oriented, consumerist spirituality, namely that this is primarily aimed at the adaptation of the individual to the societal status quo, one inevitably wonders whether this is really such a startling new feature of religion under the conditions of a neo-liberal global economy, or if this is not rather a problematic tendency which has beset all greater and smaller religions at all times. There is no doubt that Marx would have opted for the latter.

It cannot be denied that within the context of modernity, or better within the context of those impulses that modernity received from the Enlightenment, not only the subjectivity of humans but especially the self-responsibility of individual subjects were particularly emphasized. And there is no doubt that, for example, traditional Roman Catholicism has not necessarily emphasized among its members the 'logic of the subjective choice of faith'. What they had to believe was preset by the magisterium and what they had to live was preset by the Catholic milieu. There was nearly nothing to be chosen by a free subject. And yet, the religious significance of the subjective choice of faith was by no means unknown. For within the context of mission it was precisely this subjective choice of faith that was regarded and demanded as decisive for one's salvation. A subjective choice against one's present religious formation was demanded from the non-Christian or even just non-Catholic subject and was praised as spiritually crucial. Thus it was not the subjective choice itself that was seen as problematic but the eventual outcome of this choice. If this was a religion other than Catholicism, the choice was seen as wrong; but if it was made in favour of Catholicism, it was seen as salvifically decisive. This nourishes the suspicion that what lies behind many a theological critique of the modern endorsement of the subjective choice of faith are still exclusivistic positions, which in their criticism of modern subjectivity do not really reject the necessity of subjective choice itself but rather the respective outcomes of that choice.

Religious individualism, especially when it is combined with a multireligious identity, is not only often accused as being a form of consumerism, but is also readily charged with an atomistic, egocentric and a-social attitude. We find talk of 'the individualisation of responsibility with no consideration of society', of 'an ethic of self-interest', of 'treating others as means rather than ends', etc.[33] Along these lines is also the often-cited remark by Josef Ratzinger, who said in 1997 about the appeal of Buddhism in the West: 'If Buddhism is attractive, it is because it appears as a

33 Ibid., p. 21.

possibility of touching the infinite and obtaining happiness without having any concrete religious obligations. A spiritual auto-eroticism (*un autoéroticisme spirituel*) of some sort.'[34] Although this label of a 'spiritual auto-eroticism' is frequently quoted as a critique of Buddhism, it was apparently meant as a critique of certain forms of the Western reception of Buddhism and, by implication, of contemporary forms of spirituality in general in so far as these are receptive to the attraction of Eastern religions.

To emphasize the subjective choice of faith in conjunction with multireligious identity has in and of itself nothing that would suggest an atomistic, a-social or even anti-social tendency, as long as one does not subscribe to the Weberian dictum or dogma that every form of mysticism is by nature 'a-social',[35] assuming that contemporary spirituality is primarily of a mystical orientation. To my mind, there is no strong evidence for these assumptions. But one may understand 'mystical orientation' in a fairly broad sense as referring to a spirituality that is primarily driven by experiences. It was in this sense that Karl Rahner made, as early as the 1960s, the prophetic remark that

> tomorrow's religious person will be a 'mystic' – someone who has 'experienced' something – or else will be no more, for the religiosity of tomorrow will no longer be supported by a unanimous, self-evident public conviction and custom of all that would exist in advance to any personal experience and decision.[36]

In this sense it might be true that religious *bricolages* are normally driven by experiences. But again, this dependency on personal experience – because religious identity is no longer predetermined by the 'self-evident public conviction and custom of all' – does in itself not imply any a-social or atomistic tendencies, but just a clearer awareness of the subjective choice of faith.

---

34 This remark was originally made in an interview with Ratzinger published by the French journal *L'Express* on 20 March 1997. Here it is quoted after Lefebure (1998), p. 221.

35 Cf. Weber (1988), pp. 230, 366.

36 Rahner (1966), p. 22 (my translation).

Nevertheless, it is understandable that the increase in the formation of multireligious identities may be perceived as a threat to a religious sense of community. However, I think that the problem is not so much one of the individual but rather one of the community. It is not religious individualism as such that is endangering religious communities. It seems to me that at least some religious communities have serious difficulties in developing such forms of community life that would also be open to people with multireligious identities. This is particularly the case if the primary purpose of the community is in the common cultivation of a collective identity that allows no, or only marginal, forms of deviation. Communities of that kind need, for their own constitution, demarcation and differentiation from other religious communities with other collective identities. Hence the inroad of such foreign identities into the ranks of their own community, in the form of members with multireligious identities, would be perceived as erosion. But this crisis too entails an opportunity and constructive challenge, namely the creation of religious communities which do justice to the very personal, unmistakable faith-identity of their members, thereby refraining from seeing persons as means but taking them as ends in themselves.

A further frequent objection against patchwork-religiosity is of a hermeneutical nature. If one appropriates merely individual elements, patches, of certain religions, one presumably misses their genuine meaning and remains within the realm of the superficial. The outcome can only be misunderstanding, which is further increased if such elements are combined with further patches from various other religious traditions. What, so the critical question of Bettina Bäumer, would Christians feel, 'if some Hindus started celebrating the mass without understanding the totality of meaning of which the mass is a part'?[37] To be sure, Bäumer's critical remark is not directed against Hindus; what she has in mind are in fact those Christians who take over forms of meditation from Hinduism or Buddhism without at the same time appropriating the context with which these practices

---

37 Bäumer (1989), p. 37.

are connected. If the other religion is to be taken seriously, says Bäumer, one has to adopt together with the respective religious practice also its underlying premises. For Bäumer, this points us in the direction of religious bi-identities, that is, to 'sincerely and fully accept another spiritual tradition, without giving up one's own roots'.[38] However, she also admits that '(t)his vocation may be rare, and . . . not easy'. Indeed!

But let us come back briefly to less demanding vocations. I don't know whether there are in fact any Hindus who are interested in celebrating the Catholic Mass. But it is well known that the monastery of Einsiedeln in Switzerland, for example, is no longer only a popular pilgrimage site for Catholics but has, over the years, also become highly popular among Hindus who go there in order to venerate the black Madonna as a form of the goddess Kālī. Something similar is happening at other pilgrimage sites of Mother Mary, for example, in Mariastein and apparently now also in Fatima. On these occasions, Hindus also participate in the Catholic Mass.[39] So should we then really assume that this does not make any good spiritual sense because the participating ordinary Hindus do not familiarize themselves with the whole system of Catholicism? How many among the ordinary Catholics who are present on these occasions make themselves familiar with the whole Catholic system as the background of their own religious practice? I am not denying that it is a problem of patchwork-religiosity that it might remain purely superficial. But again, religiosity that remains within the borders of a specific religious tradition is not less exposed to the very same danger.

The final problem of patchwork-religiosity that I would like to address concerns the coherence of the connected patches. Here too we can observe that this problem is by no means confined to a situation where the patches stem from different religious traditions. How many people ask seriously whether everything that they personally believe coheres in a logical, systematic manner? To be sure, the search for truth obliges us not to thoughtlessly

38 Ibid., p. 41.
39 Cf. Baumann, Luchesi and Wilke (eds) (2003).

give one over to apparent contradictions and inconsistencies. In this regard future academic theology can and will have to provide far more assistance. Pursuing, as far as possible, the question of the extent to which the whole religious heritage of humanity is coherent falls under the responsibility of scientific theology – a task which can only be taken up in a presumably ongoing process of global dialogue.[40]

The issue of coherence does of course not only arise in relation to the cognitive aspects of faith. It also relates to the level of religious practice. Here we find both: On the one hand, we can have the situation that pieces from different religious traditions appear to be incompatible on the cognitive level, but nevertheless enter the religious identity of a particular person because they cohere on the non-cognitive level of 'implicit religiosity' or because they foster, despite their different practical forms, nevertheless something like a coherent spiritual attitude or *habitus*.[41] On the other hand, the practical level can, at times, also set some clear limitations to the possibilities of a multiple religiosity. The late Roger Corless who rather intensively lived as a Christian and a Buddhist (and even received formal ordinations in both traditions), admitted that due to a lack of compatibility not all religious life-forms can be combined at pleasure: 'If one were to take something like orthodox Judaism and orthodox Hinduism, it would be more difficult, and I leave others to speak about that, but it seems one would have a difficulty in knowing what to eat in that situation.'[42]

As much as it is true that not everything can be combined, it might however be equally true that there is perhaps much more room for compatibility than we would initially assume. In part we will simply have to wait to see which compatibilities may emerge from the future global interpenetration of religious traditions. Roger Corless reported how he, on the one hand, clearly separated his practice as a Buddhist from his practice as

---

40 This, of course, is the programme of the so-called 'World Theology'. Cf. P. Schmidt-Leukel (2005), pp. 486–9.

41 Cf. Schnell (2008) and Baier (2008).

42 http://www.innerexplorations.com/catew/9.htm.

a Christian, and yet, on the other hand, was eagerly waiting for
what might come out of the combination of both in one, that is
in his, person:

> I try, then, to practice Buddhist and Christian meditation on
> alternate days. I start on Sunday being the Christian day, and
> that means that Sunday, Tuesday and Thursday are Christian
> days, and then Monday, Wednesday and Friday are Buddhist
> days because in Buddhism there is no one day a week that is
> a special day. This leaves Saturday which is the time of confu-
> sion, or co-inherence. I try to practice meditation that I am
> still developing in which I invoke the presence, or realize my-
> self to be in the presence of the triune God, and the Triple
> Jewel. I invoke them first separately, and then I invoke them
> both together, and then allow them to meet, and then to sit
> in my heart, or my consciousness. . . . The next step will be
> reporting on what happens when these two traditions meet,
> and at this point I don't know what that will be.[43]

---

43 Ibid.

4

IN DEFENCE OF
SYNCRETISM

There is something like a consensus among the experts in the history of religions that all the major religious traditions in the world emerge from and develop through syncretistic processes, that is, they integrate to a varying extent elements from other religious traditions: 'every religion is syncretistic, since it constantly draws upon heterogeneous elements to the extent that it is often impossible for historians to unravel what comes from where'.[1]

However, it seems to be the case that this fact has acquired a new dimension today. To paraphrase Wilfred Cantwell Smith: The awareness of all the other religious traditions is now becoming part of the religious consciousness within each one of them.[2] This provokes two opposed reactions: On the one hand, the *fundamentalist* reaction of determining one's own religious identity (individually or collectively) in sharp contradistinction from all others, and on the other hand the *syncretistic* reaction of integrating and combining beliefs and practices from different religions. A recent representative survey on religiosity (*Religionsmonitor*) included, among others, the question of how strongly people endorse the statement 'Personally I draw on teachings

---

1 Peter van der Veer (1994), p. 208. For the syncretistic nature of Judaism, Christianity and Islam, see Eric Maroney (2006).

2 'The process of each is becoming conscious of the process of all.' W. C. Smith (1989), p. 37. On this issue, see the whole chapter pp. 21–44.

from various religious traditions.' In Germany this statement met with strong endorsement by 23 per cent and medium endorsement by another 20 per cent.[3] It is a well-known fact that, for example, a significant number of people in Christian countries engage in spiritual practices from Eastern religions like Yoga, Zen Meditation, Tai-Chi,[4] and that about 20 per cent of at least nominal Christians in the West believe in reincarnation.[5]

This, however, raises the question of how one should assess the phenomenon of syncretism from a normative perspective. Is this something to be welcomed or deplored? Should religious institutions and academic theology try to oppose and, as far as possible, resist syncretistic developments or is there a way of constructively accompanying and even benefiting from them? I will address the issue of how to assess syncretism from a primarily Christian point of view.

During the twentieth century the issue of syncretism has been discussed within Christianity mainly under the aspect of mission theology, in other words, the question was how much of cultural adaptation and accommodation was permissible without falling into an illegitimate syncretism. This discussion intensified with the emergence of inter-faith dialogue, which in part arose from the insight that non-Christian cultures could not be easily separated from non-Christian religions so that inculturation would also imply to some extent something like 'in-religionization' which requires dialogue. On the other hand, inter-faith dialogue was also perceived as a rival and threat to the missionary project. Blaming dialogue with the charge of syncretism became a weapon in the polemical defence of the missionary agenda. Today a new aspect has entered the debate: the growing presence of non-Christian religions in the predominantly Christian cultures and the corresponding phenomenon of increasing religious

---

3 Cf. *Religionsmonitor* (2008), pp. 40, 248.

4 According to the *Religionsmonitor*, meditation and meditational practice are strongly endorsed by 34% (USA) or 13% (UK) and medium endorsed by 23% (USA) or 15% (UK). Cf. *Religionsmonitor* (2008), p. 267.

5 The 2005 Gallup Poll for America (http://www.gallup.com/poll/16915/Three-Four-Americans-Believe-Paranormal.aspx) gave 20% and the Gallup Poll 'European Values', London 1983, 21%. Cf. Mischo (1992), p. 160.

bricolages and multireligious identity-formation, which I discussed in the previous chapter.

While the term 'syncretism' is often used in a neutral, predominantly descriptive fashion, it also frequently appears in a pejorative sense so that syncretism is seen 'as an illicit contamination, a threat or a danger, as taboo, or as a sign of religious decadence'.[6] While the more neutral, descriptive usage of the term is usually found within religious studies, its normative and/or contesting use is typically, but by no means exclusively, met within theology.[7] Syncretism has been explicitly rejected as a danger of interfaith encounter that is to be averted by such influential texts as the Second Vatican Council's 'Decree on Mission' (*Ad Gentes* 22) or the World Council of Churches' 'Guidelines on Dialogue' (nos. 24–29). The fear and condemnation of syncretism are so strong that they exert an inhibiting or paralysing impact on theological developments in the context of inter-faith encounter and inter-religious interpenetration.[8]

In the first part of this chapter I will introduce the case against syncretism by summarizing what I see as the four major points of criticism. In the second part I will present a qualified defence of syncretism in response to the respective charges. The aim of my defence is to contribute to a more open-minded, less fearful and indeed constructive theological approach to the phenomenon of syncretism.

The Case against Syncretism

The theological charge: corruption of truth

It was on 8 February 1991, at the second day of the Seventh General Assembly of the World Council of Churches in Canberra/Australia: The then comparatively unknown young Korean theologian Chung Hyun Kyung delivered what was to become one of the most famous and most controversial theological

---

6 Pye (2004), p. 59.
7 Cf. Droogers (1989).
8 Ibid., p. 21; Thomas (2002), p. 1086.

presentations of the twentieth century. In fact, it was more like a shamanic performance than an academic address. Accompanied by Korean and Australian Aboriginal dancers and by the sound of 'gongs, drums and clap sticks'[9] Hyun Kyung 'invoked the spirits of women and men oppressed through the ages' and also of the 'earth, air and water, raped, tortured and exploited by human greed'. In her very brief speech she called these spirits 'the icons of the Holy Spirit'. Towards the end of her address she said, 'For me the image of the Holy Spirit comes from the image of *Kwan In*', that is, the female form of the Buddhist Bodhisattva Avalokiteśvara, a representation of perfect and all-encompassing compassion, whom Hyun Kyung also called 'a feminine image of the Christ'.[10] The reaction of the audience was dramatic. As one participant put it: 'There was passionate applause, but there was also passionate silence.'[11] At the end of the conference representatives from the Orthodox Churches openly questioned their future relations with the World Council of Churches. The subsequent discussion continued for years and the main, repeatedly renewed, accusation was 'paganism and syncretism'.[12]

'Paganism and syncretism' is a combination of terms that summarizes in dense form the central theological concern about syncretism: It is seen as a 'corruption of the absolute truth'[13] because it allegedly results from the mingling of truth and lie, light and darkness, the divine and the demonic. 'Paganism' – in this context – indicates a theological view according to which the 'religions and cultures of "non-Christian" peoples came to be perceived as expressions of heathen unbelief and iniquitous superstition, the "outside world" as the kingdom of darkness . . .'. It is this view,

---

9 Cf. the report in the *New York Times*, 16 March 1991: http://query.nytimes.com/gst/fullpage.html?res=9D0CE3DA1E3AF935A25750C0A967958260&sec=&spon=&pagewanted=all.

10 The full text of the speech is available at http://www.cta-usa.org/foundationdocs/foundhyunkyung.html.

11 *New York Times* (16 March 1991) quoting Jean Caffey Lyles.

12 Cf. Ecumenical News International ENI 98-0560 (7 December 1998), http://www.eni.ch/assembly/0560.html. For a very differentiated and sensitive analysis of Hyun Kyung's speech and some reactions, see Friedli (1995), pp. 42–66.

13 Veer (1994), p. 209.

as Jerald Gort has rightly stated, that stands behind the 'massive fear of syncretism'.[14]

This is also clear from one of the most fervent tracts written against syncretism in the twentieth century. Willem Visser't Hooft, General Secretary of the World Council of Churches from 1948 to 1966, published his book *No Other Name: The choice between syncretism and Christian Universalism* in 1963. The passion with which the book was written is evident when Visser't Hooft claims that one of the lessons to be drawn from the New Testament is 'resistance to syncretism up to the point of martyrdom'.[15] He does not contest the legitimacy of theology using 'the thought-forms of the environment in which it operates'. This – so Visser't Hooft – is not 'syncretism'. 'A theology becomes syncretistic if and when in using such thought-forms it introduces into its structure ideas which change the meaning of biblical truth in its substance.'[16] The syncretistic distortion of biblical truth happens, according to him, whenever the complete uniqueness and the unique completeness of the divine revelation and redemption in Christ are drawn into question: 'To add something to Christ is really to take something away from him. Since he is the completely sufficient revelation, any attempt to improve the Gospel by the introduction of other revelations is really a denial of the gift of God.'[17] Post-Christian syncretisms are therefore to be seen as 'in fact pre-Christian'. They 'reject the liberation which the Gospel of Christ has offered to all men' and 'make man once more dependent on the impersonal cosmic forces'.[18]

Underlying Visser't Hooft's concept of syncretism is thus the idea of a radical discontinuity between the divine revelation in Christ and the non-Christian religions. In this regard, he is deeply influenced by the so-called 'dialectical theology' of Karl Barth and Hendrik Kraemer.[19] In this sense, syncretism – as a

---

14 Gort (1989), p. 37f.
15 Visser't Hooft (1963), p. 62, referring to the book of Revelation.
16 Ibid., p. 123.
17 Ibid., p. 60.
18 Ibid., p. 91.
19 Cf. Kraemer (1938), (1958).

corruption of biblical truth – is always given when the uniqueness and completeness of the divine revelation in Christ is drawn into question:

> Christianity understands itself not as one of several religions, but as the adequate and definitive revelation of God in history . . . Every time Christians use the word religion meaning something wider than Christianity, but including Christianity, they contribute to the syncretistic mood of our times . . .[20]

The spiritual charge: superficiality

In the same book Visser't Hooft adds another point of critique. Syncretism, he argues, does not really 'know of revelation'. 'It may speak of many revelations, but this very multiplicity shows that none of them are in a sense decisive and that none of them demand a definitive commitment.'[21] This alleged lack of serious commitment, that is the accusation of spiritual superficiality, is the second major charge that is frequently produced against syncretism – in particular within the context of the changing religious scene in the contemporary Western world. It was first directed against the so-called 'New Age', but by now it has become a much broader allegation related to the often stated tendency that traditional religion is more and more 'giving way' to a kind of free floating spirituality.[22] 'New Age' and contemporary alternative spirituality have been named 'hypersyncretic'[23] and 'a pot pourri of "spiritual" ideas offered in the religious supermarket'.[24] Accordingly, this spiritual attitude has been characterized as a 'pick and mix approach'[25] or as 'Religion à

---

20 Visser't Hooft (1963), p. 95.

21 Ibid., p. 89.

22 Cf. the title of the important study by Paul Heelas and Linda Woodhead (2005): *The Spiritual Revolution. Why Religion is Giving Way to Spirituality*. The conclusions of the book are based on an empirical survey in the British town of Kendal.

23 Sutcliffe (2000), p. 18.

24 Lyon (1993), p. 122.

25 Cf. Sutcliffe (2000), pp. 19, 28.

la carte'[26] – both images illustrating the 'centrality . . . of choice and consumerism'.[27]

At the centre of this critique are the individualism and eclecticism that are seen as typical for modern syncretism in general and New Age or alternative spirituality in particular. Individualism and eclecticism are often understood as reflecting the individualistic and subjectivist tendency of modernity and the consumerist nature of postmodernist capitalist societies. The 'tendency to an individualized experience of the spiritual . . . often slides' – according to Charles Taylor – 'toward the feel-good and the superficial', toward an 'undemanding spirituality' which goes for 'the more flaccid and superficial options'.[28] The consumerist attitude has, according to Jeremy Carrette and Richard King, paved the way for a much more dangerous and distorting process, which these authors describe as the 'silent takeover' of religion and spirituality by the values of an 'unrestricted market ideology' or 'capitalist spirituality' characterized by the 'atomization' of the individual, the cultivation of 'self-interest', 'utilitarianism', 'consumerism' and 'a distinct lack of interest in compassion'.[29]

A decisive part of the superficiality charge is the alleged lack of commitment. In 1994 the British sociologist Grace Davie coined the term 'believing without belonging'[30] in order to describe this aspect. Slightly more cautious, but with the same thrust, Steven Sutcliffe notes that in line with the '"supermarket" principle of contemporary spiritualities', '(c)ommitments . . . become serial, perhaps even multiple, but always provisional'.[31] The German theologian Christof Schorsch sees a logical connection between spiritual superficiality and syncretism. The indiscriminate combination and mingling of various elements from different religious traditions, without asking for their compatibility, presupposes – according to Schorsch – an uncritical, that is superficial, approach, which replaces the serious question for truth by

---

26 The term goes back to Bibby (1987).
27 Lyon (1993), p. 122.
28 Taylor (2003), p. 113.
29 Cf. Carrette and King (2006), pp. 128, 21, 114.
30 Davie (1994).
31 Sutcliffe (2000), p. 31.

subjective arbitrariness. 'To me' – says Schorsch – 'this seems to be a more or less urgent problem of all syncretisms.'[32] This takes me to my next point.

The philosophical charge: inconsistency

Hendrik Kraemer pointed out that 'syncretism', in its pejorative sense, does not just refer to 'the mixing of religious elements of different origin', but to a 'systematic attempt to combine, blend and reconcile inharmonious, even often conflicting, religious elements . . .'[33] And Robert Baird famously suggested that this is 'the only meaningful use of the concept' of syncretism: 'What could be objectionable in synthesizing religious elements which are not in conflict? It is the willingness to maintain contradictory elements side by side that has been objectionable.'[34] In a similar vein Nicholas Rescher has used the concept of syncretism for the 'attempt to "rise above the quarrel" of conflicting doctrines'.[35] The syncretist, according to Rescher, declines 'to be intimidated by mere inconsistence, he accepts mutually exclusive alternatives and revels in their very inconsistency, regarding it as a sign of the fecundity of the real'.[36] So defined, syncretism is – of course – self-refuting. For, as Rescher argues, if all positions are seen as equally valid, including the conflicting ones, then the syncretist would have to accept as equally valid also those positions which reject syncretism: 'in being over-generous, it is self-defeating'.[37] But one might very well ask whether Rescher's notion is not just an artificial construct. As Donald Baird has argued, the charge of combining inconsistent elements is usually one that is produced by an outsider, while the alleged syncretist does not see his system as 'devoid of coherence'.[38] The question for the outsider

---

32 'Und dies scheint mir ein mehr oder minder drängendes Problem aller Synkretismen zu sein.' Schorsch (1990), p. 143.
33 Kraemer (1958), p. 392.
34 Baird (2004), p. 53.
35 Rescher (1993), p. 90.
36 Ibid., p. 92.
37 Ibid., p. 95.
38 Baird (2004), p. 56.

is, therefore, whether one is inclined to accept or to reject the principles on which the alleged syncretist establishes the unity and coherence of apparently divergent elements.

It is at this point that Hendrik Vroom has further developed the charge of inconsistency. He too suggests an understanding of syncretism 'as the incorporation of incompatible beliefs from one religion by another'.[39] Vroom, however, assumes that nobody will consciously or deliberately believe openly contradictory things. The process of incorporating an originally incompatible element from a foreign religion will therefore be accompanied by a reinterpretation of the hitherto incompatible elements and this reinterpretation will necessitate a reconfiguration of the receiving belief system, if the reinterpreted elements are of some basic function within a systematic complex of beliefs. This process produces coherence but pays the price of modifying the meaning of certain beliefs and the identity of the previous belief configuration.[40] According to Vroom, contesting or rejecting syncretism is therefore legitimate for those who wish to retain the original form of certain beliefs and the identity of the original belief configuration.[41] The twist that Vroom adds to the inconsistency accusation leads me to the fourth and final charge.

The hermeneutical charge: loss of identity

According to Visser't Hooft the 'Christian Church' would lose its 'identity and integrity' if it participated in syncretistic activities.[42] For Gerald Gort, syncretism is legitimately rejected 'when two religions, belief systems, messages of salvation are merged in such a way that the essence of the one or the other or both is radically modified, changed into something different from what it was originally'.[43] The World Council of Churches' 'Guidelines on Dialogue' from 1979 specify the 'danger' of syncretism in

---

39 Vroom (1989), p. 27.
40 Cf. ibid., p. 34.
41 Cf. ibid., p. 35.
42 Cf. Visser't Hooft (1963), p. 11.
43 Gort (1989), p. 39.

three respects, which all vary the charge that it involves a loss of identity: Syncretism can be the attempt 'to create a new religion composed of elements taken from different religions' (no. 26). It can also result from attempts to express the gospel in forms taken from other cultures or religions if these lead to 'the compromising of the Gospel'. And finally, syncretism occurs when 'a living faith' is not interpreted 'in its own terms but in terms of another' (no. 27). Hendrik Kraemer contested what he called 'genuine syncretism', because in 'genuine syncretism' 'the imported or digested elements are essentially contrary to the authentic "soul" of the absorbing religion'.[44] But syncretism – whether it, consciously or unconsciously, takes the form of a symbiosis or a fully fledged amalgamation or whether it happens through acculturation, adaptation, assimilation or identification – always involves a 'transformation' or some 'shift into a new form'.[45] Whether this transformation is seen as a loss of identity or as its deepening, widening, new articulation or positive development, etc. depends entirely on how this identity is construed. This, of course, can happen in various ways: the 'authentic "soul"' of a religion that must not be changed can either be found on what Ulrich Berner[46] has called the 'element level' – that is, it can be identified with one or several religious elements of a doctrinal, practical, existential, etc. nature – or it can be found on the 'system level', that is, it could be identified with a specific configuration or a particular mode of configuring individual religious elements. However, if every reinterpretation – whether on the level of individual elements or on the level of systemic configuration – is already seen as a loss of identity, then the underlying concept of identity will be so static that any form of change would immediately imply a loss of identity. The hermeneutical charge of identity loss is therefore contingent on how much of hermeneutical latitude will be granted, and on how the boundaries are drawn that are meant to demarcate the 'authentic "soul"'. This

---

44 Kraemer (1958), p. 398.
45 Cf. Rudolph (2004), p. 82.
46 Cf. Berner (1991) and (2004), where he relates his model directly to the theological issue of determining 'identity'.

means that the fourth charge will to a significant degree derive from the assumptions underlying the first charge, that is, on the definition of something that is seen as *an*, or *the* essential truth of a particular faith.

A Qualified Defence

Before my response to each of these four charges, let me briefly clarify the nature of my defence. I am not suggesting that any of the four charges would never apply. So I do not believe that syncretism is always 'innocent'. What I deny is that the above-mentioned charges apply to syncretism as such, that is, on my view there can be and are forms of syncretism in relation to which the said charges are unjustified. However, whether syncretism is seen as innocent or not does not only depend on the kind of syncretism that we have in mind, but it also depends, to a significant extent, on the presuppositions of the accuser. The first charge is a particularly good example of this.

Against theological exclusivism

The accusation that syncretism as such involves a 'corruption of truth' derives entirely from the view that there is no salvific revelation outside Christianity.[47] But this theological exclusivism – whether in one of its traditional forms, or in the more recent forms of evangelical or 'dialectical' theology[48] – suffers from serious theological deficits.[49] This has become very clear throughout the theology of religions debate as it has been carried out within Christian theology over the last five decades. A radical

---

47 In the more recent debates, the close connection between exclusivism and the rejection of syncretism has been mentioned several times. As André Droogers put it: 'In situations of contact, exclusivist claims will give rise to accusations of syncretism . . . as their necessary complement.' Droogers (1998), p. 16. See also Berner (1991), p. 134.

48 See Visser't Hooft's (1963, p. 96) statement: 'Man's eternal destiny depends on his decision concerning the relation to this one Jesus of Nazareth.'

49 I discussed these extensively in Schmidt-Leukel (1997), pp. 99–165, and (2005), pp. 96–127.

exclusivism, according to which all non-Christians would inevitably go to hell, is at deep variance with the Christian belief in the perfect goodness of the divine reality, the 'all-encompassing salvific will of God', as Rahner called it. It is also at variance with the biblical testimony according to which Abraham, on the basis of his faith – which had not been an explicitly Christian faith – was justified in the eyes of God (Gal. 3.6–9).[50] More moderate forms of exclusivism, which acknowledge a chance of salvation for the individual non-Christian, will hardly be able to deny that the non-Christian religions have some relevance for the relationship of the individual non-Christian to God. But then this relevance might very well be of a positive kind, that is, the non-Christian religions may – to quote the Second Vatican Council – 'reflect a ray of that truth which enlightens all men and women' (*Nostra Aetate* 2).[51]

If it cannot be excluded that there is truth, goodness and holiness outside Christianity, then, as has been argued in the previous chapters, the process of receiving and adapting insights and practices from other religions into Christianity cannot *as such* be regarded as a mixing of truth and lie, good and evil, the sacred and the demonic.[52] This does not exclude that there could be forms of syncretism to which the charge indeed applies. I think the syncretism of the 'German Christians' who merged Christianity with elements from the Nazi ideology is indeed a fitting example of that sort. But there can be other forms of syncretism that do not mix light and darkness but combine truth with truth, good with good, and sacred with sacred. Whether we have reason to assume the one or the other needs to be discussed in every single case following the maxim of 1 Thessalonians 5.21: 'test

---

50 Even William Lane Craig, who produced one of the most sophisticated defences of exclusivism, had to admit that the righteous among the Old Testament figures constitute an unexplained exception to Christian soteriological exclusivism. Cf. Craig (1989), pp. 176, 186.

51 Flannery (1996), p. 571.

52 See also the position of Walter Sparn, who argues that inter-religious syncretism is justified, if that reality which Christians call 'God' is somehow present, although in different form, within the non-Christian religions. Cf. Sparn (1996), p. 283.

everything, hold fast to what is good'. Of course it remains true that we 'shall have no other gods before God' (Ex. 20.3). But what if the 'other gods' are not other gods but representations of other experiences with the same God?

The charge of a 'corruption of truth' is therefore unjustified if it is raised as a general accusation against all forms of syncretism. As such it is an expression of the aprioristic stipulation that there is no (salvific) truth of divine origin outside Christianity. It is only because syncretism allows for the opposite possibility that it is blamed in such an aprioristic and sweeping manner with the alleged corruption of truth.

The question of superficiality

Seeing exclusivism as a highly implausible and in the end untenable position implies that, for good theological reasons, one has to expect signs of the revealing and redeeming presence of the Divine throughout human history. 'All human history is *Heilsgeschichte*',[53] as Wilfred Cantwell Smith has put it, therein following closely the theological ideas of Karl Rahner. Let me repeat here what has been said in Chapter 3: If in the process of inter-religious encounter someone recognizes in some non-Christian religion what he or she understands as a sign of divine truth, as a manifestation of something good and holy, if someone hears the 'voice of God' in and through some element of a non-Christian religion, he or she is not entitled to reject this. From a spiritual perspective there is no choice. Just as Christian mission has assumed that non-Christians will hear God's call in and through the gospel and will then have the moral and spiritual obligation to respond positively to it, it will be equally true that Christians who hear God's call in and through a non-Christian religion must not close their hearts and minds. They will have to integrate the truth as recognized in the other with the truth as known from their own tradition. A lack of genuine commitment, a lack of serious commitment to God, would be to ignore, deny

---

53 Smith (1989), p. 172.

or resist God's voice – independent of where and how it has been heard. An integrative, syncretistic effort can thus be an act of true commitment to God and, once again, cannot be put under the general suspicion of superficiality.

Commitment to God may find its expression in the commitment to and practical involvement with some particular religious community or institution, but it cannot be simply identified with that. Living without a firm and/or permanent commitment on an institutional level is therefore not necessarily a sign of superficiality in one's relation to God, nor is an intensive commitment on the institutional level necessarily a sign of one's serious surrender to God.

On the institutional level, a syncretistic spirituality can take a range of different forms. There are examples of people who went to the utmost extreme in their attempt to combine within their own personal existence their commitment to God as it is mediated by two different religious traditions. Henry Le Saux, alias Swami Abhishiktananda, is without doubt someone who exerted himself in living up to the divine calling as he perceived it via the Christian and the Hindu traditions. Not everybody will be able to show a similarly radical level of seriousness. Seriousness and superficiality mark the two ends of a spectrum that can be found equally well within a syncretistic or an (at least currently) non-syncretistic spirituality. Superficiality is nothing that would necessarily result from or inevitably accompany syncretism.

That there are in fact forms of syncretism which give rise to the strong impression of superficiality, consumerism and hedonism, and turn spirituality into an object of cheap fun, exotic thrill, ridiculous absurdity, betrayal and self-betrayal, or just stupid triviality can hardly be denied. But a 'pick and mix approach' in matters of religion is not as such an expression of this phenomenon. To quote Swatos and Christiano:

> That people are more likely to want their religion a la carte does not necessarily mean that they are 'less religious.' The metaphor is helpful: first, people who order meals a la carte often actually spend more than they would have if they bought

a prix fixe meal. Of course, choosing a la carte does mean that people do not simply take whatever is dished out to them. However, it should not be assumed that as a result they will eat irresponsibly – three desserts and no veggies. People may just as often use the carte to choose wisely, passing over rich sauces and heavy starches.[54]

There are indeed signs of such a critical and self-critical sensitivity within the so-called new religious movements. Paul Heelas, for example, as a sympathetic observer of New Age, has argued that its greatest challenge for the future is 'to find ways of ensuring that it minimizes the trivialized and self-indulgent whilst at the same time not becoming too traditionalised or hierarchically authoritative'.[55] David Tacey, a committed defender of what he calls the 'spirituality revolution', acknowledges that popular spirituality is in danger of 'leaving out the hard bits, and emphasising those aspects that seem easy or desirable. The hard bits of spirituality would include sacrifice, discipline, commitment and dedication to others.'[56] From a psychological point of view, as Vassilis Saroglou has recently pointed out, the phenomenon of religious bricolage could be seen as a sign of an underlying hedonism that seeks to maximize 'the likelihood of symbolic benefits regarding spiritual needs'. But it could also be seen as an expression of 'religious maturity . . . that combines the maximum of flexibility with some coherence and integration'.[57]

It might be the case that the impression of a close connection between syncretism and superficiality derives from the fact that 'popular religion' is the field where syncretism is rife.[58] Tacey would then be right with his suspicion that it is the popularization that accounts for the superficiality.[59] Popular religion will always have its superficial elements, regardless of whether it is

---

54 Swatos and Christiano (1999), p. 222.
55 Heelas (1996), p. 214.
56 Tacey (2004), p. 141.
57 Saroglou (2006), p. 111f.
58 'Popular religion is of course a field in which syncretism is very much present . . . ' Droogers (2004), p. 226.
59 Cf. Tacey (2004), p. 141.

particularly syncretistic or not. And if the individualistic 'pick and mix approach' has an inclination towards the 'shallow and undemanding spiritual options', one should not forget, as Charles Taylor reminds us, 'the spiritual costs of various kinds of forced conformity: hypocrisy, spiritual stultification, inner revolt against the Gospel, the confusion of faith and power, and even worse'.[60]

Exploring consistency

But what about Christoph Schorsch's argument that superficiality results necessarily from the syncretistic tendency to combine heterogeneous and even conflicting elements? I do not deny that there are cases to which Schorsch's argument applies, cases where people do in fact mix religious elements without any concern for their compatibility and thus entirely on the basis of 'the individual's personal preferences varying as a function of time, mood, and context'.[61] In those cases, the total neglect of any concern for consistency would indeed be part of a gross superficiality. The question, however, is whether the philosophical charge, as we saw it in Rescher, is correct that syncretism as such is the vain attempt to synthesize the incompatible.

Dirk Mulder has rightly stated that the 'history of interreligious encounter and interpenetration provides ample evidence that "foreign elements" (in the sense of elements from a different religious, or possibly cultural, provenance) are certainly not always incompatible'.[62] But even if such a compatibility is not given – or at least not prima facie so – one can assume that syncretistic processes, whether on an individual or collective level, are driven by what Timothy Light has termed the 'Principle of Cognitive Integrity'. We may in fact hold contradictory beliefs, but

we operate as, and consider ourselves as, unitary wholes, and we talk about ourselves as single entities and about our

60 Taylor (2003), p. 114.
61 Saroglou (2006), p. 112.
62 Mulder (1989), p. 204.

societies as cohesions definable by shared characteristics. An individual who does not have this sense of integration and cannot behave as though it were there is termed abnormal. A society lacking such definition disintegrates.[63]

In this sense André Droogers is right in determining the primary function of syncretism as its inner drive to overcome contradictions by bringing about 'a new synthesis'.[64]

It has been primarily Robert Baird who has drawn attention to the fact that the individual syncretist, or syncretistic system, do not see themselves as being inconsistent. The only legitimate charge that would according to Baird allow a pejorative use of the term 'syncretism', namely the 'willingness to maintain contradictory elements side by side', therefore does not apply to the self-understanding of the syncretist. Baird cites, among others, Śaṅkara's Advaita Vedānta (and by implication Śaṅkara's neo-Hindu followers) as an example of a system that allegedly combines inconsistent elements. But as Baird points out, Śaṅkara applies certain principles in order to avoid inconsistency, in this case the principle of different levels of truth, so that what 'is true of one level is not necessarily true of another level'.[65] If one assumes that Śaṅkara's attempt is successful on his own premises, then the charge of inconsistency would be the result of the fact that the accuser does not share the premises on which consistency is achieved. The view that syncretism in general suffers from inconsistency may result from a neglect or rejection of the principles on which a syncretistic system establishes its synthesis. In any case, the accusation that syncretism is generally inconsistent seems to be unjustified. The issue of consistency needs to be discussed separately for every syncretistic process or system.

However, it would certainly overburden the ordinary believer to leave him or her with the full duty of checking the consistency or inconsistency of his or her various beliefs and practices. Although he or she does have some responsibility not to give

63 Light (2004), p. 341.
64 Droogers (1989), p. 17.
65 Baird (2004), p. 54.

oneself openly and easily to contradictory convictions, he or she will need to rely, to some extent, on the assessment of those who might be better equipped to pursue this question. I think it is one of the major tasks of future theology – and now I am speaking not only of Christian theology – to find out to what extent the religious traditions of the world share different though nevertheless compatible insights. Not every difference of belief or practice need necessarily imply incompatibility. The alleged conflict might only be an 'apparent rather than real' one,[66] depending on the respective meaning that the relevant beliefs and practices had and have. Wilfred Cantwell Smith has therefore suggested that supposedly conflicting religious truth claims should be taken as 'an invitation to synthesis'.[67] This is in line with his visionary programme of a 'world theology', that is, of a theology that will identify and embrace the insights enshrined in the whole religious history of humankind, 'a theology that will give intellectual expression to our faith, the faith of all of us . . .'[68] This programme is by nature syncretistic, and within Christianity the widespread fear of syncretism seems to be currently one of the major obstacles for not moving more decidedly and more energetically into this direction. This fear might be mostly nourished by the content of the fourth charge: the accusation that syncretism involves a loss of identity.

Creative transformation

My defence of syncretism against the charge of losing Christian identity rests on three elements. First, Christian identity must not be seen as something abstract and static. Any concept of Christian identity needs to do justice to the historical facts that there has never been anything like 'pure Christianity'[69] or the 'pure Gospel'[70] and that Christianity from its inception until the

---

66 Smith (1975), p. 156.
67 Ibid., p. 160.
68 Smith (1989), p. 125.
69 E.g. Boff (1985), p. 102: 'There is no such thing as a chemically pure Christian identity; it is always syncretized.'
70 See on this Wagner (1996), p. 79f.

present has undergone various transformations. Second, the fear of identity loss needs to be taken seriously and criteria need to be established by which one can constructively deal with that fear. And, third, it needs to be shown how syncretistic developments can bring about a transformation of identity that is not its loss but its deepening and widening.

Some theologians, among them M. M. Thomas,[71] Leonardo Boff,[72] Robert Schreiter[73] and Michael von Brück,[74] have undertaken efforts to rehabilitate syncretism – and if not the word then at least the substance.[75] In their attempts they emphasize that Christianity has always been syncretistic:[76] that during its early formation elements from various cultural and religious backgrounds entered into a synthesis and that it has undergone further syncretistic processes, in, for example, absorbing 'Hellenistic, Germanic, Celtic, Syrian "influences"'.[77] They emphasize the need for a continuous further development of Christianity resulting from its exchange with other cultures, religions and the ever changing context of each new century – a process which to their understanding inevitably involves reception, integration and adaptation and can thus be seen as syncretistic. They underline the need to actively engage concepts from a different religio-cultural context within the process of adaptation and they reject the WCC's view that a reinterpretation of one religion in terms of another would in itself constitute a negative form of syncretism.[78] In the development of a religious tradition it needs to reinterpret itself continuously and, as von Brück says, 'interpretation must match the context'[79] which today is often that of a non-Christian religion. Mutual employment of one's own

---

71 Thomas (1985).
72 Boff (1985).
73 Schreiter (1986), (1998).
74 Brück (1991).
75 Cf. Brück's (1991, p. 254) reservations regarding the term.
76 E.g. Boff (1985) p. 92: 'The Church as a structure is as syncretic as any other religious expression.'
77 Schreiter (1986), p. 151.
78 Cf. Thomas (1985), p. 396; Brück (1991), p. 252f.
79 Brück (1991), p. 253. See also Thomas (1985), pp. 392, 396.

concepts is thus inevitable. None of the four theologians, however, suggests anything like constructing a new religion. Christian identity needs to be retained, but also to be developed. They
admit the danger of losing Christian identity through syncretistic
processes;[80] they nevertheless understand this identity as something that can undergo forms of renewal and transformation,
which are not to be understood as a loss but as a deepening.[81]

So what are the criteria by which one can distinguish between
a syncretism that loses Christian identity and one that deepens it?
M. M. Thomas spoke about legitimate syncretism as a 'Christ-
centred syncretism'. But apart from saying that this implies 'a
new integration or adaptation based on Christian fundamen-
tals',[82] he remained rather unspecific. What are these 'fundamen-
tals' and who in Christianity is entitled to establish them? It was
in particular Leonardo Boff and Robert Schreiter who gave the
question of criteria a more detailed attention.

For Boff, Christian identity cannot be construed as a concept and should not be identified with doctrine. This, so Boff,
would not do justice to the fact of historical change. Identity
that can exist in and through historical change needs to be seen
'as an ever new, repeated, and preserved experience that is experienced in different ways depending on the age, place, social
class, and geopolitical situation'.[83] Christian identity, understood
as an experience, needs to be 'linked to the experience of Jesus
of Nazareth' in sharing his own experience 'of sonship and deep
fraternity'; for Jesus experienced the 'absolute Mystery' of God
as 'Father' and this 'universal paternity implies universal fraternity'.[84] Scripture and tradition do have a function in determining
which forms of syncretistic processes retain this basic form of
Christian identity and which do not. But the ground rule will
be 'that everything that aids liberty, love, faith, and theological

---

80 E.g. Boff (1985), p. 101; Schreiter (1998), pp. 65, 83.
81 Brück (1991), p. 254. Thomas (1985, p. 392) speaks of syncretistic 'synthesis' as almost 'eschatological'. Boff (1985, p. 99) asserts 'that syncretism
achieves the concrete essence of the Church'.
82 Thomas (1985), p. 392.
83 Boff (1985), p. 105.
84 All quotations: ibid., p. 102f.

hope represents true syncretism and incarnates the liberating message of God in history'.[85]

Robert Schreiter's criteria remain far more formal and are, in a sense, more addressed to the question of by whom and how Christian identity is established within the flux of time and the change of contexts. Broadly speaking, Schreiter's answer to this is: by the tradition and through the test of the time. In more detail this involves that any new contribution to the Christian tradition needs to cohere with the tradition (including its interpretation of Scripture), needs to prove itself in the context of Christian worship and Christian praxis, needs to stand the judgement of the various churches and needs to make a contribution for the sake of the wider Christianity.[86] As Schreiter says, these criteria 'have to work in consort'.[87] But as he made clear in a more recent review, they do contain a considerable degree of indeterminacy. The first criterion of cohesion with the tradition requires that one has a theory about 'what constitutes legitimate development in the articulation of faith'.[88] To my mind, this amounts to begging the question. Similarly the two final criteria, the judgement of the churches and making a positive contribution to wider Christianity, imply a certain 'theology of the Church and of the churches'.[89] But as Schreiter admits, an ecclesiology that would be acceptable to all the existing churches is by no means evident. Schreiter's criteria are to a significant extent more like rules, which refer the question of identity to the wider Christian discourse and thereby defer it. This is in line with his statement that the issue of Christian identity in connection with new syncretistic developments is one that will have to be resolved by standing the test of the time: 'I . . . use syncretism to describe the formation of religious identity, always with the understanding that at times the new identity under examination will be in accord with, and even enrich, the religious tradition; and that at other times,

---

85 Ibid., p. 104.
86 Schreiter (1986), pp. 117–21.
87 Ibid., p. 117.
88 Schreiter (1998), p. 82.
89 Ibid., p. 83.

it will not be in accord, and so must be rejected.'[90] 'The outcome
will always bear surprises . . .'[91] The closest he comes to a more
substantial definition of Christian identity, as has been suggested
by Boff, is when he speaks of the proving in Christian practice:
'"By their fruits shall you know them" has remained one of the
oldest and clearest ways for discerning Christian identity.'[92]

In a very recent discussion, Reinhold Bernhardt also subscribes
to an understanding of Christian identity as a process, which, on
the one hand, emerges constantly and in ever-new ways from
the persistent discourse within Christianity, but, on the other
hand, has its normative focus in the continuous reference to the
spirit of Jesus. Christian identity would be lost when and where
something is in clear contradiction to the spirit of Jesus, that is,
where it is at variance with freedom and love and cultivates the
opposite.[93]

Yet the demonstration that Christian identity is something
that can be compatible with change, so that transformation is
not in itself a loss of this identity, is not enough to reply to the
charge of syncretism as an identity loss. One needs to postulate
one further point, and this is that Christian identity can in fact
be enriched, can be deepened and widened, by incorporating insights from other religions. In order to do so, one needs to go
back to the argument against exclusivism. If there is a wealth
of genuine spiritual insight among all the peoples of the world
– a wealth which reflects humanity's responses to divine self-
communication – then each of these insights has the potential of
enriching and complementing all others. This, it can be argued,
is in line – and not in conflict – with Jesus' experience of 'universal paternity' and 'universal fraternity', to quote Boff again. The
best way, however, will be to point out concrete examples. The
Christian understanding of love, for instance, can be enriched by
the understanding that loving commitment is not at odds with
non-selfish detachment, but that both qualities – the one at the

---

90 Ibid., p. 64.
91 Ibid., p. 83.
92 Schreiter (1985), p. 119.
93 Cf. Bernhardt (2008), (2005). Similarly Sparn (1996), p. 282.

centre of Jesus' spirit, the other at the centre of the Buddha's spirit – can mutually qualify and enhance each other.[94] What is crucial in this final dimension of my defence of syncretism is the insight that Christian identity in itself is nothing complete, but something that is open to further and future completion by the integration of elements from other religious traditions.

Eric Maroney has described the conflict between orthodoxy and syncretism as one between stasis and flexibility. Orthodoxy is 'anti-syncretism' because of its inflexibility, while syncretism is markedly flexible and a response to 'change and crisis'.[95] But Timothy Light has famously argued that 'today's orthodoxy is the result of yesterday's mixing, and it has never been otherwise'.[96] If this is correct, then there is hope that from today's mixing some new and renewed orthodoxy will emerge.

---

94 Cf. Chapters 6 and 7 of this volume and Schmidt-Leukel (2005b).
95 Maroney (2006), p. 168.
96 Light (2004), p. 345.

5

COMPARATIVE THEOLOGY

Limits and Prospects

An Alternative to the Theology of Religions?

In 1995, Francis Clooney published his impressive survey on 'Comparative Theology' in which he summarily reviewed more than forty books – all taken as more or less examples of 'comparative theology'. In his opening sentence Clooney introduced 'comparative theology' as a new development, as 'an exciting and quickly developing field, and a relatively uncharted one'.[1] In the same year the American journal *Horizons* published an article by James Fredericks in which he presented 'comparative theology as an alternative to a theology of religions'.[2] In 2001 Norbert Hintersteiner recommended 'comparative theology' as the most suitable theological approach to the plurality of religions and reiterated Fredericks' claim of comparative theology as an alternative to exclusivist, inclusivist and pluralist theologies of religions.[3] In 2002, another young German Roman Catholic theologian, Klaus von Stosch, joined Hintersteiner and demanded – in the face of an alleged insoluble 'grunddilemma' of every theology of religions – a transition to 'comparative theology'.[4] Meanwhile, in 1999, James Fredericks published his monograph

---

1 Clooney (1995), p. 521.
2 Thus the subtitle of Fredericks (1995).
3 Hintersteiner (2001), pp. 318–20.
4 Stosch (2002), p. 294.

Faith among Faiths, where he sharpened his earlier attacks on theology of religions and at the same time increased his praise of comparative theology as the effective rescue. 'Currently', says Fredericks, 'the quest for an adequate theology of religions is at an impasse,'[5] which he feels is primarily an 'impasse over the pluralistic model'.[6] But proclaims Fredericks: 'In comparative theology, Christians will find a way beyond the current impasse in the theology of religions.'[7]

Given these strong assertions my subsequent remarks amount to some *bad news* and some *good news*. To deliver the bad news first, I'm going to demonstrate that there is neither a way out of the theology of religions nor any theological alternative to the three basic options of exclusivism, inclusivism or pluralism. The only escape from this would be in avoiding the type of questions that a theology of religions must address. But, as I will try to show, if 'comparative theology' is really taken as genuine *theology* and at the same time remains seriously *comparative*, it cannot avoid these questions. On the contrary, their urgency will become even more strident. Consequently, my bad news for Fredericks and his German followers is that 'comparative theology' will not lead out of the impasse of theology of religions but straight into it. The liberating good news, however, is that the theology of religions is not at an impasse at all. Quite contrary to what Fredericks holds, the pluralist option in particular may be seen as a promising path into the theological future, a way ahead to which comparative theology can and should make an essential contribution.

First, I will explain briefly how I understand the theology of religions and its three basic options. Second, I will show why comparative religion cannot function as an alternative to the theology of religions. And in my third and final point, I will indicate in what sense comparative theology can contribute to the theology of religions in general and to a pluralist version in particular.

5 Fredericks (1999), p. 8.
6 Ibid., p. 10.
7 Ibid., p. 10.

Theology of Religions

The term 'theology of religions' usually refers to the Christian theological reflection on the relationship between Christianity and other religions. In a broader sense, however, it could designate an analogous reflective activity in each of the religions. Basically, a theology of religions – Christian or non-Christian – must answer two questions: first, how to interpret the claims/beliefs of other religions in face of the claims/beliefs of one's own religion, and second, how to interpret the claims/beliefs of one's own religion in face of the claims/beliefs of the others. When I say, 'interpret', I take interpretation in the broad sense that encompasses understanding *and* assessment, so that this kind of interpretation asks not only for the correct meaning but also for the potential truth of the respective claims or beliefs.

The two basic questions of a theology of religions belong intrinsically together because they are mutually conditioning. To answer one of them has decisive effects on answering the other. Thus there are not really two questions, but a double question – much like an ellipse with two equally important foci. I am not saying that the 'theology of religions' is nothing more than the effort to answer this double question. Certainly there are many more related questions and sub-questions. But nonetheless, the answer to this double question is of central and basic significance. That is, in dealing with any of the related questions, one will have to face, sooner or later, this crucial double question.[8]

In order to address the double question, it is not necessary to start with a definition of 'religion'. Whatever 'religions' might be or do, they certainly entertain some beliefs – usually expressed through propositional claims but also deeply embedded in their ritual, moral, artistic, etc. practice. Among these beliefs we find factual claims, that is, assertions about what exists or what does not exist, value judgements, and practical instructions. One central religious belief, as William Christian framed it, is that there is 'something more important than anything else in the

---

8 For a broader analysis of various tasks of a Christian theology of religions, see Schmidt-Leukel (2005), pp. 31–61.

universe'.⁹ While this may be true even for the so-called 'secular religions' (the great ideologies of the nineteenth and twentieth centuries), the traditional religions assume that this 'something', which is more important than anything else in the world, is a transcendent reality; that is, it is not one of the finite realities of this world. In one way or another, religions claim to have some form of knowledge or revelation of this transcendent reality. And they not only make the value judgement that this reality is the highest good, but they also instruct people to live their lives in such a way that it properly reflects the utmost importance of ultimate reality. Let us call such a proper orientation of life, and the further eschatological hopes connected with such a life, 'salvation'. Then we can say that religions, at least the traditional ones, claim – each in its own way – to mediate a salvific knowledge or revelation of transcendent reality.

Let us now call this claimed property 'P', so that P = mediation of a salvific knowledge of ultimate/transcendent reality. Thus 'P' is a property of a religious community or tradition if this tradition not only claims such a mediation but claims so rightly, that is, if this claim is true.

In so far as the basic double question of the theology of religions is focused on the issue of religious truth claims, it can be reformulated as: Is 'P' a property of religions?

Then what follows are these logical alternatives: Either P is not a property of any religion (because there is no such thing as a transcendent reality, so that all the respective claims are false) or P can be found among the religions. If P is a property of religions, we can ask further whether P is realized only once or more than once. And if P is realized in more than one religion, we can ask whether there is something like a singular maximum of this realization or not. This leads us to a fully disjunctive classification with four different options: (0) *Atheism/Naturalism*: Salvific knowledge of a transcendent reality is mediated by none of the religions (because a transcendent reality does not exist). (1) *Exclusivism*: Salvific knowledge of a transcendent reality

---

9 Christian (1964), p. 60.

is mediated by only one religion (which will be naturally one's own). (2) *Inclusivism*: Salvific knowledge of a transcendent reality is mediated by more than one religion (not necessarily by all of them), but only one religion among them mediates it in a uniquely superior way (which again will be naturally one's own). (3) *Pluralism*: Salvific knowledge of a transcendent reality is mediated by more than one religion (not necessarily by all of them), and there is none among them whose mediation of that knowledge is superior to all the rest.

Let me now add some clarifications: (1) As I said previously, if the four options are so defined, we have a classification that is fully disjunctive and therefore *logically comprehensive*. That is, every option within the theology of religions (in so far as it entails an answer to the opening question) can be subsumed under one of the four definitions and there is no further option left. Therefore one needs to decide for one of them. (2) The first option – that is the *atheist/naturalist* one – can be excluded as a religious or theological option. It is a logical possibility, and, no doubt, a realistic one. But because it rests on the denial of a transcendent reality, it cannot be a theological option. Therefore a theology of religions has to decide between the three remaining options. (3) Every religion can theoretically define its relationship to the other religions by one of the three remaining options; that is, the suggested taxonomy is not exclusively confined to a Christian theology of religions. However, as a classification of *Christian theological options*, it would take something like the following shape:

Christian *exlusivism* would mean that saving revelation can be found only within Christianity and not within any other religion. This does not necessarily entail that all non-Christians are lost. Soft or moderate exclusivists could hold that there are ways by which God can save non-Christians as individuals (for example, through a post-mortem encounter with the gospel). But according to my definition, Christian exclusivism would deny any positive salvific role of the non-Christian religions.

In contrast to this Christian *inclusivism* would hold that non-Christian religions sometimes entail elements of revelation and grace that are capable of supporting a salvific life. But since, according to Christian inclusivism, all salvation is finally through Christ, the revelation to which Christianity testifies is, in a unique sense, superior to any other forms of knowledge of God, which, when compared to the Christian revelation, remain necessarily deficient, fragmentary, incomplete, implicit, obscure, etc.

Christian *pluralism* would hold that some other religions – usually at least the major world religions – are in a theological sense on a par with Christianity: According to Christian pluralism, they testify to the same ultimate transcendent reality, despite the different forms this testimony takes, and they do so with the same genuine authenticity and equal salvific potential.

In my subsequent reflections I will use the terms *exclusivism*, *inclusivism* and *pluralism* in the sense of these definitions only. Let me clarify: By *exclusivism* I do not mean *any type* of exclusive claim. Every truth claim is in some sense exclusive, for it excludes the truth of its logical opposite. To criticize such an exclusivism would be intellectual suicide, because a proposition that would not exclude anything would no longer have any specific meaning and would therefore become unintelligible. In this sense, therefore, each of the four defined options would be exclusivist.

Further, by *inclusivism* I do not refer to cases wherein statements about or assessments of another religion are expressed with recourse to the ideas, values, and terminology stemming from the religious tradition of the person who makes these statements. It is true that the serious study of another religion may lead to a significant widening and change of one's own religious horizon and eventually to a transformed terminology. But it also seems to be a hermeneutical law that every process of understanding and interpreting something new has to start from one's own existing conceptual framework. In this *hermeneutical* sense, each of the four defined positions would be inclusivist.

Finally, by *pluralism* I do not mean the relativistic feeling that all religions or even all world-views or value systems are somehow equally good (or equally bad) – a conclusion drawn from the premise that there would be no way of making any universal judgement at all. According to such a loose and indeed undisciplined understanding of 'pluralism', none of the four defined positions would be pluralistic. In contrast, I understand the pluralist option precisely as a value judgement of other religions – a judgement that acknowledges theologically their equal validity as ways of salvation. Moreover, *pluralism* as a distinctive option within a theology of religions is different from the theories of political or social pluralism. Within a pluralistic society there will always be a wide plurality of all kinds of world-views and religious ideas and systems. And among all these various views there will always be some that from a 'theology of religions' perspective are considered to be false, others being regarded as insufficient, and again some others that could be seen as different but equally valid. Therefore, the ethos of a pluralist society does not require a pluralistic theology of religions but the virtue of tolerance; that is, the willingness to tolerate, as far as possible, those world-views or religions one disapproves of. A pluralistic theology of religions is therefore not an expression of toleration but of appreciation. And, as such it cannot and may not replace the important social virtue of tolerance.[10]

Limits of Comparative Theology

The various theological approaches labelled as 'comparative theology' by no means share exactly the same understanding or the same concept of 'comparative theology'. What they have in common is marked by two features: first, the pursuit of inter-religious comparison – usually embedded into inter-faith dialogue – and second, the conviction that this is an adequate and fruitful form of doing theology in a multi-religious context. I think that Clooney hits the mark when he presents comparative theology as 'the doing of constructive theology from and after comparison'.[11]

The *theological* nature of the comparative activity is what distinguishes comparative theology from the purely phenomenological approach of 'comparative religion' and from its more recent sociologically oriented versions running frequently under

10 Cf. Chapter 2 above.
11 Clooney (1995), p. 522. See also Clooney (1993), pp. 4–7.

the name 'religious studies'. According to Keith Ward, comparative theology 'enquires into ideas of the ultimate value and goal
of human life, as they have been perceived and expressed in a
variety of religious traditions'. And it 'differs from what is often
called "religious studies", in being primarily concerned with the
meaning, truth, and rationality of religious beliefs, rather than
with the psychological, sociological, or historical elements of religious life and institutions'.[12]

Quite similarly, Francis Clooney states that '(a)s theology, comparative theology consists most basically in faith seeking understanding; its ultimate horizon can be nothing less than knowledge
of the divine, the transcendent', while it 'is marked by its commitment to the detailed consideration of religious traditions
other than one's own'.[13] James Fredericks chimes in with Ward
and Clooney by affirming that '(d)oing theology comparatively
means that Christians look upon the truths of non-Christian traditions as resources for understanding their own faith'.[14]

Thus the broad theological nature of comparative theology
consists primarily in its explicit interest in the question of truth.
However, there are some noteworthy differences among the comparativists when it comes to the issue of confessional theology.
According to Ward, comparative theology does not require a
'tradition-neutral investigator',[15] and will always be undertaken
'from a particular perspective'.[16] But, says Ward, comparative
theology should be 'prepared to revise beliefs if and when it comes
to seem necessary'.[17] In this regard, Clooney and Fredericks are
far more reluctant. On the one hand, Clooney does affirm that
comparative theology 'is a theology deeply changed by its attention to the details of multiple religions', but on the other hand, he
says, 'the comparativist remains rooted in one tradition'.[18] And

---

12 Ward (1994), p. 40.
13 Clooney (1995), p. 521.
14 Fredericks (1999), p. 140.
15 Ward (1994), p. 47.
16 Ward (1994), p. 49. See also Ward (2000), p. 339.
17 Ward (1994), p. 48.
18 Clooney (1995), p. 522. See also his slightly cautious remarks on Ward's
approach in Clooney (2002), pp. 25–7.

as Clooney makes clear, this sets strong and narrow limits to any possible transformation or revision of that tradition.[19] Similarly, Fredericks speaks about the 'demanding and transforming truths of other religions'[20] and 'the power of non-Christian religions to inspire new insights within us'.[21] But he warns against the danger of 'losing our commitment to the Christian tradition' and recommends like Clooney 'to remain rooted' in it.[22] Fredericks' advice is to live with the 'tension between commitment to Christianity and openness to other religious truth' and to 'resist the temptation to overcome this tension'.[23] Thus comparativists agree that the comparative reflection is undertaken from within a particular perspective and starts from a specific religious or confessional background. But they disagree on the question of how much that perspective – and thereby one's own religious background – may legitimately be transformed or revised through and as a result of the comparative reflection.

The importance of this observation will become clear when we ask about the relation between comparative theology and the theology of religions. I do not want to deny that both are different. But I strongly dispute Fredericks', von Stosch's and perhaps Hintersteiner's claim that comparative theology constitutes a real alternative to the theology of religions that could effectively avoid any of their three basic options. A clear difference between theology of religions and comparative theology is that comparative theology is dedicated to specific religious traditions and the comparison of particular texts, thinkers, ideas, rituals, etc., while theology of religions deals more with the various theological interpretations of religious diversity in general. So Fredericks has a point in stating that:

Unlike theologies of religions, comparative theology does not start with a grand theory of religion in general that claims to

---

19 See particularly Clooney (1990).
20 Fredericks (1999), p. 170.
21 Ibid.
22 Ibid.
23 Ibid.

account for all religions . . . Instead of theories about religion in general, comparative theologians are interested in studying other religions on their own terms and then exploring their own Christian faith using what they have learned about the other religions.[24]

This concreteness, that is, the specific interest in particular religions and topics, is indeed what distinguishes comparative theology from the theology of religions. And this difference marks its strength as well as its limits. The comparative theologian may start her work without any elaborated general theory of religion or without any explicit option of a theology of religions (but she might very well harbour something of that sort as an undeveloped, implicit background assumption). However, the systematic and consequent pursuit of the comparison – if it is carried out theologically, that is with a prior interest in the truth and value of the investigated religious ideas or beliefs – will sooner or later lead to a point where the question of the relationship between the non-Christian and respective Christian beliefs becomes unavoidable. Then there will emerge quite naturally the four options that either both beliefs are wrong, or that one is true and the other wrong, or that one is more adequate or comprehensive and therefore more true than the other, or that both are different but equally true. However, these four options are nothing more than the basic options within a theology of religions. And since for logical reasons there is no further option left, the comparative theologian will then have to make her choice and so enter the field of the theology of religions.[25]

As Clooney has admitted from his own experience, there is

---

24 Frederick (1999), p. 167f. See also von Stosch (2002), p. 307: 'Komparative Theologie bemüht sich nich um eine religionstheologische Vogelperspektive, sondern wendet sich dem konkreten Einzelfall und damit spezifischen Feldern der Auseinandersetzung zu. Es geht ihr nicht um Allgemeinaussagen über die Wahrheit einer oder mehrerer Religionen, sondern um das Hin- und Hergehen zwischen konkreten religiösen Traditionen angesichts bestimmter Problemfelder, um Verbindendes und Trennendes zwischen den Religionen neu zu entdecken.'
25 For an extensive discussion of the three options within a Christian theology of religions, see Schmidt-Leukel (1997) and (2005).

a point when the comparison of, for example, certain Vedānta and Christian texts will unavoidably lead to the confrontation between the Vedāntist claim that all salvation comes through knowledge of Brahman and the Christian claim that all salvation is brought about through Christ.[26] Certainly, it is not at all immediately evident whether these two claims are compatible or incompatible – and if so how. But when the comparativist starts to discuss this question she is doing theology of religions. If she attempts to avoid the kinds of questions that arise in the theology of religions (because 'comparative theology' is claimed to be the viable alternative), she must regard her work as complete whenever conflicting, or apparently conflicting, claims are laid bare. If that is the case, then she has not proceeded beyond the classical aim of 'comparative religion', namely, a purely phenomenological comparison without pursuing the issue of truth. Therefore, I hold that there is no way for comparative theology to remain comparative and genuinely theological and at the same time to avoid the type of questions discussed in the theology of religions. Avoiding them would mean that either comparative theology loses its theological character and falls back into comparative religion, or, from a certain point onwards, it ceases to continue its comparative reflection and reverts to the reiteration of confessional standpoints. In neither way would comparative theology achieve its envisioned goal. Consequently, it is not theology of religions that leads to an impasse. On the contrary, this is precisely the fate of any form of comparative theology that would deliberately close itself off from the type of discussion carried out in the theology of religions by presenting its approach as an alternative. And I cannot avoid the impression that Fredericks' suggestion that we should live with the unsolved tension between confessional commitment and inter-religious openness is nothing more than advice to nestle in and make oneself complacent at the very dead end of this impasse. There is, however, absolutely no need for comparative theology to refrain from entering the theology of religions. This leads me to my final point.

---

26 Clooney (1993), pp. 189ff.

Prospects of Comparative Theology

Not all comparativists share Fredericks' views of comparative theology as an alternative to the theology of religions. In Ward's numerous and extremely valuable contributions to comparative theology,[27] both forms of theological reflection go hand in hand, and his own standpoint oscillates slightly between an open form of inclusivism and – as he himself once called it – a 'convergent pluralism'.[28] With a few reservations, something similar could be said about the pioneering efforts of Ninian Smart and Steven Konstantine.[29] Francis Clooney, too, maintains that there is 'a path from *comparative theology* to the *theology of religions*',[30] and in his aforementioned review article on 'comparative theology'[31] he points to all the major publications on the theology of religions that were published in the period covered by his review as examples. Clooney even holds that comparative theology 'best eventuates in the inclusivist position'.[32] This is indicative of what I regard as one of the distinguishing prospects of comparative theology: by way of theologically comparing specific Christian and non-Christian beliefs, that is, by carefully investigating the hermeneutical range of their possible meaning and the epistemological range of their possible truth, the comparativist can and should attempt to argue in favour of one of the three basic options of the theology of religions. Through contributing concrete and specific case studies, comparative theology can help to increase or decrease the overall plausibility of an exclusivist, inclusivist or pluralist view.[33]

Concerning the relationship between comparative theology

---

27 Cf. Ward (1987), (1991), (1994), (1996), (1998), (2000).

28 Ward (1991), p. 175.

29 Smart and Konstantine (1991).

30 Clooney (1990), p. 72.

31 Clooney (1995).

32 Clooney (1990), p. 66; similarly ibid., pp. 64, 67, 72ff. Also Clooney (1993), p. 195f.

33 Thus I agree with Clooney's remark on the three options of a theology of religions that in order to 'be taken seriously in a comparative context, each will have to be rewritten with a far great [sic] commitment to detail and examples'. Clooney (1993), p. 194.

and theology of religions, Clooney has emphasized 'that the sequence is important, and that . . . the theology of religions comes only *later* . . .'.[34] That is, 'after comparative reading, a transition from textual/comparative theology to a theology of religions is made'.[35] I agree that this is broadly a correct description. However, the compared Christian and non-Christian texts or beliefs might already entail certain explicit or implicit assumptions about other religions. And if the comparativist starts her work from a specific religious or confessional tradition, it is doubtless the case that she, as part of her own religious background, will already be influenced by those religious convictions that have their own implications on the truth claims entailed in the beliefs of others. To bracket or exclude the implications of one's own religious presuppositions would once again mean to fall back into the business of a purely phenomenological comparison – and apart from that, there are good reasons to doubt whether such a bracketing is possible at all.[36]

In any case, if comparative theology wants to be more than comparative religion, then the comparative reflection may very well lead to a point where some of one's own religious presuppositions are seriously drawn into question, so that revision and change of these presuppositions might seem unavoidable, and the only way one could remain rooted in one's own tradition would be to suggest a significant transformation of that tradition. This is exactly what has happened to a number of Christian pluralists, particularly to those who arrived at a pluralist position after a long, intensive and utterly serious dialogue with non-Christian religions.[37] Addressing Clooney and Fredericks, Paul Knitter has therefore rightly remarked, 'While we have to be aware that we bring our theological baggage to the journey of dialogue, that doesn't mean that during the journey we may not have to rearrange, or even dispose of, some of that

---

34 Clooney (1990), p. 66.
35 Ibid. See also Clooney (1993), p. 193f.
36 Cf. Panikkar (1978), pp. 39–52; Heelas (1978); Wiebe (1981); Schmidt-Leukel (1992), pp. 106–41.
37 See on this also Schmidt-Leukel (2008b).

baggage.'[38] If proponents of comparative theology exclude, at the outset, the possibility of revision and significant transformation as a potential result of their comparative work,[39] or if they denounce such transformation as distortion,[40] then the seriousness of their endeavours as a pursuit of truth is questionable. But if comparative theology is open to revision and significant transformation, it can then make significant contributions to the type of future theology that pioneers of religious pluralism have designated as 'World Theology'[41] or 'Global Theology'[42] – that is, as Wilfred Cantwell Smith has described it, 'a theology that will interpret the history of our race in a way that will give intellectual expression to our faith, the faith of all of us, and to our modern perception of the world'.[43]

If comparative theology holds to this vision, it must keep in mind that the wider context of every particular and therefore necessarily limited comparison is nowadays a global context. Comparison should thus be carried out with the awareness that the whole picture must not only be a multi-religious one, but one that also takes into account the important insights resulting from modern scientific world-views. Once more, I think, Keith Ward has got the agenda for comparative theology right. So, in conclusion, let me quote his programmatic words:

> The religious situation of our world requires an attempt, at least on the part of those committed to reflection, to interpret traditional beliefs in the light of our ever-growing knowledge of the material cosmos, and in awareness of the many differing traditions of belief that exist about the nature of human existence in the world. One needs to ask how far traditional formulations of belief in any tradition may need to be revised

---

38 Knitter (2002), p. 236.

39 See, for example, von Stosch (2002), p. 297f, for whom the revisionist elements of a pluralist approach are sufficient to rule it out as a Christian theological option.

40 Cf. Fredericks (1999), p. 169.

41 Smith (1989).

42 Hick (1990), pp. 29–34.

43 Smith (1989), p. 125.

because of new scientific knowledge, and how much they may reflect an ignorance of other traditions of belief that may either be complementary to or be highly critical of them.[44]

---

44 Ward (2000), p. 339.

Part Two

TRANSFORMING
CHRISTIANITY

6

BUDDHISM AND CHRISTIANITY

Antagonistic or Complementary?

Some Current Sidelights

In one of his more recent publications the renowned sociologist Peter Berger presents his personal interpretation of the Christian creed. In the second chapter, where Berger speaks about belief in God, he describes his understanding of the Christian faith by contrasting it with the Buddhist doctrine of the three marks of existence (*tilakkhaṇa*), that is the teaching that all things are impermanent (*anicca*), unsatisfactory or suffering (*dukkha*) and not the self (*anattā*). According to Berger the 'Biblical faith' can be affirmed

> in a threefold *no* to the Buddha's Three Universal Truths: All reality is *not* impermanence, because at its heart is the God who is the plenitude of being in time and eternity. All reality is *not* suffering, because God's creation is ultimately good and because God is acting to redeem those parts of creation, especially humanity, where this goodness has been disturbed. And all reality is *not* non-self, because the self is the image of God, not because it is itself divine but because it exists by virtue of God's address.[1]

1 Berger (2004), p. 30.

Thus, in Berger's view, Christianity and Buddhism stand in a directly antagonistic relationship. The alleged contrast between them is seen as so deep that any similarities or apparent commonalities are profoundly affected and thereby ultimately proved to be illusory. For example, the contrast between the Christian affirmation of the self and – as Berger sees it – the Buddhist denial of the self

> helps to see the fatuous character of some recent efforts to construct a universal ethic in which Buddhist 'compassion' is equated with Christian *agape*. I would argue that, despite some similarities on the level of practical activities, the two have very little to do with each other, indeed are almost opposites.[2]

There is no doubt that with the 'recent efforts to construct a universal ethic' Berger refers to the so-called Global Ethic-Project.[3] This project is primarily, but in no way exclusively, fostered by the World Parliament of Religions and supported by a number of religious thinkers and authorities from various religious traditions,[4] for example, from the Christian side most vigorously by Hans Küng.[5] According to the self-understanding of those who are in favour of the project, a global ethic is not something that needs to be 'constructed' – as Berger says – but something that already exists within the religious traditions of the world and only needs to be brought to common and public awareness.[6] In denying – at least for Buddhism and Christianity – the existence of profound ethical commonalities and in denigrating the whole project as 'fatuous . . . efforts' Berger makes it sufficiently clear that his portrayal of the relationship between Buddhism and Christianity has significant practical consequences which do not

---

2 Ibid., p. 28.
3 Küng and Kuschel (1998).
4 Cf. Küng (ed.) (1996).
5 See Küng (1991) and (1997).
6 'A global ethic seeks to work out what is already common to the religions of the world now despite all their differences over human conduct, moral values and basic moral convictions.' Küng and Kuschel in their Introduction to Küng and Kuschel (1998), p. 7f. See also ibid., p. 18.

lie in the realm of co-operation but rather in the more traditional arena of competition.

In choosing Buddhist compassion (*karuṇā*) and Christian love (*agapé*) for illustrating the alleged contrast, Berger might also be indirectly referring to George Lindbeck's influential book *The Nature of Doctrine,* in which the American lutheran theologian Lindbeck claimed that 'Buddhist compassion' and 'Christian love . . . are not diverse modifications of a single fundamental human awareness, emotion, attitude, or sentiment, but are radically . . . distinct ways of experiencing and being oriented toward self, neighbor, and cosmos'.[7] While Berger affirms that his understanding is despite some qualifications 'most . . . at home in the tradition of liberal Protestantism',[8] Lindbeck characterizes his own views as 'postliberal'.[9] We may leave aside the question of whether the latter might have been more adequate with regard to Berger's latest approach as well.

Another publication seems to provide strong support for Berger's theory of a Buddhist–Christian antagonism. This is Paul Williams's record of his conversion (in 2000) from Tibetan Buddhism to the Roman Catholic Church. Paul Williams is Professor of Indian and Tibetan Philosophy at the University of Bristol and has been a practising Buddhist for more than twenty years. He is the author of several scholarly works on Buddhism, among them the widely used textbook *Mahāyāna Buddhism.* In his book *The Unexpected Way. On Converting from Buddhism to Catholicism,*[10] Williams expounds his view that the contrast between Buddhism and Christianity is primarily a contrast between atheism and theism, and – according to Williams – this contrast permeates even their apparent similarities:

It is the presence of God in Christianity that makes Christianity so often the exact opposite of Buddhism. . . . It is not that basically, fundamentally, Buddhism and Christianity are alike,

---

7 Lindbeck (1984), p. 40.
8 Berger (2004), p. viii.
9 Cf. Lindbeck (1984), chapter 6.
10 Williams (2002).

with Christianity adding something called 'God' ... In the
light of God, even those aspects of Christianity that seem similar to Buddhism are really quite different. There is no avoiding
the choice.[11]

Paul Williams takes it for granted that 'Buddhists do not believe
in the existence of God'. He concedes that Buddhism affirms deities or heavenly beings, but these are regarded as being part of
the Saṃsāra, the cycle of reincarnation, and that means these
gods are themselves in need of salvation. According to Williams,
Buddhism does not affirm a God who would be crucial for the
possibility of salvation or fulfilment. But this is precisely the role
of God as taught by Christianity. And therefore, at least implicitly, 'the God referred to by Christians is indeed being denied.
From a Christian point of view Buddhism is clearly a form of
atheism.'[12]

Voices like those of Berger, Lindbeck or Williams, who are emphasizing an unbridgeable antagonism of Buddhism and Christianity, may be on the rise and much welcomed by many. They
serve the widespread and growing tendency of reacting to the
increased awareness of religious diversity by re-enforcing one's
own identity *against* all others rather than creatively transforming and developing one's identity through mutual integration or
even interpenetration. But there are also numerous voices representing and manifesting the latter alternative.

First of all, as we have seen in Chapter 3, there is a growing
number of Christians who have immersed themselves so deeply
in another religious tradition that they cannot help but state for
their own religious identity a kind of 'double belonging' or 'dual
citizenship'.[13] For many centuries this has been a widespread
phenomenon in the cultures of the Far East, but it is a fairly
new development within Christianity. Those who see themselves

---

11 Ibid., p. 71.

12 Ibid., p. 26. For am extensive discussion between Paul Williams and myself
about his understanding of Buddhism, see Williams (2007) and Schmidt-Leukel
(2007).

13 Cf. Cornille (2002) and pp. 46–66 of this volume.

as 'Buddhist Christians'[14] thereby manifest, through their own daily existence, their belief in the compatibility of Buddhism and Christianity. But this existential attitude is not always necessarily accompanied by a theoretical solution, even if the 'Buddhist Christian' or 'Christian Buddhist' is a highly reflective person. For example, Sally King, a professor of philosophy and religion in the United States, says after years of identifying herself as a Quaker and a Buddhist about these two traditions:

> I no longer see them as so nearly reconcilable, but more as two languages, each of which speaks with great profundity truths of the spiritual life, yet neither of which (like any language) is really translatable into the other. In the end, all truth must be reconcilable. But I am well aware of my distance from that point.[15]

Some authors have spoken of a complementarity of Christianity and Buddhism, but in a sense which could be characterized as 'soft complementarity'. One of them was the late Ninian Smart, who is clearly to be counted among the most eminent scholars of religion in the twentieth century. Smart describes Buddhism and Christianity as 'Rivals *and* Allies'.[16] He sees them as 'complementary religions' – in the sense that they are 'not flatly contradictory, but have a major convergence of ideals', and represent 'useful critiques' of each other.[17] However, the 'very strong non-theistic emphasis' that can be found in some traditions of Buddhism creates 'a gulf' which – says Smart – 'cannot I believe be bridged'.[18] It may be worth mentioning that one of Smart's former students is the Theravāda Buddhist Gunapala Dharmasiri, who later became Professor at the Peradeniya University in Kandy, Sri Lanka. Under Ninian Smart's supervision Dharmasiri has written the philosophically strongest attack on

---

14 Cf. the personal testimonies in Kasimow, Keenan and Klepinger Keenan (2003).
15 King (2003), p. 170.
16 Emphasis mine. Cf. Smart (1993).
17 Ibid., p. 99.
18 Ibid., p. 25.

Christian theism from the standpoint of contemporary, analytically influenced Theravāda.[19] This fact might have had its impact
on Ninian Smart's scepticism about the ultimate reconcilability
of Christian theism and Buddhist non-theism.

A similar form of 'soft complementarity' has been affirmed by
the Belgian Jesuit Jacques Dupuis, who taught systematic theology at various Indian universities and latterly at the Gregorian
University in Rome. Dupuis is a pioneering figure among those
Roman Catholic theologians who seriously enter the field of
inter-faith dialogue and draw theological consequences from it.
Dupuis even became a consultor of the Pontifical Council for
Interreligious Dialogue and served as drafter for a number of important Vatican documents on inter-religious matters. However,
in 1998 he came under investigation by the Roman Congrega-
tion for the Doctrine of Faith and was finally censured in 2000.[20]
Dupuis speaks of a 'mutual but asymmetrical complementarity'[21]
between Christianity and other religions, including Buddhism.
He calls this complementarity 'mutual' because the religions can
be mutually enriched through their encounter and dialogue. But
at the same time the complementarity is called 'asymmetrical'
because 'the Christ-event represents the climax of God's personal
dealings with humankind'[22] and is as such – according to Dupuis
– without parallel.

What emerges clearly from both the proclaimers of Buddhist–Christian antagonism and the defenders of a kind of soft
complementarity is that the major obstacles for the affirmation
of a fuller complementarity are, first, the question of the alleged
Buddhist atheism and, second, the Christian claim to the unique
revelatory and salvific role of Jesus Christ. But is this gulf really
unbridgeable? There are theologians who went further and I
would now like to introduce one of them, the Sri Lankan Methodist Lynn A. de Silva.

---

19 Cf. Dharmasiri (1988).
20 Cf. Chia (2003), pp. 49–52.
21 Dupuis (2002), p. 65f.
22 Ibid., p. 66.

Buddhist–Christian Complementarity according to Lynn A. de Silva

Lynn A. de Silva was born in Sri Lanka in 1919 and died on 22 May 1982. He was trained in Bangalore, Serampore, New York and Birmingham and was ordained as a Methodist Minister in 1950. Among his numerous activities were a long-term involvement in the Sinhalese translation of the Bible, a twenty-year-long participation in the ecumenical and dialogical activities of the World Council of Churches, directorship of the Ecumenical Institute for Study and Dialogue in Colombo from 1962 until his death in 1982, and his role as the editor of the *Dialogue*, one of the first theological journals on Buddhist–Christian encounter.

De Silva's theology, particularly in his early years, has been rightly characterized as a 'translational theology'.[23] His initial goal was to translate the Christian gospel into the context of Buddhist ideas in order to make it more intelligible to Buddhists. Thus on the one hand his motivation was clearly a missionary one, but on the other hand it was also innovative in as far as de Silva was aware that such a translation would imply opening up theological thinking for the integration of whatever truth might be discovered in Buddhism.[24]

It was Paul Tillich's method of correlation which de Silva chose as the most suitable for his aims. Following this method, belief in God should be explained in relation or correlation to the basic questions of human existence. With regard to Buddhism, de Silva saw the most dense analysis of human existence provided in the *tilakkhaṇa*-teaching, that is, in the teaching on the three marks of existence. Here de Silva found those existential questions expressed to which the Christian teaching of a trinitarian God provided the answer, that is,

---

23 De Alwis (1983). On de Silva, see also Pieris (1982); Schmidt-Leukel (1992), pp. 185–202; Brück and Lai (1997), pp. 92–107; Höhensteiger (1998). Excellent material on de Silva is now also available on http://en.wikipedia.org/wiki/Lynn_de_Silva.

24 'There are deep insights in Buddhism that can enrich Christian thinking, but Christians have been afraid of having to do anything with Buddhism.' De Silva (1979), p. 1.

the *impermanence* of all life (*anicca*) is overcome by the imperishable, eternal *Father*;
the *suffering* of unredeemed existence (*dukkha*), is overcome
by the *Son*, the Redeemer;
and *not-self* (*anattā*), i.e. the fact that we lack any substantial,
eternal soul or self, is overcome by the divine *Spirit* who transforms us into persons who can live in an eternal relationship
with God.[25]

It is remarkable that Lynn de Silva had chosen the same point
of contact as Peter Berger. But for de Silva, even in the early
phase of his theological thinking, this was not meant to sub-
stantiate the thesis of Buddhist–Christian antagonism, but rather
a deep complementarity and convergence as far as the human
predicament is concerned. De Silva has emphasized this several
times, as for example in his following remark on the Buddhist
not-self or *anattā*-teaching:

Buddhism and Christianity come to the realization of non-
egoity in two different ways. Christianity begins by stressing
the greatness and majesty of God the Creator in relation to
whom man is insignificant, fragile and weak, and apart from
whom man is nothing. Buddhism begins by looking inwards
and seeing man's nothingness, and then something beyond is
sought for.[26]

This conformity between the Buddhist and Christian understanding of the human predicament has basically the structure
of seeing Buddhism as articulating the right question to which
Christianity provides the right answer. But it is not entirely as
simple as that. The fact that Buddhism had such a clear insight
into the human predicament entailed for de Silva that there was
also a kind of implicit or vague notion of the correlative answer.

---

25 The correlation of *tilakkhaṇa* and Trinity was presented in de Silva (1967),
pp. 170–203. In a less elaborated form it appeared three years earlier in de Silva's
Sinclair Thompson Memorial Lectures: De Silva (1964), Introduction, p. Hf.
26 De Silva (1979), p. 5.

Thus, as early as 1957 de Silva rejected the interpretation of the Buddha as an atheist and pointed to the famous verse in the Udāna and Itivuttaka where the Buddha proclaims that there must be an unconditioned or unborn reality in order to make salvation or liberation possible:[27]

There is, bhikkhus [monks], a not-born, not-brought-to-being, not-made, not-conditioned. If, bhikkhus, there were no not-born, not-brought-to-being, not-made, not-conditioned, no escape would be discerned from what is born, brought-to-being, made, conditioned. But since there is a not-born, not-brought-to-being, not-made, not-conditioned, therefore an escape is discerned from what is born, brought-to-being, made, conditioned.[28]

Throughout his theological life de Silva sought to elaborate more fully the correlation between the Buddhist *tilakkhaṇa*-teaching and the Christian Trinity. But despite the fact that he wrote a smaller work on salvation[29] and one on belief in God,[30] a more comprehensive treatment was only completed with regard to the third correlation, namely, that of *anattā/pneuma* or 'not-self/ spirit'. This work, called *The Problem of the Self in Buddhism and Christianity*,[31] is definitely one of the classics of Buddhist– Christian dialogue and has become widely known among those who are actively involved in this dialogue.

However, only a few have noted the significant transformation of de Silva's thought towards the end of his life. This is primarily manifested in a longer, posthumously published essay which was entitled 'Buddhism and Christianity Relativised'.[32] The title indicates a crucial change in de Silva's understanding of Buddhist–Christian complementarity. For here, the complementarity

27 See de Silva (1957), pp. 1 & 6. The source of the *Itivuttaka* verse is here wrongly identified as the *Dīgha-Nikāya*.
28 *Itivuttaka* 43. *Udâna* 8:3. Translation from Ireland (1997), p. 103.
29 De Silva (1966).
30 De Silva (1970).
31 De Silva (1975/1979).
32 De Silva (1982).

was no longer seen as one between question and answer or one between a vague and a clear answer. Now de Silva understood it as a complementarity of different aspects, and accordingly of different expressions, of the human experience of transcendent reality.[33]

The Buddhist affirmation of an unconditioned/unborn reality is primarily expressed in impersonal terms, while the Christian affirmation of the Unborn has been expressed primarily in personal terms. The reason for this is that the experience of transcendent reality has two different but equally profound aspects, which de Silva calls 'ultimacy' and 'intimacy'. If ultimacy is emphasized, religious language tends to employ impersonal expressions, and if the emphasis is on intimacy, religious language tends to be personal. The impersonal *That* of the Buddhist Nirvāṇa and the personal *Thou* of the Christian God are therefore not contradictory, but complementary. They express and they evoke different aspects of the human experience of transcendent reality.

So on the one hand intimacy and ultimacy are different and polar, but on the other hand they belong closely together. If the ultimate and ungraspable nature of transcendent reality is really experienced, this experience can take deeply intimate forms. And in every intimate experience of the transcendent there is an awareness of its ultimate and ungraspable nature. De Silva therefore points out that despite the dominance of impersonal language in Buddhism there can also be found a number of personal expressions evoking a deep sense of intimacy, while at the same time in Christianity, despite the prominence of personal God-language, there are also a number of impersonal expressions pointing towards the experience of ultimacy. Both aspects balance, correct and complement each other. In de Silva's words: 'ultimacy gives depth to intimacy and intimacy gives vitality to ultimacy'.[34] This had a significant consequence for de Silva's understanding of the Trinity, which was now presented as a theological structure that

---

33 This change was inspired by two Western Buddhist writers: Maurice Walshe and Marco Pallis.
34 De Silva (1982), p. 51.

seeks to hold ultimacy and intimacy together. In this regard – says de Silva – it has a functional equivalent in Buddhism, which is the *trikāya*-doctrine, that is, the teaching of the three bodies of the Buddha. Within the context of the Christian Trinity and the Buddhist Trikāya, Gautama Buddha and Jesus Christ are both understood as human manifestations or incarnations of the ultimate transcendent reality, that is, 'the Ultimate . . . became intimate by becoming man'.[35]

As mentioned before, de Silva's essay 'Buddhism and Christianity Relativised' was published posthumously and had been completed by de Silva just shortly before his death. So he had no opportunity to draw the full consequences from his new understanding of Buddhist–Christian complementarity. It is, however, evident that this change had become possible by the way in which de Silva now related religious language to human experience. Neither Christian God-talk nor Buddhist talk of Nirvāṇa refers directly and immediately to the transcendent reality in itself, but is related to different aspects or forms of human experiences of this transcendent reality.[36]

A hermeneutics of religious language which pays full attention to the constitutive role of human experience in our talk about ultimate or transcendent reality has become the cornerstone of several approaches which see the Buddhist–Christian relationship as a complementary one. This is particularly true for two other

---

35 Ibid., p. 55.

36 Traces of this idea can be found in much earlier works of de Silva. See, for example, his interesting remark in de Silva (1970), p. 57: 'To say that God is personal does not mean that He is *a* person. It means that He is the ground and source of everything personal.' Or, in the same book, on p. 62: 'we cannot talk of God without at the same time talking of ourselves. Whatever name we may use for "God" will be meaningless unless it points to something within us and beyond us . . . Whatever term, metaphor, analogue or image we may use to signify what we mean by God, will not be altogether satisfactory. Their meaning is bound up with the faith-community which uses them. The term Allah has significance for the Muslim community and the term Jehova to the Jewish community, but these terms may not carry meaning in a different context.' At that time, however, de Silva did not yet draw the full consequences from this insight for the relationship between Buddhism and Christianity.

Sri Lankan theologians, Aloysius Pieris[37] and Antony Fernando.[38] It is also true for my own work on Buddhist–Christian hermeneutics,[39] of which I would now like to give a brief outline.

The Complementarity of Detachment and Involvement

It is reported that Japanese people like to go to Christian churches for marriage but will consult a Buddhist priest for funerals. At first sight this might seem very strange – at least from a Western perspective. But it could be evidence of a deep intuitive understanding of what Buddhism and Christianity are all about. In my own research on the foundations of Buddhism, I came to the conclusion that for the formation of the original Buddhist worldview the most formative experience is the experience of death, or more broadly, the experience of perishableness or transitoriness, while the categories of Christian and Jewish thinking are predominantly marked by the experience of interpersonal relationship.

The importance of transitoriness within Buddhism becomes evident, among other things, through the *tilakkhaṇa*-teaching.[40] In its original form it implies that the things of the world and the components of our own existence are transitory (*anicca*), that they are thus experienced as painful and unsatisfactory (*dukkha*), and that therefore one should not cling to them, regarding them as one's own possessions, nor identify them as one's own self or as the cosmic and divine Self, that is, as the *ātman* of the Upaniṣads (*anattā*).[41]

Another piece of evidence is the perhaps most important doctrinal formula of early Buddhism, the so-called Four Noble Truths. The first Noble Truth, which gives a systematic descrip-

---

37 Cf. Pieris (1988).
38 Cf. Fernando (1981/1985).
39 Cf. Schmidt-Leukel (1992).
40 *Aṅguttara Nikāya* III, 137.
41 For example, *Mahāvagga* I, 6; *Majjhima-Nikāya* 22, etc. For a more detailed exposition of my own understanding of the early Buddhist Not-Self teaching, see Schmidt-Leukel (2006), p. 36f.

tion of *dukkha*, 'suffering', begins with the line: 'Birth is *dukkha*, ageing is *dukkha*, sickness is *dukkha*, death is *dukkha*.' Old age, sickness and death form together a triad which can be found frequently within the Buddhist canonical writings. They must be seen as a unity, as the three existential hallmarks of human transitoriness. Birth is mentioned because, within the context of the old Indian belief in reincarnation, birth means entering again and again the cycle of perishable existence. Birth is not the opposite of death, but the start and thus part of a transitory life.

As a third example I would like to mention the Buddha legend. It was the sight of an old man, a sick man and a dead man that led to Gautama's resolve to leave his home and strive for salvation, or to be more precise, to search for what is free from old age, sickness and death. Thus, transitoriness functions as a disclosure experience which exerts a formative influence on the shape of early Buddhist doctrine.

So we can say that in Buddhism the human predicament is primarily understood as an existential suffering under the transitoriness of existence. And the idea of reincarnation, the cycle of potentially endless rebirth, is not seen as a liberation from death, but quite the contrary, as the endless perpetuation of perishable life – which is the reason why it is frequently called 're-death' (*punarmṛtyu*) instead of 'rebirth' (*punarjanma*).

In Christianity the human predicament is understood as 'sin', and 'sin' can be best explained as 'broken relationship'. It is the turning away from God and one's neighbour, or as Martin Luther has framed it, the sinner, unable to love God or neighbour, is the *homo incurvatus in se ipsum*,[42] the 'human curved or crooked in on himself'.

The categories which form the Buddhist and Christian understanding of human predicament are also formative in their views of transcendent reality. In Buddhism, a frequent equivalent for Nirvāṇa *is amata* or *amṛta* meaning the 'deathless'. As such, it was proclaimed by the Buddha after his enlightenment, when he addressed the five ascetics with the words, 'the deathless is

---

42 Cf. WA 56, pp. 304, 325, 356.

found'.[43] It is therefore not permissible to render the first of the three Buddhist marks of existence (*tilakkhaṇa*) as 'everything is impermanent' – as Peter Berger and others do. Everything *within Saṃsāra*, within the cycle of rebirth and re-death, is impermanent. But Nirvāṇa is totally other. Nirvāṇa is the deathless.

In Judaism and subsequently in Christianity transcendent reality is understood as a personal God, that is as a reality that can be approached like a person, or more precisely like a merciful father. It is the experience of the fatherly divine love that liberates sinners from their curvature in on themselves and opens them up. It is in response to the divine love that human sinners are enabled to love God and their neighbour. And because God loves us even as sinners or – as Paul says – as his enemies (Rom. 5.8–10), the sign of divine love is the ability to love our own enemies. God lets the sun shine and sends rain for the righteous and the unrighteous and therefore, says Jesus in the Sermon on the Mount, we should not only love our friends but also our enemies (Matt. 5.43–48).

In this liberating love, emerging from God and reflected in human hearts, not only sin but also transitoriness and death are overcome. For according to the biblical view, 'the wages of sin is death' (Rom. 6.23). 'But love covers all transgressions' (Prov. 11.12) and nothing in the world, not even death, says Paul, can separate us from the love of God which is in Christ (Rom. 8.38f). If nothing in the world can separate us from the love of God, the love of God separates us from being under the power of this world. Receiving and responding to the love of God goes along with a kind of detachment from the world of death. We should possess the things of the world – says Paul – as though we would not, 'for the form of this world is passing away' (1 Cor. 7.29–31). Or – according to John – we are in the world but not from the world (John 17.9–19). This is the spiritual attitude of 'realized' or 'present eschatology' – living in the midst of the world in a way that has proleptically transcended it.

According to the Buddhist analysis, the reason why we suffer

---

43 *Majjhima-Nikāya* 26.

under the transitoriness of existence is that our deepest longing is for the imperishable (cf. *Majjhima-Nikāya* 26). We cling to what is perishable, driven by the deep-rooted illusion that the transitory things of the world and the impermanent constituents of our own existence could satisfy our deepest and truest longing. This wrong and deluded orientation of our existential striving is what Buddhism calls 'thirst' (*tṛṣṇā* or *taṇhā*). The joys coming from worldly possessions can only quench our 'thirst' for the moment, but they can never remove it or satisfy it for ever. This 'thirst', expressed in attachment, binds us into the Saṃsāra, the cycle of life and death, and forces us to be reborn into perishable existence again and again. Death, and suffering under death, are therefore overcome by detachment. But this is ultimately possible only through the experience of the 'deathless' reality itself. This experience was at the core of Buddha's enlightenment, and it is mediated through the teaching of the Buddha. The Buddha's teaching, emerging from his enlightenment experience, sets us on the right track and guides us to loosening our fetters. The final disappearance of 'thirst' and 'attachment', however, cannot be our work. It will be brought about by our own experience of the 'deathless', that is by our own enlightenment.[44]

If in Christianity the correlate of divine, non-selfish love is a certain separation from the world, in Buddhism it is just the other way round, that is, selfless love is the correlate of detachment. Attachment has as its innermost form the structure of clinging to oneself, of self-centredness. And thus every form of genuine love, that is, of love which does not seek in the first instance one's own gratification, implies some degree of detachment. Ideal love – according to Buddhism – would be totally detached love, and that means a form of love which is indiscriminately directed towards everyone, high or low, friend or foe. Thus in Buddhism we find the ideal of loving one's enemies in a form which is equally as strong as in Christianity, if not even stronger. Again the great model is the Buddha himself. After his enlightenment he did not disappear from the world, but in his detached, enlightened

---

44 Cf. the excellent analysis in Palihawadana (1978).

attitude he chose the life of forty-five years of active involvement, proclaiming his insight to everyone, and established the
community of his monastic and lay followers – out of compassion for the world.

Thus Buddhism and Christianity express their perception of
life in different categories which can be related to the different
emphasis that is given to the experience of transitoriness on the
one hand and the experience of interpersonal relationship on the
other hand. Nevertheless, Buddhism and Christianity coincide in
the ideal of detached love or loving detachment which is shown
in an indiscriminate way to everyone.

Conclusion

From what has been said so far, let me now draw my conclusion. On the *existential* level the complementarity of Buddhism
and Christianity is based on the complementarity of detachment
and involvement. It is here where each can enrich and spiritually
stimulate the other. For within Christianity the dominance of
involvement tends to supersede the element of detachment, and
within Buddhism the dominance of detachment carries with it
the danger of superseding loving involvement. No doubt both
traditions have their own sub-traditions in which the complementary element has been more strongly affirmed than usual:
Christian mysticism and monasticism have always emphasized
the spiritual value of detachment. And in Buddhism, particularly
in Mahāyāna Buddhism, but also to some extent in Theravāda
Buddhism, the Bodhisattva-ideal has always stood for the
supreme value of compassionate involvement. It is therefore
not surprising that Buddhist–Christian encounter has on the
Christian side inspired a revitalization of contemplative, medita-
tive practice, and on the Buddhist side it has inspired a renewed
sense of social responsibility.

On a more *doctrinal* level, the theory of Buddhist–Christian
antagonism rests on the assumption that Buddhism is a form of
atheism. But this assumption is highly questionable. There is no

doubt that Buddhism is non-theistic in the sense that it does not affirm transcendent reality as a 'personal God'. But it does affirm a transcendent reality! And contrary to Paul Williams, it affirms transcendent reality precisely as the precondition of salvation. Thus I would prefer to say that Buddhism is *non-theistic*, but it is not atheistic in the sense of materialism or naturalism.

When it comes to the various theories of 'soft complementarity', the decisive question is our understanding of religious language. If human words and concepts are capable of giving a correct description of transcendent reality, then either its portrayal as a personal being is right and its portrayal as an impersonal reality is wrong, or the other way round. But if transcendent reality is essentially beyond everything that human concepts can comprehend and human words can describe, then the immediate reference of religious language is not transcendent reality in itself, but the various forms and aspects of human *experiences* with transcendence.[45] As I tried to show, this would clearly allow for a full and symmetric rather than asymmetric complementarity of Buddhism and Christianity.

Thus we are only left with the question of Buddha and Christ. Is one of them superior or even unique? Or are both unique in some sense, but on a par as human mediators of divine reality? I think that the latter is indeed the case. This will be further explored in the next chapter.

---

45 For a philosophical elaboration of a general view of religion on the basis of such a hermeneutics, see Hick (1989).

7

BUDDHA AND CHRIST
AS MEDIATORS OF THE
TRANSCENDENT

One of the most beautiful Buddhist temples in Thailand is Doi Suthep, built high into the slope of the Suthep mountain, north-west of Chiang Mai. In former times one had to climb more than 300 steps for the final part of the way to the top, but today you can take a modern cable car to the plateau of the temple area: a wide plain of shining polished stone offering a marvellous view over Chiang Mai and the whole valley below. If you turn around, you find yourself surrounded by several smaller and bigger stupas, all covered with gold, dazzlingly reflecting and radiating Thailand's bright sunlight. Due to the enormous height, the temple plateau is at times hemmed with tattered clouds, and so you can't help thinking that you stand in the middle of a celestial palace, an effect which was probably intended by the building masters. Next to the stupas there are various Thai salas, open temple constructions and colonnades with numerous Buddha statues – the large ones in the very same dazzling gold as the stupas, the smaller ones partly in a darker, almost mystical glow of jewels and jade. Without doubt everything in this place proclaims the supramundane, not to say 'divine' nature of the Buddha. On the inner side of the wall, which circumscribes the core of the temple area, you see a series of highly poetic wall paintings depicting the Buddha legend. The picture that shows the Buddha or, more precisely, Prince Gautama, moving from home into homelessness, does not show Gautama riding on his faithful horse Kanthaka, as the text of the legend has it. Rather, it depicts Gautama *flying* on the back of his horse over a deep valley out of the world into the realm where heaven, earth, humans and here even animals meet – as if he were attracted by a powerful, invisible force.

What a difference between the presentation of the Buddha within the genuine context of religious veneration, as in this Theravāda temple, and the image of the Buddha – currently so widespread in the West – according to which the Buddha was simply a human being, free from all divine features![1] Indeed this modern view does not at all correspond to the description of the Buddha in the classical Buddhist scriptures. In the Pāli Canon, for example, it is told how the Brahmin Doṇa discovered the Buddha's footprints with the sign of the thousand-spoked wheels that were under Buddha's soles. Amazed by these footprints, the Brahmin thought: 'How wonderful and marvellous – it cannot be that these are the footprints of a human being.'[2] Doṇa followed the track until he met the Buddha. Respectfully approaching him, Doṇa asked the Buddha what kind of being he was and received the answer that the Buddha cannot be described as a celestial being, nor as a ghost, nor as a human being. These are all forms of *saṃsāric* existence – that is, beings which are still caught in *saṃsāra*, the net of constant rebirth. But the Buddha is a being who has transcended all this:

> Brahmin, those outflows whereby, if they had not been extinguished, I might have been a deva (celestial being) . . . or

---

1 Cf. Parrinder (1997), p. 246: 'modern apologists . . . say that Gautama was a man with nothing supernatural about him, and his teaching was a simple ethic which should be acceptable to the rationalistic western world. The trouble is that this is not how the Buddha is viewed, or ever has been viewed, in any of the eastern schools of traditional Buddhism, Theravāda or Mahāyāna. The Buddha is not a god, a *deva*, but he is superior to all exalted human and divine beings . . . ' For an early, but largely neglected critique of a reductive portrayal of the Buddha, see also Cheng (1981).

2 *Aṅguttara-Nikāya* 4:36. Translation from Conze (ed. and transl.) (2000), p. 104.

a human being – those outflows are extinguished in me . . . although born in the world, grown up in the world, having overcome the world, I abide unsoiled by the world. Take it that I am Buddha, brahmin.[3]

The view that the Buddha *as a Buddha* embodies or incarnates a reality which is above gods and humans, that is, a reality which essentially transcends the world of *saṃsāra*, is by no means just a later fabrication of Mahāyāna Buddhism, even if it is true that on a doctrinal level the Mahāyāna has elaborated this view more than the Theravāda has. In what follows, I would like to draw a very brief and selective sketch of this development and relate the Buddhist understanding of incarnation to its Christian parallel. Thereby I will explore the possibility of seeing both, Buddha and Christ, as incarnations of that transcendent reality which is the basis of our salvation.

On the Buddhist Belief in Incarnation

It is told in the Pāli Canon[4] that the Buddha, after his enlightenment, was hesitant at first to proclaim the insight he had received. But then god Brahmā intervened and showed the 'Exalted One' that the sentient beings would be lost if they were deprived of the help contained in the Buddha's teaching. The Buddha felt compassion with the beings and so he decided to preach the Dharma, the Buddhist teaching. According to another version, also told in the Pāli Canon,[5] it was Māra, the evil tempter, who tried to prevent the Buddha from teaching. Māra declared to the Buddha that, since he had now completed the path and attained the highest goal, it would be appropriate to leave the world. But the Buddha replied that he would not depart this world until holy conduct is solidly established – that is, until the Dharma is well taught and the Buddha's followers are able to pass it on.

---

3 Ibid., p. 105.
4 Cf. *Mahāvagga* I,5,1–3.
5 Cf. *Dīgha-Nikāya* 16,3,34f.

In both of its versions this narrative emphasizes the point that the Buddha had achieved through his enlightenment everything he could aspire to for himself; thus all his activity *after* the enlightenment was entirely and exclusively motivated by altruism. Only for the sake of the sentient beings, out of perfect compassion, the Buddha proclaimed the Dharma, the eternal truth he had found. I suppose that behind this tradition stands the well-documented ancient Indian conviction according to which a sage or an enlightened one maintains silence.[6] Therefore someone like the Buddha who spent forty-five years as an itinerant preacher could by no means be regarded as enlightened. In any event, as late as the seventh century CE the Buddhist philosopher Dharmakīrti still found it necessary to take issue with this objection. He replied with what had already been the point in the two narratives of the Pāli Canon, namely, that the Buddha was perfect in wisdom *and* in compassion, and that the perfection of compassion had been the sole motivation for his preaching.[7]

However, the Buddhist tradition went even further and this already at an early stage. The story wherein Māra tempts the Buddha to depart from the world after his enlightenment probably alludes to religiously motivated suicide, a practice not unusual in the Buddha's day.[8] Hence, not only Buddha's preaching activity but the whole of his existence following his enlightenment must be seen as an expression of his compassion and his propagation of the Dharma. And this means the whole of his existence as a 'Buddha', because Gautama became a Buddha (a 'fully awakened one') only through his enlightenment. Thus in the Pāli Canon the Buddha is repeatedly identified with the Dharma: 'Seeing the Dharma' says the Buddha 'one sees me, seeing me one sees the Dharma'.[9] It is worth noting that at least in some places the tenor is that the Buddha thereby points away from himself and

---

6 Cf. *Saṃyutta-Nikāya* 10,2.

7 Cf. *Pramāṇavārttika* II, 142–6, 280–2. Cf. Vetter (ed. and transl.) (1984), pp. 50–2, 169–71.

8 This is testified to in, e.g. *Saṃyutta-Nikāya* 4:23; 54:9; *Majjhima-Nikāya* 145.

9 Cf. *Saṃyutta-Nikāya* 22,87; *Itivuttaka* 92.

towards the exclusive significance of the Dharma.[10] But precisely this significance is manifested in the lives of those who are seized by the Dharma. The 'visible Dharma' – says the Pāli Canon – is the life of a person who has become entirely and lastingly free from greed, hatred and delusion. And, the text continues, the life of such a person is also the 'visible Nirvāṇa'.[11] The lives of the enlightened ones are, so to say, 'nirvāṇized'. They have 'plunged into the deathless, have achieved it completely, have taken it for free and enjoy the highest peace' (the 'deathless' is a standard Buddhist epithet for the Nirvāṇa).[12]

In this context one needs to bear in mind that according to the traditional Buddhist view Nirvāṇa is not merely a mental state, the state of the enlightened one. Nirvāṇa is rather understood as an 'unconditioned' (*asaṃskṛta*), 'transcendent' (*lokottara*) reality,[13] whose existence is the condition of the possibility of salvation. Thus it is said in the Pāli Canon:

> There is, monks, a not-born (*ajātaṁ*), a not-brought-to-being (*abhūtaṁ*), a not-made (*akataṁ*), a not-conditioned (*asaṅkhataṁ*). If, monks, there were no not-born, not-brought-to-being, not-made, not-conditioned, no escape would be discerned from what is born, brought-to-being, made, conditioned. But since there is a not-born, a not-brought-to-being, a not-made, a not-conditioned, therefore an escape is discerned from what is born, brought-to-being, made, conditioned.[14]

In this sense two of the most influential works of traditional Theravāda Buddhism, the *Milindapañha* and Buddhaghosa's *Visuddhi Magga*, present the following argument: In order to be a deathless

---

10 On this, see the relevant remarks of Lambert Schmithausen (2000), p. 263.

11 Cf. *Aṅguttara-Nikāya* 3,54–6 (I 157–9).

12 *Khuddaka Pāṭha* 6:7.

13 The point has been very clearly made in some excellent recent studies as for example: Moti Lal Pandit, 'Nirvāṇa as the Unconditioned', in Pandit (1993), pp. 312–39; Makransky (1997), particularly pp. 85–108; Collins (1998), pp. 161–85; Harvey (2004), pp. 180–97.

14 *Udāna* 8:3; and *Itivuttaka* 43.

reality, Nirvāṇa needs to be unconditioned. For everything that is subject to conditioned origination is also subject to death and decay. And since it is unconditioned, Nirvāṇa cannot be merely a mental state. For as the mental state of the enlightened one, it would be conditioned, that is, it would arise as the result of completing the Buddhist path. Therefore the state of the enlightened one must be understood as the attainment of a transcendent reality which exists independently from this achievement. Hence it is the existence of this unconditioned reality that makes enlightenment, which is the liberation from the world of conditioned existence, at all possible.[15] With this in mind, the concept of the 'visible Nirvāṇa' could be interpreted as follows: The enlightened one, freed from the roots of all evil and motivated exclusively by perfect compassion, is imbued with, and hence transparent to, the unconditioned reality of Nirvāṇa, which in itself transcends all conditioned reality and all human understanding.

These beginnings of a Buddhist belief in incarnation were further developed with the rise of Mahāyāna Buddhism. In the still relatively early, but at the same time extremely influential *Lotus-Sūtra*, which became formative for all of East-Asian Buddhism, the earthly Buddha is portrayed as the temporally limited manifestation of a supramundane and virtually eternal[16] Buddha-reality. In the *Lotus-Sūtra* this reality is named the 'Father of the World' who for the sake of the deluded beings manifests or incarnates among them in order to show them the path towards enlightenment.[17] Obvious are the parallels to the *avatāra-*

---

15 Cf. *Milindapañha* 269f; *Visuddhimagga* 507–09.

16 The *Lotus-Sūtra*, chapter 15 (in Kumārajīva's version: chapter 16) is slightly ambiguous as to the Buddha's eternity. On the one hand, it still speaks of an attainment of the Buddhahood. On the other hand, it says that this 'attainment' took place in an immeasurable past and that the Buddha's life is never ending. In East Asian Buddhism it was and is taught that the Buddha of the *Lotus-Sūtra* is in fact eternal. Cf. Williams (1989), p. 151f.

17 *Saddharmapuṇḍarīka Sūtra* (Sanskrit version) 15:21–3:

So am I the father of the world, the Selfborn, the Healer, the Protector of all creatures . . .

What reason should I have to continually manifest myself? When men become unbelieving, unwise, ignorant, careless, fond of sensual pleasures, and from thoughtlessness run into misfortune, concept of the *Bhagavadgītā*, which was composed at about the same time as the *Lotus-Sūtra*.[18]

The Buddhist belief in incarnation is fully developed in the later mahāyānistic doctrine of the 'Three Buddha Bodies' (*trikāya*).[19] 'Body' (*kāya*) refers here to the respective form or level of reality or effectivity within the complex reality of the Buddha. The earthly Buddha represents the 'Transformation Body' *(nirmānakāya)* – so-called either because of the impermanence of this form of reality or because of its relative unreality, which is to say, a form of existence which in comparison with the unconditioned ultimate reality resembles an illusion. Following the track traced by the *Lotus-Sūtra*, the earthly Buddha of the *nirmānakāya* is further regarded as the manifestation of a supramundane Buddha whose form of reality is designated as 'Enjoyment Body' (*sambhogakāya*). The name 'Enjoyment Body' probably refers on the one hand to Buddhahood as it is enjoyed by the Buddha as the fruit of his own striving and on the other hand to Buddhahood as an enjoyment for the others in so far as the Buddha's existence is basically understood as an altruistically motivated pro-existence.[20] However, the ultimate basis (*āśraya*) of the human and the supramundane Buddha is the inconceivable, ineffable transcendent reality, which in the context of the 'Three

---

Then I, who know the course of the world, declare: I am so and so, (and consider): How can I incline them to enlightenment? how can they become partakers of the Buddha-laws? (Kern (transl.) 1963, p. 309f)

18 See *Bhagavadgītā* 4:6–8:
Though I am unborn, and My self is imperishable, though I am the lord of all creatures . . . I come into (empiric) being through My power (*māyā*).
Whenever there is a decline of righteousness and rise of unrighteousness . . . then I send forth (create incarnate) Myself.
For the protection of the good, for the destruction of the wicked, and for the establishment of righteousness, I come into being from age to age. (Radhakrishnan and Moore (eds) (1989), p. 116)
The parallels between the *Lotus-Sūtra* and the *Bhagavadgītā* have already been pointed out by H. Kern (1963), p. XXVf.

19 On the *trikāya*-doctrine, see Gadjin Nagao, 'On the Theory of Buddha-Body (*Buddha-kāya*)', in Nagao (1991), pp. 103–22; Griffiths (1994); Tauscher (1998), pp. 93–118, 247–51; Makransky (1997).

20 Cf. G. Nagao (1991), p. 108.

Buddha Bodies' is called the 'Dharma Body' (*dharmakāya*, also called *svābhāvika-kāya* = 'Essential Body'). In contrast to the two other bodies, the *dharmakāya* is not a 'form' of existence, but a 'formless' (*arūpa*) reality. The 'Transformation Body' and the 'Enjoyment Body' are both called 'Form Bodies' (*rūpakāya*) because they are conceivable and even visible – the human Buddha through human eyes, the supramundane Buddha through meditational vision. But the *dharmakāya* is in a radical sense inconceivable and ineffable. It is the ultimate true reality transcending, underlying and permeating everything,[21] accessible only through the two form bodies.

The dynamics of the 'Buddha Bodies' doctrine can be interpreted as the twofold movement of ascent and descent.[22] The ascent begins with the human Buddha through whom an understanding of the divine Buddha as his supramundane ground is won. And this supramundane Buddha needs to be transcended too towards its ultimate ground, the ineffable, truly eternal or timeless[23] reality of the *dharmakāya*. But at the same time this

21 Paul Harrison (1992) has warned strongly against an understanding – or, as he thinks, misunderstanding – of the *dharmakāya* as 'a kind of Buddhist absolute' (p. 44). Harrison has produced impressive philological evidence that at least in pre-Mahāyāna, early Mahāyāna and partly middle Mahāyāna usage *dharmakāya* should be understood as either Buddha's embodiment in his teaching or as the Buddha's equipment with the 'body', i.e., with the full range of those attributes and features that are particular to a Buddha. However, Harrison seems to interpret the *dharma as teaching* in a quite modern, purely propositional sense, and not in the traditional sense according to which the *dharma* is an eternal truth or law discovered by the Buddha and reflected or mediated in his teachings. Moreover, Harrison seems to neglect the fact that the attributes of the Buddha are traditionally understood along the lines of the idea of the 'visible *dharma/nirvāṇa*' and hence as expressive of an ultimate, unconditioned reality. For a critique of Harrison's interpretation of the early Mahāyāna usage of the term *dharmakāya*, see Makransky (1997), pp. 373–5, n. 12. For Makransky the 'study of Buddhist understanding of *dharmakāya* could instigate rewarding new lines of inquiry into the nature of God; and I believe the reverse to be equally rewarding' (ibid., p. 370, n. 13).

22 Cf. G. Nagao, 'The Bodhisattva Returns to this World', in Nagao (1991), pp. 23–4.

23 See, for example, the *Ch'êng-wei-shih-lun* (chapter 14): 'The pure realm of the Dharma is said to be eternal because it is devoid of origination, devoid of cessation, and by nature unchanging.' Cook (transl.) (1999), p. 359. While the eternal or timeless nature of the *dharmakāya* is undisputed, the eternity of the

movement of ascent can also be seen as a movement of descent. That is, the human Buddha is a manifestation or incarnation, an *avatāra* (literally 'descent') of the supramundane Buddha, and the supramundane Buddha, the Buddha of the 'Enjoyment Body', is a manifestation, a concretizing or an 'outflow' *(niṣyanda)*[24] of the absolute Buddha, the *dharmakāya*.

The motif of descent has played a significant role in the ideas of some Buddhist thinkers; for example, in the work of T'an-luan who lived in China from 476 until 542. In accordance with the Indian Mahāyāna tradition T'an-luan understood the formless *dharmakāya* as the true basis and ground of the two form bodies. But he interpreted this distinction as two different modes of the one *dharmakāya*. The '*dharmakāya* as suchness' is the *dharmakāya* in its inconceivable, absolute reality. And the '*dharmakāya* as skilful means' is the *dharmakāya* as it is manifest in the two form bodies in order to make itself accessible. According to T'an-luan, these two modes of the *dharmakāya* are different, but not separable, are one, but not identical.[25] In the thirteenth century, this idea was adopted by Shinran Shōnin (1173–1262), the founding figure of the Japanese Jōdo-Shin Shū.[26] According to Shinran, the inconceivable '*dharmakāya* as suchness' manifests itself as the '*dharmakāya* as skilful means' in the form of Amida Buddha, the supramundane Buddha of limitless, all-encompassing compassion; in turn, Amida Buddha is manifested or incarnated as Gautama Buddha, in order to guide

---

saṃbhogakāya is similarly ambiguous as the eternity of the Buddha in the *Lotus-Sūtra* (see n. 16 above). Sometimes the eternity of the *saṃbhogakāya* is affirmed (as e.g. in the *Ch'êng-wei-shi-lun* 14, cf. Cook 1999, p. 361), sometimes eternity is attributed genuinely only to the *dharmakāya*, while the *saṃbhogakāya* is somehow expressive of this, as for example in *Mahāyānasaṃgraha*, chapter 10 (cf. Keenan (transl.) 1992, p. 120). Nagao (1991, p. 110) has rightly said of the *saṃbhogakāya* that it 'has the two aspects of being at once transcendental and phenomenal, and at once historic and super-historic'.

24 Cf. Nagao (1991), p. 110 and p. 250, n. 17 (with references).

25 Cf. T'an-luan's Commentary on Vasubandhu's Treatise on the Pure Land (Ching-t'u lun) as quoted in Shinran's *Kyōgyōshinshō* part IV. Cf. Shinran (1973), p. 189f. See also the translation in Shinran (1997), p. 165.

26 Cf. Hee-Sung Keel (1995), pp. 154–82; Schmidt-Leukel (1992), pp. 605–54 and (1998).

the beings towards their salvation. In other words, the inconceivable transcendent reality is revealed to us as the mind of infinite loving kindness finding its metahistorical expression in the figure of Amida and its historical expression in Gautama Buddha. Thus despite the inconceivability of the ultimate in itself, it can be determined in the mode of revelation as 'great compassion' (*mahākaruṇā*). 'The aspiration for Buddhahood', says Shinran,

> is the aspiration to save all beings. The aspiration to save all beings is the mind that grasps sentient beings and brings them to birth in the Pure Land of happiness. This mind is the mind of ultimate equality. It is great compassion. This mind attains Buddhahood. This mind is Buddha.[27]

From this vantage point let us look back on the portrayal of Gautama Buddha in the Pāli Canon:[28] In his proclamation of the Dharma, Buddha indiscriminately embraced everyone, whether brahmin, king, prince, merchant, farmer, or servant, whether high, low or outcast, wealthy or poor, man or woman. He publicly honoured the leper Suppabuddha by offering him the seat on his right-hand side.[29] He did not turn down the invitation to dinner in the house of the prostitute Ambapālī, even as some noblemen tried to hold him back.[30] He spoke highly of the drunkard Sarakāni as of someone who had attained the first stage of holiness.[31] And he did not even hesitate to seek a personal encounter with the cruel mass-murderer Aṅgulimāla. After he succeeded in converting him, he admitted him to the order despite the public displeasure this caused.[32] The Buddha was critical of the caste

---

27 'Passages on the Pure Land Way (*Jōdo monrui jushō*)', in Shinran (1997), p. 314.

28 I refer here to the image of the Buddha as sketched in the canonical scriptures, not to the character-features of the historical Buddha, about whom we have no certain knowledge apart from his reflection in the mirror of faithful veneration. The same needs to be said with regard to the character-features of Jesus.

29 Cf. *Udāna* 5:3.

30 Cf. *Dīgha-Nikāya* 16: 2,4–20.

31 Cf. *Saṃyutta-Nikāya* 55:24f.

32 Cf. *Majjhima-Nikāya* 86.

system and proclaimed that people should be judged only by their spiritual and moral achievements, not by their descent.[33] He confirmed that women are in principle spiritually equal to men and established as a result the order of nuns.[34] When he met Panthaka, a man expelled from house and home, the Buddha put his arm tenderly around him, comforted him with kind words, gave him a linen cloth for washing his feet and admitted him to the community.[35] With his own hands the Buddha washed and tended a monk who suffered from fatal diarrhoea and was neglected by his fellow monks. They were admonished by the Buddha with the words: 'Whoever, monks, would wait upon me . . . should wait upon the sick.'[36] He instructed the children not to harm animals[37] and rejected the Vedic animal sacrifices as cruel and useless.[38] He taught a loving-kindness that does not exclude anyone, a loving-kindness that is forbearing and forgiving and includes even the worst enemy.[39] When a war once threatened to break out over a shortage of water, the Buddha actively intervened and managed to reconcile the hostile tribes thereby preventing the pending carnage.[40] What real love means, he said, can be seen from a mother who protects her child with her life.[41] The image of the Buddha in the Pāli Canon is summarily stated in the words of the lay-follower Jīvaka: 'I have heard that Brahma lives with love. But I saw with my own eyes that the Venerable One (the Buddha) is always living with love.'[42]

---

33 Cf. *Sutta-Nipāta* 116–42, 546–94; *Dhammapada* 383–423; *Majjhima-Nikāya* 84.
34 Cf. *Cullavagga* 10:1.
35 Cf. *Theragātha* 557–66.
36 Cf. *Mahāvagga* 8:26,1–4.
37 Cf. *Udāna* 5:4.
38 Cf. *Dīgha-Nikāya* 5; *Sutta-Nipāta* 284–315.
39 Cf. *Sutta-Nipāta* 1:8; *Majjhima-Nikāya* 21.
40 Cf. *Jātaka* 536.
41 Cf. *Sutta-Nipāta* 149.
42 Cf. *Majjhima-Nikāya* 55.

On the Christian Belief in Incarnation

The portrayal of Jesus in the Gospels bears some strikingly similar features to the image of the Buddha. Jesus, too, addressed his message of the forthcoming kingdom of God to people from all strata of society, to men and women, to Jews and non-Jews, to the scribes and to the simple, to the rich and to the poor, to the insiders and to the outsiders of society such as tax-collectors, prostitutes and drunkards. He accompanied his message of the saving and liberating reign of God by symbolic acts of healing and exorcism, and lived a life in service of others, again symbolically expressed by the washing of his disciples' feet. He encouraged a life of non-violence, and as the central rule of God's kingdom he proclaimed and practised forgiving love, which includes even one's enemies and finds its highest expression in sacrificing one's life for one's friends.

Jesus' life, as portrayed in the Gospels, was entirely determined by his understanding of and his complete dedication to the kingdom of God. But Jesus did not put himself in God's place. Wolfhart Pannenberg sums up what is nowadays an uncontroversial view in serious biblical scholarship:

> At the heart of the message of Jesus stood the Father and his coming kingdom, not any dignity that Jesus claimed for his own person that would thus make himself equal to God (John 5.18). Jesus differentiated himself as a mere man from the Father as the one God. He thus subjected himself to the claim of the coming divine rule, just as he required his hearers to do. He could even reject the respectful title 'good Master' (Mark 10.18 par.), with a reference to God alone as good.[43]

Quite early and rather quickly, however, the professions of faith went beyond Jesus' own self-understanding, such that the Gospel of John could already speak about Jesus as the 'word' or *logos* 'made flesh'. One decisive reason for this may have to do with Jesus' own message of the kingdom of God. Jesus, as

---

43 Pannenberg (1994), p. 372.

Joachim Gnilka says, 'did not merely proclaim the coming reign of God; it also became an event in him, linking his message, his work, and his person'.[44] In principle this view is corroborated by the Jewish historian Geza Vermes. In Jesus' understanding, says Vermes, God's rule on earth is realized in that humans fulfil the divine will. Hence the two petitions of the Lord's Prayer must be seen in close conjunction: God's kingdom comes by letting God's will be done.[45] According to Vermes, the guiding idea behind Jesus' understanding of God's kingdom was the imitation of God – to be merciful to one another, just as God is merciful to us (Luke 6.36).[46] In this sense Jesus' life reflected the love of God. To quote Vermes:

> The 'neighbours' he is to love as himself often turn out to be the outcasts of society, whose company he does not merely accept but positively seeks. . . . He treats them as friends . . . But his behaviour should cause no surprise. He is simply imitating in his personal conduct what he understands to be the conduct of the Father towards those of his children who return to relation with him from a state of irrelation.[47]

It is not difficult to see how from this the following conclusion, as expressed by Gnilka, can be drawn:

> Since the kingdom of God denotes God establishing God's gracious reign, the presence of the future reign of God in Jesus' ministry ultimately means that God is actually at work in him and that in Jesus God's love itself could be experienced.[48]

---

44 Gnilka (1997), p. 255.
45 Cf. Vermes (1981), part II.
46 Cf. Vermes (1993), pp. 157ff, 200ff.
47 Vermes (1981), p. 44.
48 Gnilka (1997), p. 254 (translation amended). The German original reads: 'Weil Gottesherrschaft besagt, daß Gott seine gnädige Herrschaft aufrichtet, beteutet die Gegenwärtigkeit der zukünftigen Gottesherrschaft im Wirken Jesu letztlich, daß Gott unmittelbar in ihm wirkt, die Liebe Gottes selbst in ihm erfahrbar wurde.' Gnilka (1990), p. 258.

In this light the metaphor of the divine word made flesh makes good sense: Jesus embodies in his life and work what God is to us. In Jesus it becomes clear that 'God is love', as declared in the first letter of John (1 John 4.8). The word that is metaphorically spoken to us by God gains a concrete, relevant, perceptible, or even – as also said in the first letter of John (1 John 1.1) – 'tangible' form in the life and person of Jesus.

This is, however, precisely what prohibits a simple identification of Jesus and God, demanding instead a dynamic, high-contrast correlation that retains both the real representation of God in the life of Jesus and, at the same time, the genuine difference between Jesus, the human, and God. This has found a startling expression in the paradoxical word of the letter to the Colossians calling Jesus 'the image of the invisible God' (Col. 1.15). That is, God remains the 'invisible' reality which transcends all our finite perception and conception, and yet what God is to us finds in Jesus a visible and conceivable image.

As Christian belief in incarnation developed further, this tense correlation was clearly in danger of being dissolved for the sole benefit of its divine pole. It is therefore important and should not be underestimated that the theological development did not come to a halt when the Council of Nicaea (325) exclusively emphasized Jesus' substantial unity with God. Indeed, it led to the Council of Chalcedon (451), which balanced and in a sense amended Nicaea by adding that Jesus is not only of one substance with God but also of one substance with humans.[49] However, the question of how one should understand the relationship between the divine and the human natures of Jesus, and in particular, how it would be possible to affirm Jesus' divine nature without denying his true humanness, was left unanswered.

Pluralist Perspectives

To be sure, there are a number of differences between Jesus and Gautama, differences regarding the context, the content, and in

---

49 Cf. Kelly (1977); Young (1983).

a sense the grammar of their life and their teachings, and, of course, differences between the faithful interpretation of their person as the Christ, the 'Anointed One', and as the Buddha, the 'Enlightened' or better 'Awakened One'. But there are also some startling structural parallels in the formation of the Buddhist and Christian belief in incarnation, as in the interpretation of the Buddha and the Christ as mediators of transcendent reality: Gautama embodies the Dharma which he taught, and Jesus embodies the kingdom of God which he proclaimed. Seen from the perspective of their followers, both Jesus and Gautama are actual expressive figures of that ultimate reality to which they refer through their message, their work and their life. The Buddha appears to his adherents as the 'visible Nirvāṇa' and the Christ appears to his adherents as the visible 'image of the invisible God'. In both cases, this seems to provide the starting point for the further development of the respective concepts of incarnation. In this context I would like to underline two things:

(1) The immediate foundation for the incarnation belief does not consist in a corresponding self-understanding of Jesus or Gautama. Jesus did not understand himself as the human incarnation of the second person of a trinitarian God[50] any more than Gautama saw himself as the 'Transformation Body' (*nirmāṇakāya*) of a three-bodied Buddha-reality or cosmic *trikāya*. Rather, both were pointing beyond themselves: Jesus to the Father whose coming reign he lived and proclaimed, and Gautama to the Dharma he lived and proclaimed. In both cases the formation of incarnation belief begins with the religious experience of those for whom Jesus and Gautama became the decisive mediators of their own respective relation to transcendent reality. It was the disciples of Jesus who experienced Jesus as the mediator of God's presence, and it was the disciples of Gautama for whom he became the personified Dharma and the 'visible

---

50 As Reinhard Hübner has shown, the doctrine of the Trinity was neither implicitly nor explicitly characteristic for the origins of Christianity, and did not develop before *c.*150 CE. Moreover, its first proponents were accused of the heresies of ditheism and tritheism. Cf. Hübner (1996). For an outline of the development from the monotheism of Jesus to the later Christian doctrine of the Trinity, see Ohlig (1999).

Nirvāṇa'. Belief in incarnation is thus grounded in the principle of a real-symbolic mediation, that is, the symbol pointing away from itself to the symbolized from which it is different, while at the same time making the symbolized present through the symbol itself. This is, as Roger Haight rightly emphasizes, the crucial and lasting core of the incarnation idea.[51]

(2) What enabled Jesus and Gautama to become mediators of a salvific relation to a transcendent reality for their disciples was, of course, the fact that Jesus and Gautama lived their own lives out of such a close relationship with transcendence: in Jesus' case, his complete self-surrender to the Father and His will; in Gautama's, his utmost striving for Nirvāṇa and his loving, selfless, nirvāṇized life after his enlightenment. However, the logic of incarnation belief entails that this was not merely Jesus' and Gautama's own achievement, but something that originated in the transcendent reality *itself*. Within the Christian context this is expressed by the affirmation of the full divinity of the Spirit with whom, according to scriptural testimony, Jesus was filled and who lay at the foundation of his work. Within Buddhism the doctrine of the Buddha-Nature or Buddha-Germ (*tathāgatagarbha*) fulfils a similar function.[52] In the face of the question as to how it is possible at all that a deluded being enmeshed in greed and hatred could become a Buddha, Mahāyāna Buddhism responds with the belief in a potentiality or inclination within every being: an embryonic Buddha-Nature, rooted in nothing else than in the unconditioned reality of the 'Dharma-Body' (*dharmakāya*) itself.

Inevitably, this confronts us with the issue of the uniqueness of incarnation. The Buddha-Nature of all beings enables them to unfold this fully and become Buddhas. Could something similar

---

51 Cf. Roger Haight (1992) and (1999).

52 For a brief overview over the doctrine of Buddha-Nature, see Williams (1989), pp. 96–115. For a more comprehensive treatment, see Ruegg (1969) and (1989); King (1991); Hookham (1991). A translation of the short, but highly influential *Tathāgatagarbha Sūtra* is offered by Grosnick (transl.) (1995). The perhaps most important scripture on Buddha-Nature, the *Ratnagotravibhaga* has been translated in Jikido Takasaki (1966) and more recently in Fuchs (transl.) (2000).

be said within Christianity about the divine Spirit? According to Romans 8.14, 'all who are being led by the Spirit of God are sons of God'. In a modern theological anthropology, for example, in the thought of Karl Rahner, the gift of the Spirit is not understood in a particularist manner but as the gracious presence of God in the life of *all* people. The perfect way in which Jesus resonated with the Spirit therefore represents, as Rahner said, the '*highest* instance of the actualization of the essence of human reality, which consists in this: that man is in so far as he abandons himself to the absolute mystery whom we call God'.[53] Given such a conception, the idea that Christ had two natures can no longer jeopardize his true humanity. On the contrary, the universal presence of the divine Spirit in the depth of everyone's existence is exactly the precondition for the full actualization of what it means to be truly human. This, however, allows for the possibility of something like a 'gradual incarnation', according to which everyone incarnates or embodies the presence of God, in so far and to the degree that he or she resonates in his or her life with the divine Spirit. But why should we then not seriously reckon with the possibility that there are several 'highest instances' of such an 'actualization of the essence of human reality', that is with the possibility of several incarnations so conceived?[54]

Concretely: What impact does the Christian belief in the divine incarnation in Jesus have on Christians' response to the Buddhist belief in Buddha as the 'visible Nirvāṇa' or the incarnation of the 'Dharma-Body' (*dharmakāya*)? Will the belief that God was in Christ help Christians to accept or even affirm the Buddhist belief in incarnation, or will it oblige them to deny that Buddha embodied the *dharmakāya*? The answer to this question depends not only on what type of incarnation concept is presupposed and whether this allows in principle for the possibility of several incarnations or not. It will also depend on whether Christians can identify the reality that they see embodied in Jesus with the

---

53 Rahner's emphasis. Rahner (1978), p. 218.
54 See also Knitter (1985), pp. 186–94, where Knitter raises similar questions regarding Karl Rahner's Christology. For an example of a clear version of a gradual understanding of incarnation, see Hick (1993), particularly pp. 99–111.

reality that Buddhists see embodied in the Buddha. Is it possible, from a Christian perspective, to identify the reality called 'God' with the reality called '*dharmakāya*'?

First of all, it needs to be stated soberly that historically and phenomenologically 'God' and '*dharmakāya*' are not identical. The connotations they carry within their respective systems and their historical genealogies are simply too different. But, despite those undeniable differences, they can be seen as 'functional equivalents'. Within their own and different contexts they both serve as pointers towards an unconditioned, transcendent reality, which is the ultimate source of salvation or liberation. Whether this entails that they are pointing towards the *same* ultimate reality, can not be established in any objective and unquestionable sense, of course. The response to this question can only be given by the members of the respective religious communities themselves on the basis of specific criteria prescribed by their own traditions. From a Christian point of view the two most important criteria may be that any functional equivalent to God can be seen as genuine, (1) if it does not entail idolatry, that is, if it does not confound the ultimate with any finite and man-made reality (Ex. 20.4); and (2) if it is intrinsically linked to the evocation of selfless love, as stated in 1 John 4.7: 'Everyone who loves . . . knows God.' I suggest that the *dharmakāya* complies exceptionally well with these two criteria and that therefore Christians can and should regard it as a genuine equivalent – that is, as a concept which points indeed to the very same transcendent reality known to Christians under the concept of 'God'. Again, this does not mean that *dharmakāya* and *God* are the same, but that they refer in different ways to the same reality which transcends them both.

Could such a view meet with consent from Buddhists? Can Buddhists identify the Christian God as a genuine equivalent to the *dharmakāya* and hence see Jesus as an authentic incarnation? José Cabezón has argued that what is objectionable from a Mahāyāna Buddhist perspective is not 'the claim that Jesus is the incarnation or manifestation of a deity' but rather 'the Christian characterisation of the deity whose manifestation Jesus is said to be'.[55] According to Cabezón, this could neither be the God of the Hebrew Bible, who has too many morally objectionable features,[56] nor 'the God of later Christian theological speculation', since from a Buddhist point of view such a God does not exist.[57] Alternatively Jesus could be understood along the lines of the 'Three Bodies' doctrine as 'a *nirmāṇakāya* – that is, as the physical embodiment of an enlightened being'.[58] But this, says Cabezón, would still leave us with the question as to how to explain the contradictions between the teachings of Jesus and the traditional Buddhist doctrines. Nevertheless Cabezón indicates that this problem might be solved with recourse to the Buddhist doctrine of 'skilful means' (*upāya*) – the idea that in face of the inconceivability and ineffability of ultimate reality all teachings are at best only provisionally or relatively true if and in so far as they can be used to guide people to enlightenment.[59]

A similar approach has been adopted by three other Buddhist thinkers. Alfred Bloom,[60] Masao Abe,[61] and John Makransky[62] have, each in his own way, argued that, as Bloom

---

55 Cabezón (2000), p. 24. Additionally, Cabezón rejects 'the claim that Jesus is unique in being such a manifestation' (ibid.). This criticism has been frequently advanced by Buddhists (cf. Schmidt-Leukel (ed.) 2001, p. 29), and coincides with the view of those Hindus who accept Jesus as an *avatāra*, but not as the only one. However, as I tried to show, incarnation can also from a Christian perspective be conceived such that it no longer entails an inevitable claim to uniqueness.

56 'The God of the Hebrew Bible is a jealous one that demands the undivided loyalty of its followers, it demands of them blood sacrifice, it is partial and capable of seemingly malevolent actions, to the point of even engaging in violent reprisals against those who refuse to obey its will . . . Those who would identify Jesus with the God of the Hebrew Bible make him heir to a divine legacy that is, from a Buddhist viewpoint, at the very least of questionable worth.' Cabezón (2000), p. 25.

57 'There is no god who is the creator of the universe, who is originally pure and primordially perfected, who is omnipotent and who can will the salvation of beings. Jesus, therefore, cannot be the incarnation of such a God.' Ibid., p. 26. For the attempt to show that those traditional Christian ideas have far more in common with the Buddhist understanding of ultimate reality than Cabezón admits, see my essay, Schmidt-Leukel (2005d).

58 Cabezón (2000), p. 26.

59 Cf. Pye (1978); Cabezón (1994).

60 Cf. Bloom (1992).

61 Cf. Abe (1985).

62 Cf. Makransky (2003).

says, the 'Gods, Buddhas, and spiritual beings or symbols are manifestations from the *Dharmakāya* . . . in order to guide beings to Enlightenment'.[63] Hence, 'other religions, each in their own historical and spiritual development', could be interpreted 'as means' in the Buddhist sense of *upāya*. Makransky states, quite similarly, that 'viewed from within the Mahāyāna doctrine of skilful means, non-Buddhist traditions *do* originate in or fully express, in their own ways, the Absolute realized on the Buddhist path . . . Buddhahood is speaking through the world, and through the various religions'.[64] Abe too employs the 'Three Bodies' scheme in order to provide a Buddhist interpretation of religious diversity. He assigns to the level of the *nirmāṇakāya* any 'historical religious figure that is the center of faith', such as Gautama, Krishna, Jesus, Muhammad, or Moses; and to the level of the *saṃbhogakāya* any 'personal God who is supra-historical but has a particular name and virtue', such as Amida, Ishvara, Yahweh or Allah.[65] The level of the *dharmakāya* is represented by what Abe calls 'formless emptiness' or 'boundless openness'. This is linked to the other two levels or 'bodies' as their 'ultimate ground', and 'dynamically reveals itself both in terms of personal "God" and in terms of "lords", that are historical religious figures'.[66]

I wish to highlight two observations with regard to these Buddhist proposals. First, each of the three Buddhist thinkers uses a conceptuality specific to his own particular sub-tradition in order to give a clearer profile or specification to the understanding of the Ultimate or *dharmakāya*. For Alfred Bloom, who is a Pure Land Buddhist, the *dharmakāya* is primarily qualified as Amida Buddha,[67] while the Zen Buddhist Masao Abe qualifies the *dharmakāya* as 'boundless openness', a term that is specific to the Zen Buddhist tradition and goes back to Bodhidharma.[68] Makransky speaks about the *dharmakāya* more generally (but

---

63 Bloom (1992), p. 26.
64 Makransky (2003), p. 358. See also Makransky (2005).
65 Abe (1985), pp. 182–7.
66 Ibid., p. 184.
67 Cf. Bloom (1992), p. 26f.
68 Cf. Dumoulin (1994), pp. 90ff.

again typically for the Tibetan tradition to which he belongs) as 'Buddhahood'.

Second, all three point out that ultimate reality is beyond all concepts, and that therefore, even their tradition-specific conceptuality needs to be transcended. But this is precisely what the idea of 'skilful means' entails, so that it is again their Mahāyāna Buddhist background that enables and encourages such a view. The Buddhist affirmation that all language is at best only 'an approximation of the highest truth' might be, as Bloom indicates, the specific Buddhist contribution to inter-religious dialogue in face of those 'traditions which may be more literalist or objectivist in character'.[69] Makransky says explicitly that Buddhism is not superior in having the better concepts for the absolute, but quite the contrary because it displays 'a fuller knowledge of the ways that persons mistake their representations for absolute reality . . .'[70] Hence, Buddhism is provided with 'a fuller awareness of how its representations (all of which are relative, conceptual constructs) may be used to undercut, rather than reinforce, the human habit of absolutising what is not absolute and clinging to it'.[71] Similarly, Abe insists that his designation of the ultimate as 'Boundless Openness' should not be misread as the affirmation of a conceptual superiority, but as the invitation to all religions to go beyond their specific traditional forms of representing the ultimate, so as to be able to accept all forms as manifestations of 'formless emptiness'.[72]

As can be seen from these statements, some Buddhists are indeed prepared to identify the reality that Christians see incarnate in Jesus as a manifestation of the *dharmakāya* if and in so far as the Christian God can be understood along the lines of 'skilful means' (*upāya*) – which is to say, if the Christian God serves the purpose of leading to enlightenment as understood by Buddhists by fostering the process of non-attachment, whether on the existential level of transcending self-centredness or on the

---

69 Bloom (1992), p. 29.
70 Makransky (2003), p. 359.
71 Ibid., p. 359.
72 Cf. Abe (1985), pp. 184–90.

epistemological level of transcending all clinging to concepts. Given that Mahāyāna Buddhism understands its own concepts too as 'skilful means', this entails – as it seems – a conditioned acceptance of the Christian God as functionally equivalent to Buddhist concepts of the ultimate.

It may be true that Mahāyāna Buddhism, more than any other religious tradition, has affirmed the need for transcending all concepts. And while it is certainly true that Christianity has always had a strong and influential tradition of apophatic or negative theology, affirming that God is beyond everything that humans can conceive of, this has hardly functioned as a criterion in the assessment of other religions. But I think that the ancient criterion of non-idolatry, that is, of making no image of God, could and should be understood as referring to our conceptual and theological images of God as well.[73]

In any case, the fact that the criteriological emphasis of Buddhism and Christianity in their assessment of other potential mediators of transcendence is different, does not necessarily entail a claim to superiority.[74] For, as I argued in the previous chapter, the Buddhist emphasis on the fostering of non-attachment and the Christian emphasis on the fostering of love can be seen as complementary and mutually qualifying. Detachment without loving involvement would not be a sign of liberation but at best a form of indifferent complacency. And loving involvement without detachment seems but a barely concealed form of self-centredness.[75] If therefore detachment and loving involvement are indeed complementary and mutually qualifying, then both the Buddha and the Christ can be recognized by Buddhists and by Christians as authentic mediators of salvific transcendent reality – a recognition that would transform and enrich the followers of both.

---

73 This has been forcefully argued in Wilfred Cantwell Smith (1987).

74 I agree with Alfred Bloom that one 'does not necessarily intend the denigration of another faith if one's understanding of the ultimate and essential unity of faith is seen through the prism of one's own faith'. Bloom (1992), p. 26f.

75 Something similar has already been expressed by Buddhaghosa (fourth/fifth century CE) in the *Visuddhimagga* IX (p. 325), where he describes the 'great beings' (*mahāsatta*) as combining unswerving love (*mettā*) with perfect equanimity (*upekkhā*).

8

UNIQUENESS

A Pluralistic Reading of John 14.6

Uniqueness Confessed

'Why do you look at the speck that is in your brother's eye, but do not notice the log that is in your own eye?' (Matt. 7.3) – this is one of the striking sayings of Jesus, so typical for him. It hits us and touches us at the bottom of our hearts because of the moral and psychological truth in it. It is not only true of particular specks and logs. It implies the very general observation that we usually have a much sharper eye when it comes to a critical analysis of others than for a critical analysis of ourselves. So before I start my reflections on Christology, I'd like to sharpen our awareness by throwing a brief glance at a classical Buddhist discourse on Buddhology. Detecting the 'speck' in Buddhology might help sensitize us to the 'log' in Christology.

A major source of the early formation of traditional Theravāda Buddhist doctrines is the *Milindapañha*, 'The Questions of King Milinda'.[1] It is composed as a long series of dialogues between the Indo-Greek king Milinda (Menander, second century BCE) and the Buddhist monk Nāgasena. In one of these dialogues

---

1 As usual, it is difficult to date the origin of the work. Its oldest parts (chapters 1–3) may have been composed as early as the first century BCE, while the rest of the work seems to contain later additions, perhaps from the hands of Ceylonese revisers. Cf. T. W. Rhys Davids, 'Introduction', in Rhys Davids (1963), Part I, pp. XI–XLIX; Bechert (1985).

Nāgasena expounds the Theravāda teaching that there can be only one Buddha at one time in each aeon or world system.[2] But King Milinda questions this doctrine with the argument:

Already by the appearance of one Buddha has this world become flooded with light. If there should be a second Buddha the world would be still more illuminated by the glory of them both.[3]

To this the Buddhist monk Nāgasena replies:

This world system, O king, is a one-Buddha-supporting world; that is, it can bear the virtue of only a single Tathāgata. If a second Tathāgata were to arise the world could not bear him, it would shake and tremble, it would bend, this way and that, it would disperse, scatter into pieces, dissolve, be utterly destroyed.[4]

If two Buddhas were to arise in one world, Nāgasena continues,

then the passage (of Scripture) that the Buddha is the chief would become false, and the passage that the Buddha takes precedence of all would become false, and the passage that the Buddha is the best of all would become false. And so all those passages where the Buddha is said to be the most excellent,

---

2 Cf. *Aṅguttara-Nikāya* I, 15, 10. Basically all Buddhist schools teach that there were, are and will be many Buddhas. But this is said against the background assumption that there is an infinite number of worlds in chronological sequence and in different spacial locations. At issue is therefore whether there can be more than one Buddha per world. Parts of Nāgasena's explanation clearly entail that there can be only one Buddha per world (e.g. *Milindapañha* IV, 6, 5: 'This world system . . . is a one-Buddha-supporting world . . . '), while other parts affirm that there can be only one Buddha at a time. The traditional Theravāda concept is that the next Buddha will only appear after the community that was established by Siddhārtha Gautama has completely declined and the Dharma is entirely forgotten. Each Buddha, therefore, makes a new start in a world where no soteriological community exists and the Dharma is unknown. Nāgasena's assumption seems to be that as long as the Dharma is still proclaimed there cannot be a second Buddha, i.e. within a religious 'world' there can be one only.

3 Rhys Davids (1963), Part II, p. 47 (*Milindapañha* 237).

4 Ibid., p. 48 (*Milindapañha* 237).

the most exalted, the highest of all, the peerless one, without an equal, the matchless one, who hath neither counterpart nor rival – all would be proved false.

. . .

Of other things also, whatever is mighty in the world is singular. The broad earth is great, O king, and it is only one. The ocean is mighty, and it is only one. Sineru, the king of the mountains, is great; and it is only one. Space is mighty, and it is only one . . . Wherever any one of these spring up, then there is no room for a second. And therefore, O king, is it that only one Tathāgatha, an Arahat Buddha supreme, can appear at one time in the world.[5]

Nāgasena's explanation clearly testifies to what could be called the *logic of exaltation*. If the Buddha is praised by the scriptures as 'the highest of all' and if the scriptures are right, then by logical implication there cannot be a second. But it is easy to recognize that this argument is in a sense self-produced: the Buddha must be unique for those who praise him as the highest. And within this particular universe of praise he surely is unique. But can this claim be extended beyond that particular world, that is the world of Theravāda Buddhist faith? Look at Nāgasena's examples: the earth, the ocean, mount Sineru – we know that all of these are unique only within the narrow boundaries of Nāgasena's ancient Indian world-view. But nowadays we are well aware that neither the ocean is unique, nor high mountains, nor the earth, nor perhaps even the space if space is understood as a function of a particular universe and if there might be a plurality of worlds. Within the boundaries of a certain religion or – as we could say – a certain universe of religious experience, the Buddha might very well be as unique as the earth is for us. But within a wider context of inhabited worlds, that is in the context of various religious realms, there might be others and among these we will find ourselves, that is, Christianity, and Jesus Christ as the one whom we exalt as the 'highest of all' or as the only one – expressed in statements

---

5 Ibid., p. 50f. (*Milindapañha* 239).

ascribed to him like: 'I am the way, and the truth, and the life, no one comes to the Father, but through Me' (John 14.6).

Religiously, our current situation is marked by a global inter-religious encounter which has just begun, which proceeds gradually but constantly, which cannot be stopped and which implies – in the long run – massive consequences which are hardly to be estimated. This might be compared to an interstellar exchange, to the meeting and intersecting of large galaxies. In such a situation a range of new and unexpected phenomena occur, among which is the possibility not only of penetrating and understanding another religious universe but of seeing our own world through their eyes – reminiscent of the first fascinating pictures of the earth, the 'blue planet', as seen from space – or conversely, of seeing the broader world – the various universes of faiths – from the different perspectives of each of them.[6]

It is in this context that I present some reflections on John 14.6. I will not argue as a biblical scholar since this is simply not my field; hence I am not able to discuss competently any of the details or intricacies of the proper interpretation of John's Gospel, for example, the degree of Gnostic influence or more specifically the Gnostic or non-Gnostic (Jewish) origin or background of the metaphors 'way', 'truth' and 'life' in our verse. I will take them in a rather broad sense and my reflections will be determined by a systematic approach – however, by the approach of a systematic theology that is carried out in the horizon of our growing knowledge and understanding of other religions and of the inevitable process of a hermeneutical 'Horizontverschmelzung' (H. G. Gadamer), that is, of the fusion of the different traditional horizons of our interpretative attempts.

Uniqueness Challenged

From a Christian point of view the crucial issue is the status of Christianity in relation to other religious traditions. This entails

---

6 Cf. Grünschloß (1999); Coward (2000); Gort, Jansen and Vroom (eds) (2006).

two fundamental and interrelated questions: First, how does Christianity understand and assess the other religions in the light of its own teachings? Second, how does Christianity understand and assess itself in the light of the other religions? It is obvious that the answer to each one of these two questions has immediate implications for the answer to the other one. The theological discussion of these two questions has come to be called 'theology of religions'. Over the last four decades it has developed into one of the most heated theological debates carried out on a worldwide level. The various standpoints that theologians have taken are frequently grouped into three different classes: exclusivism, inclusivism and pluralism. This classification has become the object of some criticism during recent years. I feel that it is still a very helpful taxonomy, but one which is, however, in need of a more precise formulation.[7] As I define it, *exclusivism* is the conviction that salvific knowledge of a transcendent reality is mediated by only one religion (which will naturally be one's own). *Inclusivism* is the conviction that salvific knowledge of a transcendent reality is mediated by more than one religion (though not necessarily by all of them), but that only one religion mediates that knowledge in a uniquely superior way (this again, will naturally be one's own religion). Pluralism shares with inclusivism the conviction that salvific knowledge of a transcendent reality is mediated by more than one religion (though not necessarily by all of them) but, unlike inclusivism, it holds that there is none among them whose mediation of that knowledge is superior to all the rest. In other words, there is no 'single highest' among the religions, so that at least some of them are different but equally valid paths of salvation.

If we add a fourth possible position, the position of *atheism/naturalism*, according to which salvific knowledge of a transcendent reality is mediated by none of the religions (because there is no transcendent reality), we arrive at a classification that is complete due to its fully disjunctive character: either religions mediate salvific knowledge or they do not. If they do, then either

---

7 Cf. Schmidt-Leukel (2005c).

only one of them does or more than one does. If more than one, then either only one does in a uniquely superior form, or there are several doing this differently but equally well. Every theory addressing the question of whether religions mediate salvific knowledge of transcendence falls necessarily under one of these four categories. There is no further option left. Either one avoids the question (and thus ceases to do 'theology of religions') or one has to make a choice. The *atheist/naturalist* position runs counter to the claims of all religions and is therefore not a 'theological' or religious option (note: this does not entail that it is no option at all). The choice a *religious* interpretation of religious diversity has to make is thus between exclusivism, inclusivism and pluralism.

It may be the case that religious diversity does not challenge each religion in exactly the same way – but it does constitute a challenge to each of them. The challenge arises from the fact that as more and more members of each religion acquire a deeper understanding of other religions they are learning how to see their own tradition through the others' eyes. This inevitably sheds new light on one's own tradition and therefore requires a reconsideration of one's previous self-understanding – whatever this might have been. In this process of reconsidering and reinterpreting one's own religion in relation to the others, each religion needs to make a choice between the three basic options.

A number of religious thinkers (though still a comparatively tiny minority) in all the major religious traditions are currently moving towards a pluralistic view, as developed from within their own specific religious background.[8] This is possible because each religious tradition seems to have important doctrinal resources – or should I say: living fountains of insight – which not only permit but in fact call for such a move. But each religion also has strong traditions of either exclusivistic or inclusivistic claims hinging on specific doctrines and kerygmatic formulas. These need to be addressed and openly discussed by those who tend

---

8 Cf. Hick and Askari (eds) (1985); Knitter (ed.) (2005). For an overview of pluralistic positions in non-Christian religions, see Schmidt-Leukel (2005), pp. 171–5.

towards a pluralistic understanding of religious diversity. Within Islam, for example, there is the understanding of Muhammad as the 'seal of the prophets' (Sura 33.40) and the corresponding claim that the Qur'an is revelation in its most superior form. In Judaism there is the belief in a special election and a kind of superior covenant. In Buddhism there is the claim that the Noble Eightfold Path is 'the only way' so that 'there is no other' (*Dhammapada* 273f). In Hinduism there is the quasi-pluralist claim that only Hinduism possesses the suitable doctrines to acknowledge the fundamental unity and equality of religions (which, of course, makes Hinduism the *primus inter pares*). And in Christianity there is, as noted, John 14.6, which is quoted again and again when Christian pluralists are scolded by their exclusivistically and inclusivistically minded brothers and sisters. For them and their counterparts in the other religions, as John May rightly states,

> the 'truth' embodied in their ritual and expressed in myth or doctrine is an absolute value directly bound up with the possibility of 'salvation'. . . . The thought that there could be alternative systems of belief and ways of being religious that would question the uniqueness of their own certainties is, strictly speaking, inconceivable.[9]

Within the framework of this chapter there is neither space nor need to recall the arguments which, from within the Christian tradition, count against an exclusivist or an inclusivist view and at the same time in favour of a pluralist one.[10] But it may be worth offering some reflections on how a Christian pluralist might understand the words of John 14.6, which seem so obviously to deny any sound possibility of a Christian *and* pluralistic theology of religions. How can those who are convinced that *life* – even and in particular holy or eternal life – always exists in a rich manifoldness, that *truth* – even and in particular the truth

---

9 May (2000), p. 55.
10 For an extensive and detailed discussion of these arguments, see Schmidt-Leukel (1997) and (2005), pp. 96–162.

of God – always exists in a variety of human reflections, and that there are 'as many *ways* to God as there are human beings',[11] respond to a statement like John 14.6?

Uniqueness, an Interpretation not a Quotation

The first part of my answer to this question is based on the nowadays almost common exegetical judgement, that – to quote Geza Vermes –

> the so-called Gospel of John . . . reflects, not the authentic message of Jesus or even the thinking about him of his imme-diate followers, but the highly evolved theology of a Christian writer who lived three generations after Jesus and completed his Gospel in the opening years of the second century A.D.[12]

When it comes to the 'historical' or 'real' Jesus and the question of his authentic self-understanding, most biblical scholars, as far as I can see, agree that his message was theocentric and that he clearly distinguished himself from the one God in whom he be-lieved and whom he addressed as 'Father'. Wolfhart Pannenberg – who may not count as a suspect witness because he is both most interested in defending the high Christology of Nicaea and Chalcedon and a vigorous opponent of pluralist theology – sum-marizes the findings of biblical research as follows:

> At the heart of the message of Jesus stood the Father and his coming kingdom, not any dignity that Jesus claimed for his

---

11 Emphasis added. This was the startling answer given by the then Cardinal Josef Ratzinger when he was asked how many ways are there leading to God. The full interview sequence reads: '"Wie viele Wege gibt es zu Gott?" "So viele, wie es Menschen gibt. Denn auch innerhalb des gleichen Glaubens ist der Weg eines jeden Menschen ein ganz persönlicher. Wir haben das Wort Christi: Ich bin der Weg. Insofern gibt es letztenendes einen Weg, und jeder, der zu Gott un-terwegs ist, ist damit auf irgendeine Weise auch auf dem Weg Jesu Christi. Aber das heißt nicht, daß bewußtseinsmäßig, willensmäßig alle Wege identisch sind, sondern im Gegenteil, der eine Weg ist eben so groß, daß er in jedem Menschen zu seinem persönlichen Weg wird."' Ratzinger (1996), p. 35.
12 Vermes (2001), p. 6.

own person that would thus make himself equal to God (John 5.18). Jesus differentiated himself as a mere man from the Father as the one God. He thus subjected himself to the claim of the coming divine rule, just as he required his hearers to do. He could even reject the respectful title 'good master' (Mark 10.18 par.), with a reference to God alone as good.[13]

The portrait of Jesus in the synoptic Gospels, that is, the portrait of Jesus who, like every devout Jew, strictly rejects even the remotest move of identifying himself with God, is very different from the self-presentation of Jesus in the Gospel of John. 'I am the way, and the truth, and the life; no one comes to the Father, but through me' belongs to the so-called *ego eimi*-sayings, that is, a group of sayings all starting with the words 'I am', which are so typical of the portrayal of Jesus in the Gospel of John, as in, for example, 'I am the bread of life' (6.35), or 'I am the resurrection and the life' (11.25) or 'I am the door; if anyone enters through Me, he shall be saved' (10.9), the last of which is perhaps the closest parallel to our verse in so far as it has the same 'through Me' (*di' emou*) regarding salvation. Through these 'I am'-sayings Jesus is indeed put very close to God.[14] This is perhaps most obvious in John 8.58 where Jesus says 'Truly, truly, I say to you, before Abraham was born, I am'. Here we find the Johannine theme of pre-existence, which of course also makes it clear that the 'I' in the 'I am'-sayings cannot be simply identified with the human being Jesus. 'Before Abraham was, I am' connects the 'I am'-sayings with the prologue of John's Gospel. This prologue introduces Jesus as the one in whom and through whom the divine *logos* 'became flesh, and dwelt among us' (1.14) in order to reveal the invisible God (1.18). This explains why the Jesus of John's Gospel almost identifies himself with the Father in such sayings as: 'I and the Father are one' (10.30) or 'He who has seen Me has seen the Father' (14.9). I add 'almost' because even John lets Jesus say 'The Father is greater than I' (14.28).

The *ego eimi*-sayings in John's Gospel are with all historical

---

13 Pannenberg (1994), p. 372.
14 For the following, see Vermes (2001), pp. 41–55.

probability not quotations of Jesus' own words but theological interpretations which try to spell out his meaning as a divine revealer in the eyes of the early Christian Church. Jesus' life and Jesus' message were focused on the kingdom of God. Out of his own experience of God's presence, and informed by the Jewish tradition to which he belonged and in which he lived, he interpreted God's rule (God's 'kingdom') as marked by boundless mercy, as the presence of a divine love which should be answered and reflected in the twofold commandment to love God and one's fellow human being. In so far as Jesus submitted his own life to God's merciful reign, he realized the kingdom of God in his own person. In living his own life as a perfect reflection of the Father's love Jesus became a mediator of God's presence for his disciples, a human image of the invisible God (Col. 1.15). The developing interpretation of Jesus as a human mediator of God's loving presence reaches its first climax in the Gospel of John and the Johannine portrait of Jesus as the human manifestation of the divine Logos.

Uniqueness, an Interpretation Reinterpreted

If this brief sketch is at all close to a correct historical placement of John's Gospel and the Johannine Jesus, what does this mean for a Christian theology of religions? How, in particular, should we understand the second half of John 14.6, 'no one comes to the Father, but through Me'? The meaning of the words 'through Me' is far from clear. Without doubt, it is a strong instance of metaphorical language, as is also evident in the same 'through Me' in: 'I am the door; if anyone enters through Me, he shall be saved' (10.9). But if 'through Me' is metaphorical language, how should we translate it?[15]

Christian *exclusivists* usually translate this phrase as pointing to the crucifixion in the sense that, through his self-sacrifice,

---

15 Cf. the exciting but very fragmentary notes in Thomas Merton's Asian Diary (19 November 1968) where he attempts to interpret the 'I am the door' in terms of the Buddhist 'emptiness' alluding to the Zen motif of the 'gateless gate' (*mumonkan*) (Merton 1999, p. 285).

Christ has made salvation possible and that this salvation is only available through its explicit proclamation and the corresponding belief in the Christian gospel.[16] Christian *inclusivists* usually emphasize that the words 'I' and 'Me' when spoken by the Johannine Jesus refer to Jesus in so far as he manifests the divine Logos. These words are meant as expressions of the Logos who is incarnated in Jesus but whose revealing and saving activity is neither confined to Jesus nor to the Christian Church, but 'enlightens every man' (John 1.9).[17] This is the ancient patristic teaching of the *logoi spermatikoi*, the 'germs of the Logos', which led countless people among the non-Christians to a saving, but fragmentary knowledge of God, while the fullness of the Logos has appeared only in Jesus Christ. According to Christian inclusivism, 'through Me' therefore means that salvation is possible only through the Logos, that is, only through divine self-disclosure – a self-disclosure that encompasses all humanity, but finds its unique climax in Jesus, so that the chance of salvation is highest within the orbit of Christianity.

How then may a Christian *pluralist* interpret John 14.6? First of all, the Christian pluralist will not deny that divine truth, eternal life, and the way to the 'Father' can indeed be found through Jesus and the proclamation of the gospel. A Christian pluralist will not deny Jesus' status as a genuine mediator of God's saving presence, but he or she will deny that Jesus is the only mediator or that Jesus is a mediator who is uniquely superior to all the others. So, a Christian pluralist also sees the Way, the Truth and the Life in Jesus, but as exemplified and represented in him. To quote Paul Knitter's famous thesis: 'The uniqueness of Jesus' salvific role can be reinterpreted in terms of *truly* but not *only*.'[18]

Against exclusivists, a pluralist will thus reject the idea that salvation was enabled through the crucifixion, and will hold that all salvation depends (in Christian terms) on God's grace alone, which would cease to be grace if Jesus had to pay the full price

---

16 Cf., for example, Geivett and Phillips (1995).
17 Cf., for example, Pinnock (1997), pp. 77–9.
18 Knitter (1997), p. 7.

for the debt of our sins by the sacrifice of his life.[19] Salvation or God's grace is therefore not constituted by the crucifixion but represented or expressed by it[20] in so far as the crucifixion marks the consumption of Jesus' life, lived as a reflection of God's love up to its most radical consequence. Together with Christian inclusivists, pluralists will hold that the revealing and saving activity of the Logos is not confined to Jesus Christ or the Christian Church.[21] Like inclusivists, pluralists can interpret the phrase 'through Me' as referring to the divine Logos. But they will deny that the fullness of the Logos can be found in Jesus alone.

A two-natures Christology, as classically formulated by the Council of Chalcedon, does not necessarily contradict a pluralist interpretation of Jesus (as I will show in more detail in Chapter 9). A real human being can be the medium of nothing less than the Logos, that is, the communication of the real divine reality. Precisely because of the true humanity of the mediator – with all the specific human limitations – the finite medium cannot exhaust the infinite God, so that the reality which Jesus mediates is *totus deus* (fully God) but not *totum deum* (the fullness of God), as Christian tradition has constantly reaffirmed. This leaves room for the assumption of other finite mediators of the same infinite reality.[22] However, if Jesus need not necessarily be seen as the only mediator, is he not nevertheless a very specific one, being unique not as a divine mediator as such but in the specific form in which he made God present to us? I think that this can be acknowledged without any hesitation. How, then, shall we specify his uniqueness in comparison to other unique mediators? But who are the 'we'? I think that 'we' Christians assume too quickly something like a natural hermeneutical privilege on the correct understanding of Jesus' specific role. Jesus belongs to humankind – as do the Buddha, Muhammad, and others. It is for all humanity – while drawing on various religious traditions

---

19 Cf. Hick (1993), p. 127.
20 Cf. Ogden (1992), pp. 84–99.
21 Cf. Hick (1977), p. 181.
22 For the discussion of other possible mediators, see John Macquarrie (1995).

– to say what Jesus might mean to them, and in which sense they would possibly see something unique in him. This is an exciting new discourse and belongs to the fascinating phenomena that occur when the religious galaxies intersect. As Gregory Barker shows in his tremendously important book *Jesus in the World's Faith*,[23] this discourse is well underway.

A Christian pluralist, however, can and will presumably understand Jesus as a *normative* exemplar of what a genuine mediation of divine presence is like. For this, one might point to the first letter of John which derives from the life of Jesus the crucial criterion that 'everyone who loves is born of God and knows God' (1 John 4.7) and that 'anyone who does not practise righteousness is not of God' (1 John 3.10). Nevertheless, to acknowledge the normativity of Jesus does not exclude – as Roger Haight rightly remarks – 'the possibility of other saviour figures of equal status . . . who may also reveal something of God that is normative'.[24]

Yet, it might very well be the case that such a pluralist reading of John 14.6 falls short of what the author of the Gospel wanted to express. Maybe John wanted to claim more. Maybe he wanted to say that Jesus has a completely unique role regarding salvation, that he is 'the most excellent, the most exalted, the highest of all, the peerless one, without an equal, the matchless one, who hath neither counterpart nor rival'. Do you remember these words? These are from Nāgasena's statement about the Buddha quoted at the beginning of this chapter. If this gives us the clue – that is, if it indicates that the uniqueness of Jesus is proclaimed out of the logic of exaltation – then a pluralist can agree once more, without taking such words too literally, knowing that a claim for uniqueness born out of an entirely justified exaltation is anything but unique.[25]

---

23 Barker (ed.) (2005).
24 R. Haight (1992), p. 281. For a balanced and careful treatment of the question of Jesus' normativity, see also R. Haight (1999), pp. 403–10. On the issue of suitable criteria for mutual inter-religious assessment, see Bernhardt and Schmidt-Leukel (eds) (2005).
25 'A claim to uniqueness is not unique.' W. C. Smith (1987), p. 64.

9

CHALCEDON DEFENDED

A Pluralistic Re-Reading of the Two-Natures Doctrine

Christian theology of religions can either be understood in a more practical or in a more theoretical sense. When understood in a practical sense, it means theological reflection about social interaction and living together with members of other religions. But when understood in a theoretical sense, it includes a twofold question: How does Christianity make sense of the existence of other religions, and how does Christianity make sense of itself in the light of the presence of other religions? Thus theoretical theology of religions has to correlate Christian doctrines with the awareness of the existence of other religions. Or more precisely, other religions have to be interpreted in relation to Christian beliefs, and Christian beliefs have to be looked at again in the light of the beliefs of other religions. Wilfred Cantwell Smith has nicely expressed that task by his aphorism: 'We explain the fact that the Milky Way is there by the doctrine of creation, but how do we explain that the Bhagavad Gita is there?'[1] The following considerations belong to that theoretical kind of theology of religions, and they are about one specific Christian belief, the belief in the divine incarnation in Jesus and its dogmatic elaboration as the two-natures doctrine.

---

1 Smith (1976), p. 16.

Incarnation, in a Christian context, basically means that the 'word became flesh', that God's revealing self-disclosure took shape in and through Jesus of Nazareth. This, of course, did not happen at Jesus' birth or at his conception. Celebrating Christmas as the beginning of the incarnation is only done so retrospectively. For incarnation happened through and throughout Jesus' life and death as a human being who lived and died in such a way that he became the 'image of the invisible God' (Col. 1.15; see also 2 Cor. 4.4). This double aspect of the incarnation, the visible image that is a real human being, and the invisible mystery of God, has been traditionally expressed in the Chalcedonian two-natures doctrine[2] and in what follows I will look at this from the perspective of a pluralistic theology of religion.

Frequently the belief in incarnation, particularly in its Chalcedonian form, is cited as an argument against a pluralistic theology of religions, or more precisely, as an argument against the compatibility of a pluralistic position with Christian theology. At first sight the arguments for such an incompatibility seem very strong. For instance, in 1967 Karl Rahner wrote that it is the belief in divine incarnation in Jesus Christ which makes it impossible for a Christian to consider other religions as being of equal value, since it would follow from belief in incarnation that 'Christianity alone is founded by God himself through Christ and is therefore the absolute religion designed for all humankind.'[3] In the writings of John Hick we find a very similar assertion: 'the incarnational doctrine' to which – says Hick – it is 'integral . . . that there has been (and will be) no other divine incarnation . . . makes Christianity unique in that it, alone among the religions of the world, was founded by God in person'.[4]

Therefore, while developing his pluralistic hypothesis, John Hick has strongly criticized the incarnation doctrine and allowed only its understanding as myth and metaphor. The two-natures

---

2 For the historical context of the Christological decisions of the Council of Chalcedon (451 CE), see Kelly (1977); Young (1983).

3 Die 'einzige von Gott durch Christus selbst gestiftete, absolute, für alle Menschen bestimmte Religion ist.' Rahner (1967), p. 355f.

4 Hick (1985), p. 34.

doctrine of Chalcedon in particular has become a major target of his sharp attacks, for this doctrinal development can rightly be seen as the most elaborate expression of a literal belief in incarnation. But the consequence of this is that many Christians today feel sure that the pluralistic theology of religions and Christian belief are incompatible. For they consider the incarnation doctrine and its Chalcedonian elaboration to be indispensable to Christianity.

Now, for anyone understanding him- or herself as a Christian pluralist that situation leaves only two possibilities: One would be to argue that belief in incarnation (or at least its Chalcedonian version) is not essential to Christianity – and there are of course Christian churches that still reject Chalcedon. The other route would be to question the putative incompatibility of incarnation belief and religious pluralism. In what follows I try to take up this latter alternative.[5] I think there are some good arguments showing that (1) a purely metaphorical interpretation of incarnation remains insufficient, that is, it still leaves open the question of two natures; (2) therefore there is a sense in which Chalcedon can be meaningfully interpreted and defended; and (3) such a reading of Chalcedon fits very well into a pluralistic option within the Christian theology of religions. This may at first sound like a theological conjuring trick, but it is in fact intended as a serious and constructive proposal.

Beyond Metaphor

In his contribution to *The Myth of God Incarnate* Hick introduced into the debate the question of the logical character of Christological language.[6] This aspect is fundamental for Hick's argument, which might be summarized as: Talk about incarnation can either be understood literally or metaphorically. If understood literally it will lead to the following dilemma: Either the claim of divine incarnation in Jesus conflicts with his true

---

5 For a similar approach, see Haight (2005).
6 Hick (1977).

humanity, as for example in the various *logos-sarx* concepts (a human body with a divine soul), or if you try to safeguard his genuine human nature you run into the paradoxical utterances of Chalcedon. In the first case the claim of incarnation would conflict with Jesus' own self-understanding, since he decisively differentiated himself as a true human being from the one true God (cf. Mark 10.18). And it would also conflict with the synoptic records, which picture Jesus – despite his exorcisms and miraculous healings – nevertheless as a true man with typical human limitations. But in the second case – trying to safeguard true humanity – one has to face the enigma of how anyone could remain a true man when at the same time the true God is incarnate in him. According to Hick we get the 'insoluble problem . . . of a being who is both divinely omniscient and humanly fallible, divinely omnipotent and humanly limited, eternal and yet born in time, omnipresent and yet locally physical'.[7] Thus Hick interprets the two-natures doctrine of Chalcedon as expressing the 'idea of someone having both a fully divine nature, i.e. having all the essential divine attributes, and at the same time a fully human nature, i.e. having all the essential human attributes'.[8] However, Chalcedon only *asserts* that Jesus is truly God and truly human, it does not *explain* how this is possible. But this, Hick claims, makes it an unintelligible and meaningless utterance.

For Hick the alternative lies in a metaphorical understanding. Whereas the idea of incarnation makes no sense when taken literally, it nevertheless 'makes excellent metaphorical sense'.[9] When understood metaphorically the conflict with Jesus' own self-understanding and the earliest biblical witness to him as a genuine human being disappears. And the Chalcedonian formula, together with all its logical problems, becomes superfluous, because this formula is clearly based on a literal understanding of incarnation. However, what does it mean exactly to understand incarnation metaphorically? What is the literal meaning behind such a metaphorical reading? Hick mentions three aspects:

---

7 Hick (1991), p. 208.
8 Hick (1993), p. 48.
9 Ibid., p. 12.

(1) In so far as Jesus was doing God's will, God was acting through him on earth and was in this respect 'incarnate' in Jesus' life; (2) In so far as Jesus was doing God's will he 'incarnated' the ideal of human life lived in openness and response to God; (3) In so far as Jesus lived a life of selfgiving love, or *agape*, he 'incarnated' a love that is a finite reflection of the infinite divine love.[10]

These statements are not meant to be metaphorically but literally true. The appropriateness of the incarnation metaphor depends, according to Hick, on the literal truth of these three statements. At a different place he summarizes what he considers to be the non-metaphorical meaning behind the incarnation metaphor as 'something like this: that Jesus was so open and obedient to God that God was able to act through him in relation to those whom Jesus encountered'.[11] Repeatedly Hick has illustrated this non-metaphorical meaning by the inspiration Christology of Geoffrey Lampe[12] and the paradox-of-grace Christology of Donald Baillie.[13]

I think that by these statements Hick undoubtedly does cover what today is affirmed by most New Testament scholars as the result of historical research: What Jesus had taught and what he practised in his own life emerged from his deep and intimate experience of God. And by living what he taught about the merciful reign of God, his followers were able to experience the *basileia tou theou*, the kingdom or reign of God, in the life and person of Jesus himself. For them, Jesus himself became the paradigm of God's kingdom, the *autobasileia*, the kingdom in person, as it was later expressed by Origen.[14] But does that really mean abandoning a literal understanding of incarnation? I do not think so. Hick sticks to the belief that it was truly God who was present in the life of Jesus. And he clarifies that presence in a twofold

---

10 Ibid., p. 105.
11 Hick (1991), p. 207.
12 Cf. Lampe (1977).
13 Cf. Baillie (1961).
14 Origen in his Commentary on Matthew (books 12:34f and 14:7).

way: First, God was present *to* Jesus, that is, Jesus experienced the presence of God and let his life be governed by that. Second, God was present *through* Jesus to others, that is, Jesus became God's 'agent' and 'the divine reality was mediated through him to others'.[15] However, these statements do preserve the basic idea and justifiable root of the incarnation doctrine in a *literal* sense: The true God being present *in* (in Jesus' experience) and *through* (in the disciple's experience mediated through Jesus) the life of a true human being.

It seems that Hick is willing to concede that this divine presence in and through a true human being indicates two senses of a literal understanding of incarnation. In his Christological monograph *The Metaphor of God Incarnate* he refers to six different senses of incarnation that had been pointed out by Sarah Coakley, and accepts the first two of them: He does not deny an understanding of incarnation 'that affirms God's involvement in human life', and equally he does not deny incarnation in the sense 'that in the life of Jesus God was involved in a particular and specially powerful and effective way', so that 'Jesus was not just an ordinary man, but one whose relationship to God has a universal significance'.[16] Exactly these two basic forms of incarnational divine presence have again been reaffirmed by Hick in the context of his pluralist hypothesis. For instance in a response in his American Festschrift he emphasized that 'according to the . . . (pluralist) hypothesis the Real is present to us in and through everything, but most importantly . . . through other finite persons . . .'[17]

Thus I think that Hick's seemingly non-incarnational Christology is in fact still very much an incarnational one, or to put it differently, that behind the metaphorical interpretation of the incarnation doctrine a literal one reappears. If that is true, this must have consequences for the evaluation of the Chalcedonian two-natures doctrine as well as for the clarification of the relationship between belief in incarnation and the pluralistic option

---

15 Hick (1988), p. 177.
16 Hick (1993), p. 9.
17 Hick (1991b), p. 242.

in the theology of religions. Let me first explain the consequences for the interpretation and evaluation of Chalcedon.

Chalcedon Reaffirmed

If it is truly God who was present in the life of Jesus and whose presence was mediated through Jesus to others, and if this mediator was truly man, then we have the problem of the two natures: How is it possible that the infinite God is present in and through[18] a finite medium, a true human being? To my mind, this is and remains a genuine mystery. But does this make it a meaningless utterance? Not every affirmation of a mysterious relation between two very different realities is meaningless. For example, it is and remains very mysterious, as Thomas Nagel has impressively shown,[19] how it is possible for a physical reality like the sounds of our language or the printed signs in a book to be the medium of something very different, namely intellectual content or meaning. Actually one could say – following Nagel and Chalcedon – that every book and every word has two natures: the material nature of the sign and the immaterial nature of the meaning. How they are related to each other and how this relation is possible remains in fact deeply puzzling. Another example of a meaningful but mysterious two-natures case can be taken from Hick's own writings. In his *Death and Eternal Life* he remarks – while defending mind/brain interaction – that this

---

18 Hick – in his appreciative but also critical discussion of Roger Haight (in the 2nd enlarged edition of *The Metaphor of God Incarnate*, 2005, pp. 161–73) – has expressed reservations about the formula that God is encountered 'in and through' Jesus, at least in so far as the 'through' could easily be equated with the 'in' and thus 'authorize the traditional dogma that Jesus had two natures' (ibid., p. 169). But it needs to be asked whether there could be any genuine experience of God by human beings at all without the implication of some sort of ontological presence or immanence of the Divine *in* the finite. From a pluralist perspective, I would hold, it is not the ontology of Divine immanence that is at stake but the question whether that should apply only to Jesus. Pluralists can argue that it is precisely the general Divine immanence that makes the special role of mediatorship as we find it in Jesus, but not only in him (!), possible at all. On this, see the final section of this chapter.

19 Cf. Nagel (1987), chapter 5.

'interaction of body and mind, as entities of basically different kinds, is unique and utterly mysterious'.[20] One final example will bring us back to Christology: In a debate, Stephen Davis charged Hick with being inconsistent in rejecting Chalcedon as an insoluble paradox, but accepting at the same time Donald Baillie's paradox of grace as a possible illustration of the literal meaning behind the incarnation metaphor. Hick responded that the paradox of grace, that some freely done acts are at the same time caused by divine grace, has to be accepted, even though we do not understand it, because 'it happens' or better, because it is a given in our experience, whereas 'the God-manhood of Jesus with his divine and human natures, is not an observed fact . . .'[21] But if my thesis is correct, that Hick's putatively non-incarnational interpretation is still incarnational enough to create the two-natures problem, then this response seems very doubtful: For Hick does attest that the presence of God in and through the life of Jesus was *experienced*. So at least for Jesus' disciples there was the experience of a reality of a truly divine reality mediated by a truly human being. This experience seems to be on the same level as the experience of the paradox of grace, and thus it could and should be accepted in the same manner.

Therefore it seems clear to me that finally Hick does not and cannot avoid incarnational thinking, that in this sense a purely metaphorical interpretation is insufficient, so that in the end the problem of the two natures persists: How is it possible that there is a real divine presence in and through the life of a real human being? I think that this remains utterly mysterious, but nevertheless, that this is not a meaningless mystery. But Chalcedon says more than just that there are two natures encountered in and through the life of Jesus. It goes beyond that in also saying something about the *relation* between the two natures, namely that neither of them becomes diminished by the presence of the other, but that they are both present without confusion and without separation. With that, of course, the matter becomes much more difficult. Chalcedon might be rightly charged with being mean-

---

20 Hick (1990), p. 120.
21 Hick (1988b), p. 34.

ingless if its doctrine of two natures had to be understood exclusively in the way that Hick has done, namely that having two natures means to combine all the essential divine and human attributes in *one person*. However, is that really the only possible way to interpret Chalcedon? The Chalcedonian formula affirms that the 'property of each nature' is 'preserved and coalescing in one *prosopon* and one *hypostasis* – not parted or divided into two *prosopa*. . .'.[22] But is the point of union to which the fathers of Chalcedon refer by the terms *prosopon* and *hypostasis* identical with a modern or contemporary understanding of 'person' in the sense of the unique individual subject of will and cognition? This is hardly the case if one follows the post-Chalcedonian condemnation of monotheletism, that is the rejection of the doctrine that Jesus Christ had only one single will. If – as the Church affirmed after Chalcedon – the two natures imply *two wills*, a divine will and a human will, one would presumably have to conclude that in a modern sense of 'person', as the unique subject of volition, the post-Chalcedonian Church did in fact imply two 'persons'.[23] In addition, it is more than doubtful that the *logos* as the second 'person' of the Trinity could be understood in a modern sense of 'person' which would amount to tritheism. The alternative is, of course, to see the divine 'persons' as 'roles', as different ways in which God is revealed to us. And this understanding of 'person' as 'role' is more in line with the original meaning of 'person' (the mask that the actor used in the classical Greek drama, in other words, the 'role' he played) than the modern understanding of the concept. Taking these two aspects into account, we cannot say that Chalcedon ascribed the conflicting properties of the two natures to one and the same person (in any modern sense of the word 'person').

Be that as it may, from a contemporary systematic perspective we are free to interpret Chalcedon in such a way that it reflects and corresponds to the original God-experience of Jesus himself, and the experience of his disciples and ourselves that God

22 Kelly (1977), p. 340.
23 See also Rahner's related considerations in his *Foundations of the Christian Faith*, § 6:7c (Rahner 1978).

was and still is mediated through the life of Jesus to his follow-ers. This kind of interpretation has been masterfully sketched by Roger Haight in his lucid essay 'The Case for Spirit Christology'. According to Haight, double-nature is characteristic of any medi-ation of the infinite God through a finite medium or *symbol*: 'the symbol both makes God present and points away from itself to a God who is other that itself'. For Haight 'the doctrine of Chal-cedon mirrors this dialectical structure'.[24]

In this light, Chalcedon represents the very welcome warn-ing that the divine presence in the life of Jesus does not mean, and cannot mean, that Jesus was not a true and real human be-ing. On the contrary, Jesus was 'like us in all things except sin' (Chalcedon). I call it a welcome warning, because it enables us to understand Chalcedon in such a way that it remains consistent with modern historical insights into the earliest scriptural wit-ness about the true humanity of Jesus. Therefore I would suggest as a hermeneutical principle for any modern reading of Chal-cedon that the divine nature of Jesus has to be understood in such a way that it does not diminish the true humanity of Jesus – rather than the other way around.

'. . . not a singularity'

Nevertheless, there is still the question of whether it makes sense to say that someone is truly and really human if a divine real-ity or nature is also present in him (or her). I think it does, if we understand human nature as something that is open for just that, for responding to and mediating the divine presence. It is not alien or contradictory to human nature to be a vehicle or medium of divine immanence. This seems to be the basic idea behind those modern Christologies that try to show that Jesus is not *essentially* different from all other human beings – which would automatically draw his true humanity into question – but that he is only different *in degree*. You can find that idea also

---

24 Haight (1992), p. 263. The same idea is also developed more fully in Haight (1999), particularly p. 205.

in the Christology of Karl Rahner, who spoke of Jesus as the 'unique and *highest* instance of the actualization of the essence of human reality' or as 'the most radical culmination of man's essence'.[25] However, if it is really in no way alien to human nature to be the vessel of divine immanence, if it is even, as Rahner says, 'the actualization of the essence of human reality', then it appears very implausible that this should have happened only once. Rather this conception leads to the idea that, when talking about incarnation, we are not – as Hick rightly says – 'speaking of something that is in principle unique, but of an interaction of the divine and the human which occurs in many different ways and degrees in all human openness to God's presence'.[26] Or to quote John Macquarrie, 'that incarnation was not a singularity or anomaly in world history but is a constant characteristic of God's relation to his creation. There are, one may say, degrees of incarnation.'[27] This allows very well for the consequence that Christian theology can interpret the mediators and saviour figures of other religious traditions on roughly the same model. Moreover, it is not difficult to point out debates within other religions that structurally resemble the Chalcedonian problem, for example, the long Islamic debate about the created or uncreated nature of the Qur'an, or the early Buddhist debate about the real humanity of the Buddha despite the nirvāṇic realization which lifted him above gods and men.

A pluralistic theology of religions can recognize in these debates basically the same structure of a transcendent Reality that must be somehow immanent or incarnate in a finite reality in order to be effectively mediated by that finite reality. And so, if we don't abandon Chalcedon, it can help us both to accept the divine immanence or presence in and through other mediators, but, equally so, to remain aware that those other mediators and media share in themselves a truly human nature, with all its limitations! As Chalcedon says, this human nature of the media and mediators should not be confused with the divine reality that

---

25 Rahner (1978), p. 218 (Rahner's italics!).
26 Hick (1993), p. 109.
27 Macquarrie (1995), p. 149.

is mediated through them, nor should it be separated from the mediated transcendent Reality – neither in a reductionist nor in a docetist manner. To quote Keith Ward:

> if 'incarnation' is the temporal expression of an eternal and infinite reality in a particular human life and social context, there may be other different modes of expression, none of which will exhaust the divine reality and none of which contains the fullness of truth on its own.[28]

To sum up: For a Christian and pluralistic theology of religions it is not the idea of incarnation and the consequent two-natures doctrine that create serious problems. What really conflicts with religious pluralism is the idea that incarnation happened only once and only in Jesus. But, as I tried to show, it is exactly this assumption that becomes highly implausible if we follow a modern reading of Chalcedon and accept that incarnation is not in conflict with the general possibilities of true human nature.

---

28 Ward (1991), p. 11.

EPILOGUE

10

FOUR FROGS

Studying Religion with a Religious Interest

Asking about the particular purpose of religion is misunderstanding religion, argues the Buddhist philosopher Keiji Nishitani in his well-known work *Religion and Nothingness*.[1] For a number of things we can, and have to, ask what their purpose is in relation to us, thereby making ourselves the centre and *telos* of their function. Religion, however, crosses this perspective by putting our own existence into question. Only with the inverted question 'For what purpose do I exist?' will a genuine understanding of religion become possible.[2]

Today religion is made the subject of religious studies or *Religionswissenschaft* under a range of different functional interests. Its moral, political, social, economical, cultural, geographical, aesthetical, psychological, etc. functions are all investigated in the various academic disciplines that deal with religion. But if Nishitani is right and if religion is the field where we humans seek to understand the purpose of our own existence – on the basis of its radical questioning – this crucial feature of religion is not properly envisaged if religion is studied solely from a functionalist perspective. But if religion is studied with the kind of existential interest that corresponds to the religious quest itself, the various answers that religions have given in response to this

---

1 Nishitani (1983), pp. 1ff.
2 Ibid., p. 3.

quest will be automatically related to our current and, in the end, to one's own present individual situation. An existential leap is taken over the gap of history and religion is perceived, indeed actualized, as a challenge to or even the resolution of one's own existential quest. Joseph Cahill has characterized this approach as the 'theological dimension' in religious studies, a dimension that is indispensable to an adequate understanding of religion and marked by 'immediacy and ultimacy': *immediacy* in that the student of religion becomes 'directly addressed' and *ultimacy* in that this address confronts him/her with a claim to 'an absolute validity and unconditional transcendence'.[3]

In what follows I would like to exemplify this approach by reflecting on four brief texts and poems – all of which happen to take the frog's relationship to water as a metaphor by which they establish the purpose and nature of human life. At the same time these four frogs tell us something about the historical development and transformation of religious ideals, starting from the ancient period of the Vedic religion, leading over its radical questioning through the Indian Śramaṇa-movements, as they are documented in early Buddhism and in the Upaniṣads, going on to the transformation of the Buddhist religious orientation within Mahāyāna Buddhism and particularly within the fusion of Mahāyāna Buddhism and Daoism as it is manifest in Zen Buddhism, and finally to the changes that the encounter with this type of Buddhism elicits within Christianity.

The Vedic Frog

> Our thoughts bring us to diverse callings, setting people apart:
> the carpenter seeks what is broken, the physician a fracture,
> and the Brahmin priest seeks one who presses Soma.
> O drop of Soma, flow for Indra. . . .
> I am a poet; my Dad's a physician and Mum a miller with
> grinding-stones. With diverse thoughts we all strive for wealth,
> going after it like cattle.

---

3 Cahill (1982), p. 109. This, of course, reflects the existentialist motifs of Kierkegaard's 'Gleichzeitigkeit' and Tillich's 'ultimate concern'.

O drop of Soma, flow for Indra.
The harnessed horse longs for a light cart; seducers long for a
woman's smile; the penis for the two hairy lips, and the frog
for water.
O drop of Soma, flow for Indra. (Ṛg Veda 9:112:1, 3–4)[4]

The ancient parts of the Vedas, particularly the hymns (saṃhitā)
of the Ṛg-Veda, were probably composed by around 1200 BCE.[5]
In them we encounter a religious life that is of a startlingly this-
worldly nature. There is a pantheon of deities to whom people
offer their prayers, their worship and most importantly their sacrifices. While some of the early Vedic texts throw up philosophical
questions of a remarkably metaphysical depth, the fundamental
orientation is rather practical and marked by the overall assumption that all life, including that of gods and humans, is clamped
into the framework of a cosmic order (ṛta or dharma) which
determines the nature and duties of all beings. In providing the
gods with the due sacrifices, humans can expect from them that
they in turn provide whatever humans need and properly long
for. The gods are offered gifts like milk, butter and curd, grains
like rice and barley, and also more valuable things like domestic
animals, sometimes even very precious ones like good and costly
horses. Another oblation is Soma, a stimulating and apparently
hallucinogenic drink. As the fire (Agni) transports the oblations
to the invisible realm of the gods, the intake of Soma allows the
worshipper a glimpse into their heavenly world. So both Agni
and Soma are themselves seen as powerful deities who mediate
between the divine and the human realm. In return for the sacrificial gifts, the gods are asked for this-worldly benefits: male
offspring, material wealth, good health, military victory, protection against catastrophes and misery, etc. Artha, that is power
and wealth, is seen as a perfectly legitimate goal in life for which
one can – and in fact has to – ask the help of the gods. Artha is
the condition for well-being (yogakṣema) and in particular for
the enjoyment of sensual pleasure, kāma. The later tradition

4 Doninger O'Flaherty (transl.) (1981), p. 235.
5 Brockington (1998), p. 7.

summarizes Vedic religiosity in listing three principal goals of life: *dharma*, the cosmic order which one has to observe and uphold; *artha*, the wealth and power which one rightly acquires within the boundaries of *dharma*, and *kāma*, the sensual and specifically erotic pleasure that one is enabled to enjoy through obtaining *artha*.

Artha and *kāma* as the natural and perfectly legitimate goals in and of human life are reflected within the above quoted verses from the *Ṛg-Veda*: we all strive for wealth and sex as much and as naturally as the frog longs for water. This striving is built into the nature of creatures by the creator from whose very being the creation emerges – as the famous *Kāmasūtra* teaches in its opening verses.[6] The persuasion of the religious specialist, the Brahmin, is seen as being on the same level ('the Brahmin priest seeks one who presses Soma'); he strives for Soma in order to be in contact with the gods. The longing for the gods is as much part of natural life as the longing for sex, wealth and power. Perhaps our text even suggests that the gods too are subject to this kind of natural desire, in their case, a desire for the sacrificial oblations. The recurrent refrain 'O drop of Soma, flow for Indra' may very well indicate that Soma is something that the gods too are longing for.

If the gods are as much in need of sacrifice as humans are in need of divine help to fulfil their longing for wealth and pleasure, the gods seem to be something like penultimate beings. But what might that mean? It might mean that they are part of a larger whole, part of a greater cosmic reality as much as human beings are, just in a somewhat different way and on a different plane. This understanding paves the way for the view that is taken in the Upaniṣads and the early Buddhist scriptures where the gods are explained as *saṃsāric* beings, as beings who transmigrate through the cycle of constant rebirth and re-death (*saṃsāra*).

6 *Kāmasūtra* 1:1–5: 'We bow to religion, power, and pleasure [that is, *dharma, artha, kāma*; P.S-L] . . . For when the creator emitted his creatures, he first composed, in a hundred thousand chapters, the means of achieving the three aims of human life, which is the vital link with what sustains those creatures.' Cf. Vatsayana Mallanaga (2002), pp. 1f, 181.

As such, they are by no means transcendent or ultimate but they are this-worldly beings, only that 'this world' is larger and more complex than just the visible earthly sphere with which we are usually familiar. Indeed, the boundaries between gods and humans blur: humans can be reborn as gods and gods can be reborn as humans, or both may descend to lower forms of existence such as animals, ghosts or even denizens of various hells.

Seeing the gods as penultimate and conditioned can also take the form of explaining them as a human fabrication. This position is assumed by the Cārvākas, the earliest genuinely atheistic/materialistic school of thought of whose existence we know. Later some of their views were summarized as:

> There exists here no cause excepting nature.
> The Soul is just the body . . .
> There is no world other that this; there is no heaven and no hell; the realm of Śiva and like regions are invented by stupid imposters of other schools of thought.
> The enjoyment of heaven lies in eating delicious food, keeping company of young women, using fine clothes, perfumes, garlands, sandal paste, etc.
> The pain of hell lies in the troubles that arise from enemies, weapons, diseases; while liberation (*mokṣa*) is death which is the cessation of life-breath. . . .
> The wise should enjoy the pleasures of this world through the proper visible means of agriculture, keeping cattle, trade, political administration, etc.[7]

The Cārvākas still stick to the early Vedic life goals of *artha* and *kāma*, but these are now completely severed from any religious context – something that makes their views astonishingly modern. Hence, the Vedic frog, both in its religious and its materialistic variant, confronts us with an existential option that is by no means outdated. We can live a religious life in that we rely on the gods or on God primarily in order to obtain this-worldly

---

7 From a summary of the Cārvākas's views in Śaṅkara's *Sarvasiddhāntasaṅgraha*, quoted from Radhakrishnan and Moore (eds) (1989), p. 235.

benefits, understanding our religious performance as a kind of advance payment that should earn us the due reward. But from this understanding the step to an atheist position is not that great. It focuses on the same life goals but sees their fulfilment as entirely dependent on human effort and/or the incalculable incidents of a world that only knows of natural causes. The overall regulating cosmic order, the *dharma*, becomes then the physical mechanism of a by and large soulless world.

But not everybody will see the Vedic goals of wealth/power and sensual enjoyment as satisfying. With the various Śramaṇa movements arising in India between the seventh and fifth centuries BCE, the Vedic frog was radically questioned and replaced by a different one.

The Śramaṇa Frog

> In this body, which is afflicted with desire, anger, covetousness, delusion, fear, despondency, envy, separation from the desirable, union with the undesirable, hunger, thirst, senility, death, disease, sorrow, and the like, what is the good of enjoyment of desires?
> And we see that this whole world is decaying, as these gnats, mosquitoes, and the like, the grass, and the trees that arise and perish. . . .
> In this sort of cycle of existence (saṃsāra) what is the good of enjoyment of desires, when after a man has fed on them there is seen repeatedly his return here to earth?
> . . . In this cycle of existence I am like a frog in a waterless well. (*Maitrī Upaniṣad* 1:3–4)[8]

The Śramaṇas ('strivers') propagated new religious ideals and lifestyles guided by the new religious goal of salvation/liberation (*mokṣa, vimuktī*). Not only did the religious traditions of Jainism and Buddhism have their origins in Śramaṇa movements, but the ideas and practices of the Śramaṇas also had a strong influence

---

8 Ibid., p. 93f.

on a number of Upaniṣadic texts and through them they shaped to a considerable extent the further development of Hinduism. The *Maitrī Upaniṣad*, from which the above quotation is taken, not only displays many features typical of the Śramaṇas; more specifically, it shows a clear Buddhist influence, as can be seen from the above quotation itself which repeats a well-known formula from the first of the Buddhist 'Four Noble Truths' ('separation from the desirable, union with the undesirable').

A major new idea associated with the Śramaṇas is the belief in rebirth or better re-death. The exact origins of the belief in reincarnation are still obscure, but it did not exist at the time when the early parts of the Vedas were composed. The idea of repeated birth and death, of a potentially endless cycle of reincarnation (*saṃsāra*), was forceful enough to render the Vedic goals of *artha* and *kāma* pointless and meaningless. All wealth, all possessions, all sensual enjoyments are impermanent – even on the level of the gods, for they too are caught in the cycle of *saṃsāra*, will have to die at the end of their heavenly existence and will be reborn into some new form of transitory life. Moreover, the idea of perpetual repetition uncovers the deceiving quality of sensual enjoyment. The satisfaction that arises from *artha* and *kāma* is in itself transitory. Its enjoyment is only for the moment and soon after human desire seeks for other and new forms of satisfaction. No lasting peace or fulfilment can be found in pursuing these goals. Striving for *artha* and *kāma* is, in a sense, short-sighted. It is in vain, for no lasting satisfaction can ever be gained from them. 'In this cycle of existence I am like a frog in a waterless well' – as the *Maitrī-Upaniṣad* says in direct opposition to the verses from the *Ṛg-Veda* quoted earlier.

So where does the Śramaṇa frog find his water? It is here that the belief in an ultimate transcendent reality comes in and with it the conviction that our real striving – the striving that can never be satisfied by *artha* and *kāma*, by the goods and pleasures within the *saṃsāra* – goes after this ultimate and can therefore find its lasting satisfaction, its imperishable peace, only in reaching the transcendent goal. Siddhārtha Gautama explains the motive of his spiritual search thus: 'being myself subject to ageing, sickness, death, sorrow, and defilement, having understood the danger in what is subject to ageing, sickness, death, sorrow, and defilement, I seek the unageing, unailing, deathless, sorrowless, and undefiled supreme security from bondage, Nibbāna'.[9] Reaching the Ultimate is what salvation/liberation means and with the Śramaṇas this becomes the new goal in life. But through the various Śramaṇa movements the new goal became so convincing that it was incorporated into the Vedic and then Hindu tradition: it was added to the previous life-goals of *dharma*, *artha* and *kāma* as the supreme and final goal: *mokṣa* (liberation).

The various Śramaṇa groups differed in how they conceived the Ultimate. Although there is the frequent affirmation that Ultimate Reality exceeds human conception and expression, it is nevertheless sometimes hinted at in more personalistic terms and on other occasions with impersonal concepts and metaphors. But there is a general agreement that the end of suffering, or to be more precise, the end of unsatisfactoriness can only be found through the knowledge and experience of this Ultimate Reality.

The dissatisfaction with the more mundane goals of life and the corresponding search for ultimate satisfaction, final liberation, lasting peace as coming from a transcendent reality are typical features that the religions which arose from the Śramaṇa movements (Jainism, Buddhism, Hinduism) share with other religions of the so-called Axial Age: 'ordinary human existence' is perceived as 'defective, unsatisfactory, lacking' and 'something fundamentally different' is sought for, 'an ultimate unity of reality and value' which allows for a final liberation/salvation.[10] This reflects a fundamental human orientation that is significantly different from 'the Vedic frog': The feeling that there should be – must be – more to life than the smaller or greater enjoyments of ordinary existence. This existential orientation too is not confined to a limited period of the past. Augustine's masterly phrase *inquietum est cor nostrum, donec requiescat in te* ('our heart is restless, until it repose in Thee') echoes an existential condition

---

9 *Majjhimanikāya* 26,13. Ñāṇamoli and Bodhi (2001), p. 256. 'Nibbāna' is the Pāli word for 'Nirvāṇa'.
10 Cf. Hick (1989), p. 32f, referring to Karl Jaspers.

felt by many people today although they might be less confident than Augustine in identifying that what they are somehow looking or hoping for as a divine 'Thee' or even as the 'Thee' of the Christian God.

The Zen Frog

The old pond, ah!
A frog jumps in:
The water's sound! (Matsuo Bashō (1644–94))[11]

Although its roots can be firmly identified in the ideas, goals and practices of the Śramaṇas, Buddhism – like all other major religious traditions – went through a number of significant changes and transformations. With the emergence of the so-called Mahāyāna ('great' or 'eminent vehicle') form of Buddhism, not only the understanding of the relationship between the ultimate and the penultimate reality changed, but also – and correspondingly – the understanding of the Buddha and of the religious ideal.[12] With the conviction that none of our concepts can grasp reality as it truly is, Saṃsāra became as mysterious as Nirvāṇa and therefore ultimately indistinguishable from it. 'Buddha' signified far more than just an individual being who had achieved the highest enlightenment and established a religious community (*saṅgha*). Increasingly the term 'Buddha' referred to various levels on which the ultimate reality manifests itself: ranging from the cosmic ground of everything over its instantiation in supranatural figures and human beings to the true nature of all reality (Buddha-Nature, *tathāgatagarbha*).[13]

Most crucial in relation to Buddhist practice was the new idea that ideally everybody can and should strive to become a Buddha, that is, that all should follow the path of the Bodhisattva (a being on its way to Buddhahood). To reach this goal, a Bodhisattva

---

11 Suzuki (1973), p. 238.
12 Cf. Schmidt-Leukel (2006), pp. 94–126.
13 On this, see also Chapter 7 in this book.

needs to develop wisdom and compassion. While wisdom is focused on the transconceptuality (or conceptual 'emptiness') – and therefore non-duality – of Nirvāṇa and Saṃsāra, compassion realizes a non-duality of self and others: Striving for the (spiritual and material) well-being of others is the way of realizing one's own true Buddha-Nature, that is of realizing one's true existential determination. As a result, altruism is now seen as a major goal in life, genuine fulfilment as arising from selfless care:

> All those who suffer in the world do so because of their desire for their own happiness.
> All those happy in the world are so because of their desire for the happiness of others.[14]

The altruistic Bodhisattva does not leave the world of Saṃsāra; he or she remains active in it for the sake of all others, thereby realizing a (in the words of the later Mahāyāna tradition) 'non-static' or 'dynamic Nirvāṇa' (*apratiṣṭhita nirvāṇa*), a Nirvāṇa present in the midst of Saṃsāra.

When Mahāyāna Buddhism reached China, its ideas about the Buddha-Nature as our and everything's true nature were further refined under the influence of Daoism and its own understanding of 'nature' and of 'naturalness' in the sense of 'spontaneity' or 'non-action' (*wuwei*). As Malcolm David Eckel so aptly said: '"Nature" in the Indian tradition was a world to be transcended, while in East Asia it took on the capacity to symbolize transcendence itself.'[15]

All of these just roughly sketched developments go into Ch'an or Zen Buddhism. This is nicely illustrated by the last three of the ten 'oxherding pictures'. The eighth picture shows an empty circle indicating – as the commentary explains – a reality beyond enlightenment and non-enlightenment, that is beyond the distinction of Nirvāṇa and Saṃsāra. The ninth picture expresses

---

14 Śāntideva, *Bodhicaryāvatāra* 8:129; Crosby and Skilton (transl.) (1995), p. 99.
15 Eckel (1997), p. 339.

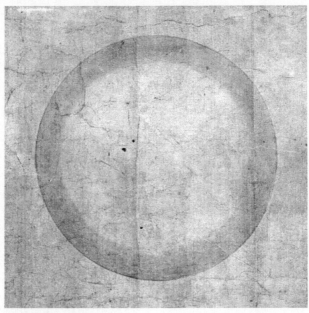

Ox-herding picture no. 8.

the state of true naturalness, of realizing one's true nature, that which is not-made and cannot be made (the Daoist term 'non-action' is explicitly used), by depicting a scene from nature. Finally, the tenth picture refers to the Bodhisattva ideal, to the belief that true enlightenment consists in working among the ordinary people for their enlightenment. 'I visit the wineshop and the market, and everyone I look upon becomes enlightened' – says the commentary on the last picture.[16]

This now brings us to the 'Zen frog' or more specifically to Bashō's frog, which is without doubt the most famous of our four frogs.

16 Pictures 8, 9 and 10 of the so-called 'Ox-herding pictures' by the fifteenth-century Japanese Rinzai Zen monk Shubun. They are said to be copies of originals, now lost, traditionally attributed to Kakuan, a twelfth-century Chinese Zen Master. Museum of Shokoku-ji Temple. In the public domain because its copyright has expired. Licence at http://commons.wikimedia.org/wiki/Image:Oxherding_pictures,_No._8.jpg (analogously Nos. 9 and 10). The commentary is available from several sources, e.g. http://www.deeshan.com/zen.htm or http://www.terebess.hu/english/bulls.html.

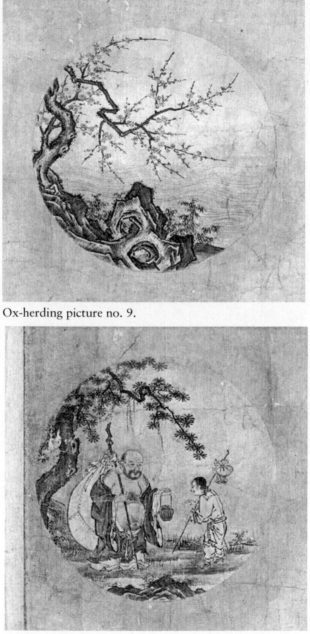

Ox-herding picture no. 9.

Ox-herding picture no. 10.

It is usually assumed that the great Japanese poet Matsuo Bashō (1644–94) composed this short poem (*haiku*) (see above, p. 181) during a period of intensive Zen training. That Bashō was crucially influenced by Zen is beyond doubt and many interpreters have regarded particularly this short haiku as a masterly expression of the spirit of Zen. However, the interpretations of this haiku vary as much as its translations into English or other Western languages.[17] A number of translators have inserted into their translation a notion of silence or of breaking the silence through the sound of the water, as, for example, in the following translation by Nobuyuki Yuasa:

> Breaking the silence
> Of an ancient pond,
> A frog jumped into water –
> A deep resonance.[18]

The famous German scholar Wilhelm Gundert – although his own translation is closer to the original and refrains from inserting the motif of silence – has nevertheless suggested an interpretation that makes use of the same motif: 'What is life other than a noise that breaks the silence, a noise of foolish origin and soon to pass?'[19] And Heinrich Dumoulin, following Gundert, sees in this an expression of 'the final meaning of reality'.[20]

Against the idea of 'breaking silence' as the central motif of Bashō's poem Takiguchi has argued that

> frogs are noisy in spring, when this haiku is believed to have been composed, because of the mating season. They are a symbol of the merriment, colour, noises, life (sex) and bustling movements of spring – a celebration of life on earth . . . Why, then, should the scene of Basho's haiku be doctored and

---

17 For various other translations and a commentary by Robert Aitken, see http://www.bopsecrets.org/gateway/passages/basho-frog.htm
18 Bashō (1983), p. 32.
19 'was ist dies Leben anders als ein Geräusch, das die Stille durchbricht, närrischen Ursprungs und gleich vorüber?' W. Gundert (1929), p. 123.
20 Dumoulin (1990), p. 353.

philosophised into one of stillness, loneliness, quietude and tranquillity?[21]

Given that the notion of silence is absent from the original text, Takiguchi's point seems to be strong.

What is, however, beyond dispute is Bashō's innovative step taken in the first line. Opening the poem with 'the old pond' was apparently chosen against the more traditional suggestion of opening it with the words 'the mountain roses'.[22] In a very early work on the style of Bashō's poetry, written by Bashō's disciple Shiko, Shiko comments on his master's choice of 'the old pond' that this opening line 'being simpler, contains more truth in it. It is only he who has dug deep into the mystery of the universe that can choose a phrase like this.'[23]

In his classic *Zen and Japanese Culture* Daisetz Suzuki also rejected an interpretation of Bashō's poem based on the (absent) motif of silence. For Suzuki the old pond does not refer to 'solitude and tranquillity'[24] but to

the other side of eternity, where timeless time is. It is so 'old,' indeed, that there is nothing more ancient. No scale of consciousness can measure it. It is whence all things come, it is the source of this world of particulars, yet in itself it shows no particularization . . . And this intuitive grasp of Reality never takes place when a world of Emptiness is assumed outside our everyday world of the senses; for these two worlds, sensual and supersensual, are not separate but one.[25]

If we take, once more, the water, the 'pond', that the frog longs for – and into which he happily jumps – as an expression of human existential longing, does Bashō's Zen frog confront us with

21 Susumu Takiguchi, 'A Contrarian View on Basho's Frog Haiku', p. 5. http://www.worldhaikureview.org/5-1/whch/essay_takiguchi_dreams.htm
22 Cf. ibid., p. 15f.
23 Quoted from Bashō (1983), p. 32. Takiguchi refers to the same remark (cf. Takiguchi, p. 16).
24 Suzuki (1973), p. 240.
25 Ibid., p. 241.

a new kind of this-worldliness? In a sense, yes. But it does not seem to be a fall back to the understanding of human striving as presented by the Vedic frog. It is rather the this-worldliness of a radically transformed understanding of the world. It presupposes a world in which Saṃsāra is non-different from Nirvāṇa, a world in which, as Suzuki says, 'these two worlds, sensual and supersensual, are not separate but one'. This view of the world and of life in it presupposes that the Absolute cannot be known apart from the relative, 'the everyday world of the senses', but equally so that 'our life, lived in the realm of the relativities, loses its meaning altogether'[26] if it does not realize its non-duality with the Absolute. The water that the frog longs for is at hand, the 'old pond' is right there. One does not need to look for it in some indefinite 'beyond' nor should it be confused with the shallow reward of sensual gratification in and of itself. The water is found in living out one's true nature, naturally and spontaneously, but this true nature is nothing else than the Bodhisattva's Buddha-Nature, 'the treasure store of wisdom and the great wealth of widely caring for one another' – as it is expressed in the influential *Tathāgatagarbha Sūtra*.[27] When life is lived for the sake of others immanence is transcended without losing this immanence. Thus it does not exclude that the Bodhisattva 'visits the wineshop and the market' as it does not exclude that the sounds made by the frogs and the water is 'a celebration of life on earth'. The frog is one with the water.

The Buddhist–Christian Frog

The frog
sat
on the lily pad
not waiting. (Frances S. Adeney)[28]

---

26 Ibid., p. 243.
27 Cf. Grosnick (transl.) (1995), p. 99.
28 Adeney (2003), p. 16. Reproduced by kind permission of Continuum International Group.

The final frog brings us back to the topic of this book: It is a Buddhist–Christian frog because it appears in a haiku written by the Christian theologian Frances S. Adeney[29] expressing a spirituality that is significantly influenced by the practice of a Buddhist-type of meditation (most closely to the Zen practice of 'just sitting', *shikantaza*) which Adeney learned at the Trappist Gedona monastery in Java. Adeney describes the differences of her newly acquired Buddhist meditation practice from Christian forms of silent meditation, with which she had been familiar before, as follows:

(1) It was not focused on an interchange between God and my-self. I was not listening for God's voice. I was not bringing my concerns to God. I was simply entering a place of silence. (2) It was not predicated on specific ideas about God or thoughts from writings in the Bible. I did not need to frame this time of silence with religious meanings. (3) It was not focused on an outcome. I neither expected nor did I ask for any changes in myself or the world.[30]

This practice led her to experience 'the intensity of deepened consciousness, the passing of time without awareness of its passing, the stillness of little breath, and the sense of etherealness of oneself and one's surroundings. . .'.[31] It allowed her 'to explore the deeper reaches of myself' and helped her in the 'process of letting go of attachments'.[32]

All of these features have an unmistakably Buddhist taste and many Buddhists will easily recognize central characteristics of their own practice in them. But in addition Adeney emphasizes that through this practice she is 'entering and becoming part of God's presence'. 'More than once I had experiences that were "sightings" if not meetings with the Divine.'[33] Her frog haiku

---

29 Frances S. Adeney is currently (2008) William A. Benfield, Jr Professor of Evangelism and Global Mission at the Louisville Presbyterian Theological Seminary.
30 Adeney (2003), p. 16.
31 Ibid., p. 18.
32 Ibid., p. 18f.
33 Ibid., p. 16.

testifies to one such experience: She had been on her way to the Gedona monastery and after a longer journey through the Indonesian countryside arrived there a bit early when the nuns were still having their mid-morning prayers:

> Rather than entering, I seated myself by a small pool at the foot of the chapel steps. The sun brightened the lily pads in the dark pool, and I noticed a green frog sitting on one of them. Just sitting.
>
> I decided to sit like that, allowing the sun to warm my back, staying quite still, completing my journey to this place of silent retreat. I felt that I need not go further. I had come there to be in silence. I need not enter the chapel and join the singing of the Psalms. I need not wait for the sisters to come out of the chapel. I could begin. There was nothing to wait for. I sat still with the unmoving frog. The sounds of singing became distant. The mountain faded away. The whole world became the pond and me; I and the pond became the whole world.[34]

It is this 'not waiting' that connects Adeney's frog with Bashō's frog. It doesn't really matter whether the frog jumps into the water or enjoys 'just sitting' in the middle of the pond – both happen 'spontaneously', 'naturally', as uncalculated 'non-action'; the frog is part of the pond and the water is at hand anyway. 'Entering silence' says Adeney 'is like drinking from a deep well of cool water. I don't think about it. I don't analyze what exactly happens or why this mystical water quenches my thirst. I come and drink.'[35] Identifying herself with the frog, she describes her experience of the Divine on this particular morning as oneness: 'The whole world became the pond and me; I and the pond became the whole world.' 'Not waiting' is the point: There is nothing to wait for because everything is already there. One can let go of any attachments.

But as much as the 'not waiting' links Adeney's frog with the Buddhist tradition it raises the question of whether this 'not

---

34 Ibid., p. 17.
35 Ibid., p. 19.

waiting' might not put it into a sharp contrast with the Christian tradition. Is waiting not essential to Christianity whose
Holy Scripture ends with the Greek equivalent for *marana tha*
– 'Come, O Lord' (cf. Rev. 22.20), expressing the Christian
waiting for the final eschatological fulfilment, and whose central
prayer pleads: 'Your kingdom come!'? 'Not waiting' – is this not
seriously distorting Christianity's eschatological nature? Is the
Buddhist–Christian frog perhaps an impossibility?

Christian 'waiting' can also be called 'hope' – and hope, as
Paul famously taught, is one of the three central Christian virtues
(or can we call them *pāramitās*, Bodhisattva perfections?): faith,
hope and love (1 Cor. 13.13). 'And hope does not disappoint'
(Rom. 5.5), writes Paul. During a Christian–Buddhist dialogue
at the University of Glasgow in 2004 about the peace potential of both religions, the Sri Lankan Bishop and peace activist
Kenneth Fernando emphasized 'the message of hope' as 'one of
the important contributions Christians must bring to any peace
process. We never give up because we know that we will win.
Christian hope is the assurance that God is at work, that he
reigns.'[36] The Zen Buddhist Roshi and peace activist Hozan Alan
Senauke took up this point. He quoted the tradition according
to which the Buddha, despite his repeated serious attempts, had
been unable to prevent his own clan, the Śākyas, being attacked
and wiped out by a hostile army (Jātaka 465). 'Buddhist teachers
. . .', Senauke said, 'encourage us to have "no gaining idea", to
practise good without attachment to an outcome.'[37] So is hope,
is Christian hope or 'waiting' a form of attachment, a clinging
to the outcome? Fernando replied that struggling for peace and
justice need to be sustained by hope: 'How else can we carry on
in the face of seeming defeat?' and added his assumption, 'that
Zen Buddhism too provides sources for such hope'.[38]

Eschatological motives are indeed by no means absent from

36 K. Fernando (2005), p. 253.
37 Senauke (2005), p. 256.
38 K. Fernando (2005b), p. 252. His significant recommendation to make
the question of possible sources of hope in Buddhism and Christianity a topic of
further research has so far (at least as far as I am aware) not been taken up.

Buddhism. Most frequently they are linked to the idea of pure Buddha Lands, the kind of Buddhist paradisial worlds that Buddhas create by their boundless mercy and their good karmic energies, or – with a more millennialist or utopian twist – to the expectation of the coming of the future Buddha Maitreya.[39] In the latter context the eschatological hope can even take shapes that are reminiscent of the prophetic tradition in the Bible, as, for example, in the following text that speaks of an all-encompassing peace immediately preceding the advent of Maitreya:

> No one will stir up quarrels because of villages, towns, wealth, crops, fields, property or soil; all human beings will be handsome, with beautiful bodies, (and will be) loving and pleasant to each other. Crows will become friendly with owls, cats with mice, deer with lions, mongooses with snakes, lions with deer . . .[40]

On the other hand, Christian eschatology is not only future-oriented but has a dimension which has been called 'realized' or 'present eschatology': The 'kingdom', or better 'reign of God', is not only something to be expected and waited for in the future. It is already present, at least initially so, and carries within itself precisely the kind of dynamism that pushes and leads towards its future completion. The 'kingdom comes', has started to come, through and in as much as humans submit themselves to God's reign. This is the connection between the two lines of the 'Our Father': 'Thy kingdom come' and 'Thy will be done . . .'

Yagi Seiichi has interpreted the relation between present and future eschatology in the light of the Mahāyāna Buddhist logic of mutual interdependence according to which everything is conceptually/essentially constituted in dependence on everything else, or, as Yagi puts it, 'that no existing being is composed simply and exclusively of the constitutive parts which belong to

---

39 On both aspects, see Collins (1998), pp. 287–574. Unfortunately Collins' careful study covers only the Pāli tradition.
40 From the *Māleyyadevattheravatthu*; cf. Collins (1998), p. 623.

itself alone'.[41] Yagi calls this mutual inherence 'front-structure' and shows that it also applies to entities or processes in time. In a piece of music, for example,[42] moving forward in a linear fashion, performed as a diachronic succession of tones, each tone is not only qualified by preceding, present and following ones but also by movements, tempi, instruments, etc. and, finally, by the piece as a whole (and vice versa). So even in linear processes there is the circular structure of mutual interdependence, which, in a sense, does not only make the future dependent on the present but also allows the future to have its qualifying impact on the present. Analogously, the reign of God realizes itself not only by shaping the future through the present but also by shaping the present through the future via the mode of anticipation. However, a final, fulfilled reign of God would bring 'history to a close' and replace it by a new world.[43] Within the world of history it therefore remains necessarily utopian. But this does not exclude that every single expression of the Transcendent within history can legitimately be seen as an anticipation of the eschatological fulfilment, as an advent of the future in the here and now.[44]

Taking into account the inner unity between future and present eschatology Christian hope is not just an act of waiting. It is rather an expression of what is already found in the present by understanding this as something that carries an inner promise, prediction or anticipation of something infinitely greater, by taking it as a partial representation of the whole which is seen not only from a synchronic but also from a diachronic perspective. If the world as a whole is not separate from an ultimate reality that shows itself to us and in us through wisdom and compassion, this partial representation of the whole can assume the quality of a sacramental representation of the ultimate and as such be a sign of hope. If all attachment bears the mark of self-centredness, then this kind of hope is not a form of attachment; quite the contrary, it encourages and enables oneself to let go of oneself.

---

41 Yagi (1990), p. 76.
42 Cf. ibid., pp. 126ff.
43 Ibid., p. 137.
44 Cf. ibid., p. 137f.

This representational structure of anticipation lies at the bottom of the Bodhisattva-ideal: the Bodhisattva-vow. In the vow (*praṇidhāna*) the person following the Bodhisattva-path commits him-/herself to save all beings 'however innumerable sentient beings are' and to overcome all evils 'however inexhaustible the defilements are'. It doesn't really matter whether the Bodhisattva will be ever able to achieve these goals. What matters is that the utopian eschatological perspective of the vow qualifies every single act of a smaller or larger contribution to the salvation of others and the overcoming of evil as a step on that Bodhisattva path. It gives these acts their distinctive meaning. It makes them, in this sense, signs of hope.

The 'not waiting' of the Christian–Buddhist frog is not a distortion of Christianity's eschatological nature. It is a reminder of the unity between future and present eschatology. More importantly, it is an invitation to allow the future becoming present by entering this state of 'not waiting'. As Frances Adeney testifies, the practice of 'entering silence deepens my faith and calls from me a compassion for others and an appreciation of their worth and ways'.[45] Once more there is evidence that loving involvement and selfless detachment complement each other. Therefore, the Buddhist–Christian frog is not an impossibility but a genuine existential option.

---

45 Adeney (2003), p. 18.

REFERENCES

Abe, Masao (1985), 'A Dynamic Unity in Religious Pluralism: A Proposal from the Buddhist Point of View', in J. Hick and H. Askari (eds), *The Experience of Religious Diversity*, Aldershot: Gower, pp. 163–90, 225–7.

Adeney, Frances S. (2003), 'How I, a Christian, Have Learned from Buddhist Practice, or "The Frog Sat on the Lily Pad . . . Not Waiting"', in Rita M. Gross and Terry C. Muck (eds), *Christians Talk about Buddhist Meditation – Buddhists Talk about Christian Prayer*, New York and London: Continuum, pp. 15–19.

Ahlstrand, Kajsa (2007), 'Boundaries of Religious Identity: Baptised Buddhists in Enköping', in J. D'Arcy May (ed.), *Converging Ways? Conversion and Belonging in Buddhism and Christianity*, St Ottilien: EOS, pp. 155–64.

Askari, Hasan (1991), *Spiritual Quest. An Inter-Religious Dimension*, Pudsey: Seven Mirrors.

Baier, Karl (2008), 'Spiritualität und religiöse Identität', in: R. Bernhardt and P. Schmidt-Leukel (eds), *Multiple religiöse Identität*, Zürich: Theologischer Verlag Zürich, pp. 187–218.

Baillie, Donald (1961), *God Was In Christ*, London: Faber and Faber (1st edition 1948).

Baird, Robert (2004), 'Syncretism and the History of Religions', in Anita M. Leopold and Jeppe S. Jensen (eds), *Syncretism in Religion: A Reader*, London: Equinox, pp. 48–58.

Bashō (1983), *The Narrow Road to the Deep North and other travel sketches*. Translated from the Japanese with an introduction by Nobuyuki Yuasa, New York: Penguin Books.

Barker, Gregory A. (ed.) (2005), *Jesus in the World's Faiths: Leading Thinkers from Five Religions Reflect on His Meaning*, Maryknoll, NY: Orbis.

Barth, Karl (1945), *Eine Schweizer Stimme 1938–1945*, Zollikon-Zürich: Evangelischer Verlag.

Baumann, M., Luchesi, B. and Wilke, A. (eds) (2003), *Tempel und Tamilen in zweiter Heimat: Hindus aus Sri Lanka im deutschsprachigen und skandinavischen Raum*, Würzburg: Ergon Verlag.

Bäumer, Bettina (1989), 'A Journey with the Unknown', in T. Arai and W. Ariarajah (eds), *Spirituality in Interfaith Dialogue*, Geneva: WCC Publications, pp. 36–41.

Bechert, H. (1985), 'Einleitung', in *Milindapañha: Die Fragen des Königs Milinda*, Herausgegeben und teilweise neu übersetzt von Nyanaponika, Interlaken: Ansata, pp. 15–22.

Berger, Peter L. (2004), *Questions of Faith: A Skeptical Affirmation of Christianity*. Oxford: Blackwell.

Berner, Ulrich (1991), 'Syncretismus und Inkulturation', in Hermann Siller (ed.), *Suchbewegungen. Synkretismus – Kulturelle Identität und kirchliches Bekenntnis*, Darmstadt: Wissenschaftliche Buchgesellschaft, pp. 130–44.

Berner, Ulrich (2004), 'The Concept of "Syncretism": An Instrument of Historical Insight/Discovery?', in Anita M. Leopold and Jeppe S. Jensen (eds), *Syncretism in Religion: A Reader*, London: Equinox, pp. 295–315.

Bernhardt, Reinhold (2005), 'Die Polarität von Freiheit und Liebe: Überlegungen zur interreligiösen Urteilsbildung aus dogmatischer Perspektive', in R. Bernhardt and P. Schmidt-Leukel (eds), *Kriterien interreligiöser Urteilsbildung*, Zürich: Theologischer Verlag Zürich, pp. 71–101.

Bernhardt, Reinhold (2008), '"Synkretismus" als Deutekategorie für multireligiöse Identitätsbildungen', in R. Bernhardt and P. Schmidt-Leukel (eds), *Multiple religiöse Identität*, Zürich: Theologischer Verlag Zürich, pp. 271–94.

Bernhardt, Reinhold and Schmidt-Leukel, Perry (eds) (2005), *Kriterien interreligiöser Urteilsbildung*, Zürich: Theologischer Verlag Zürich.

Bernhardt, Reinhold and Schmidt-Leukel, Perry (eds) (2008), *Multiple religiöse Identität*, Zürich: Theologischer Verlag Zürich.

Bibby, Richard (1987), *Fragmented Gods: The Poverty and Potential of Religion in Canada*. Toronto: Irwin Publications.

Bloom, A. (1992), 'Shin Buddhism in Encounter with a Religiously Plural World', in *The Pure Land* (New Series), nos. 8–9, pp. 17–31.

Bochinger, Christoph (2008), 'Multiple religiöse Identität im Westen zwischen Traditionsbezug und Individualisierung', in R. Bernhardt and P. Schmidt-Leukel (eds), *Multiple religiöse Identität*, Zürich: Theologischer Verlag Zürich, pp. 137–62.

Boff, Leonardo (1985), *Church, Charisma and Power: Liberation Theology and the Institutional Church*, London: SCM Press.

Brockington, J. L. (1998), *The Sacred Thread: Hinduism in its Continuity and Diversity*, Edinburgh: Edinburgh University Press.

Brück, Michael von (1991), *The Unity of Reality: God, God-Experience and Meditation in the Hindu-Christian Dialogue*, New York: Paulist (1st German edition 1986).

Brück, Michael von (2007), 'A Theology of Multiple Religious Identity', in J. D'Arcy May (ed.), *Converging Ways? Conversion and Belonging in Buddhism and Christianity*, St Ottilien: EOS, pp. 181–206.

Brück, Michael von and Lai, Whalen (1997), *Buddhismus und Christentum: Geschichte, Konfrontation, Dialog*, München: C.H. Beck.

Buber, Martin (1991), *Tales of the Hasidim*, New York: Schocken Books.

Cabezón, J. I. (1994), *Buddhism and Language: A Study of Indo-Tibetan Scholasticism*, Albany, NY: SUNY Press.

Cabezón, J. I. (2000), 'A God, but Not a Savior', in R. M. Gross and T. Muck (eds), *Buddhists Talk about Jesus. Christians Talk about the Buddha*, New York: Continuum, pp. 17–31.

Cahill, Joseph (1982), *Mended Speech: The Crisis of Religious Studies and Theology*, New York: Crossroad.

Carrette, Jeremy and King, Richard (2006), *Selling Spirituality: The Silent Takeover of Religion*, London and New York: Routledge.

Cheng, Hsueh-li (1981), 'Buddha, Man and God', in *Dialogue* (N.S.) 8: 54–68.

Chia, Edmund (2003), *Towards a Theology of Dialogue: Schillebeeckx's Method as Bridge between Vatican's Dominus Jesus and Asia's FABC Theology*, Bangkok: Edmund Chia.

Chittick, William (1994), *Imaginal Worlds: Ibn al-'Arabī and the Problem of Religious Diversity*, Albany, NY: SUNY Press.

Christian, William A. (1964), *Meaning and Truth in Religion*, Princeton: Princeton University Press.

Clooney, Francis X. (1990), 'Reading the World in Christ: From Comparison to Inclusivism', in Gavin D'Costa (ed.), *Christian Uniqueness Reconsidered: The Myth of a Pluralistic Theology of Religions*, Maryknoll, NY: Orbis, pp. 63–80.

Clooney, Francis X. (1993), *Theology after Vedanta: An Experiment in Comparative Theology*, Albany, NY: SUNY Press.

Clooney, Francis X. (1995), 'Comparative Theology: A Review of Recent Books (1989–1995)', *Theological Studies* 56: 521–50.

Clooney, Francis X. (2002), *Hindu God, Christian God: How Reason Helps Break Down the Boundaries between Religions*, Oxford: Oxford University Press.

Cobb, John (1999), *Transforming Christianity and the World: A Way beyond Absolutism and Relativism*. Edited and introduced by Paul Knitter, Maryknoll, NY: Orbis.

Collins, Steven (1998), *Nirvana and Other Buddhist Felicities*, Cambridge: Cambridge University Press.

Conze, Edward (ed. and transl.) (2000), *Buddhist Texts Through the Ages*, reprint, Oxford: Oneworld.

Cook, Francis H. (transl.) (1999), *Three Texts on Consciousness Only*, (BDK English Tripitaka 60-I,II,III), Berkeley, CA: Numata Center for Buddhist Translation and Research.

Cornille, Catherine (ed.) (2002), *Many Mansions? Multiple Religious Belonging and Christian Identity*, Maryknoll, NY: Orbis.

Cornille, Catherine (2003), 'Double Religious Belonging: Aspects and Questions', *Buddhist–Christian Studies* 23: 43–9.

Cornille, Catherine (2005), 'Conditions for the Possibility of Interreligious Dialogue on God', in A. Lande and W. Jeanrond (eds), *The Concept of God in Global Dialogue*, Maryknoll, NY: Orbis, pp. 3–18.

Coward, Harold (2000), *Pluralism in the World Religions: A Short Introduction*, Oxford: Oneworld.

Craig, W. L. (1989), '"No Other Name": A Middle Knowledge Perspective on the Exclusivity of Salvation Through Christ', *Faith and Philosophy* 6: 172–87.

Crosby, Kate and Skilton, Andrew (transl.) (1995), Śāntideva, *The Bodhicaryāvatāra*, Oxford: Oxford University Press.

Davie, Grace (1994), *Religion in Britain since 1945: Believing without Belonging*, Oxford: Blackwell.

Dawkins, Richard (2007), *The God Delusion*, paperback edition, London: Black Swan.

De Alwis, Brian (1983), 'Christian-Buddhist Dialogue in the Writings of Lyn [*sic*] A de Silva', *Dialogue* (New Series) 10: 33–8.

De Silva, Lynn A. (1957), *Belief in God* (C.P.C.L. Pamphlets, no. 2), Colombo.

De Silva, Lynn A. (1964), *Creation, Redemption, Consummation: In Christian and Buddhist Thought*, Chiengmai.

De Silva, Lynn A. (1966), *Why Can't I Save Myself? The Christian Answer in Relation to Buddhist Thought* (Dialogue Publications No. 1), Colombo.

De Silva, Lynn A. (1967), 'Buddhist–Christian Dialogue', in Herbert Jai Singh (ed.), *Inter-religious Dialogue*, Bangalore, pp. 170–203.

De Silva, Lynn A. (1970), *Why Belief in God? The Christian Answer in Relation to Buddhism* (Dialogue Publications No. 2), Colombo.

De Silva, Lynn A. (1975), *The Problem of the Self in Buddhism and Christianity*, Colombo: Ecumenical Institute for Study and Dialogue (new edition, Basingstoke: Macmillan, 1979).

De Silva, Lynn A. (1979), *Emergent Theology in the Context of Buddhism*, Colombo: Ecumenical Institute for Study and Dialogue.

De Silva, Lynn A. (1982), 'Buddhism and Christianity Relativised', *Dialogue* (New Series) 9: 43–72.

Dharmasiri, Gunapala (1988), *A Buddhist Critique of the Christian Concept of God*, Antioch: Golden Leaves (first published Colombo: Lake House Investments, 1974).

Doninger O'Flaherty, Wendy (transl.) (1981), *The Rig Veda. An Anthology*. Selected, translated and annotated by Wendy Doninger O'Flaherty, London: Penguin Books.

Drehsen, V. and Sparn, W. (eds) (1996), *Im Schmelztiegel der Religionen: Konturen des modernen Synkretismus*, Gütersloh: Gütersloher Verlagshaus.

Droogers, André (1989), 'Syncretism: The Problem of Definition, the Definition of the Problem', in J. Gort, H. Vroom, R. Fernhout and A. Wessels (eds), *Dialogue and Syncretism: An Interdisciplinary Approach*, Grand Rapids: Eerdmans/Amsterdam: Rodopi, pp. 7–25.

Droogers, André (2004), 'Syncretism, Power, Play', in Anita M. Leopold and Jeppe S. Jensen (eds), *Syncretism in Religion: A Reader*, London: Equinox, pp. 217–36.

Dumoulin, Heinrich (1990), *Zen Buddhism: A History. Vol. 2: Japan*, New York and London: Macmillan.

Dumoulin, Heinrich (1994), *Zen-Buddhism: A History. Vol. I: India and China*, New York: Macmillan, Simon & Schuster.

Dupuis, Jacques (2002), 'Christianity and Religions: Complementarity and Convergence', in C. Cornille (ed.), *Many Mansions? Multiple Religious Belonging and Christian Identity*. Maryknoll, NY: Orbis, pp. 61–75.

Eckel, M. D. (1997), 'Is there a Buddhist Philosophy of Nature?', in M. E. Tucker and D. R. Williams (eds), *Buddhism and Ecology: The Interconnection of Dharma and Deeds*, Cambridge, MA: Harvard University Press, pp. 327–49.

Fernando, Antony (1981), *Buddhism and Christianity: Their Inner Affinity*, Colombo: Ecumenical Institute for Study and Dialogue (also published as *Buddhism Made Plain: An Introduction for Christians and Jews*, Maryknoll, NY: Orbis 1985).

Fernando, Kenneth (2005), 'Buddhism, Christianity and their Potential for Peace: A Christian Perspective', in P. Schmidt-Leukel (ed.), *Buddhism and Christianity in Dialogue. The Gerald Weisfeld Lectures 2004*, London: SCM Press, pp. 215–34.

Fernando, Kenneth (2005b), 'Response to Hozon Alan Senauke', in P. Schmidt-Leukel (ed.), *Buddhism and Christianity in Dialogue. The Gerald Weisfeld Lectures 2004*, London: SCM Press, pp. 250–2.

Feuerbach, Ludwig (1988), *Das Wesen des Christentums*, Stuttgart: Reclam (first published in 1841).

Flannery, Austin (ed.) (1996), *Vatican Council II: The Basic Sixteen Documents*, New York: Costello, Dublin Dominican Publications.

Fredericks, James L. (1995), 'A Universal Religious Experience? Comparative Theology as an Alternative to a Theology of Religions', *Horizons* 22: 67–87.

Fredericks, James L. (1999), *Faith among Faiths: Christian Theology and Non-Christian Religions*, New York: Paulist Press.

Friedli, Richard (1995), 'Synkretismus als Befreiungspraxis: Asiatische und afrikanische Modelle im Dialog', *Dialog der Religionen* 5: 42–66.

Fuchs, R. (transl.) (2000), *Buddha Nature: The Mahayana Uttaratantra Shastra by Arya Maitreya*, Ithaca: Snow Lion Publications.

Geivett, R. D. and Phillips, W. G. (1995), 'A Particularist View: An Evidentialist Approach', in D. L. Okholm and T. R. Phillips (eds), *More Than One Way?*, Grand Rapids, Zondervan Publishing House, pp. 213–45.

Gnilka, Joachim (1990), *Jesus von Nazaret*, Freiburg i.Br.: Herder.

Gnilka, Joachim (1997), *Jesus of Nazareth: Message and History*, Peabody: Hendrickson Publishers.

Gort, Jerald D. (1989), 'Syncretism and Dialogue: Christian Historical and Earlier Ecumenical Perceptions', in J. Gort, H. Vroom, R. Fernhout and A. Wessels (eds), *Dialogue and Syncretism: An Interdisciplinary Approach*, Grand Rapids: Eerdmans/Amsterdam: Rodopi, pp. 36–51.

Gort, Jerald D., Jansen, H. and Vroom, H. (eds) (2006), *Religions View Religions: Explorations in Pursuit of Understanding*, Amsterdam and New York: Rodopi.

Gort, Jerald D., Vroom, H., Fernhout, R. and Wessels, A. (eds) (1989), *Dialogue and Syncretism: An Interdisciplinary Approach*, Grand Rapids: Eerdmans/Amsterdam: Rodopi.

Greive, G. and Niemann, R. (eds) (1990), *Neu glauben? Religionsvielfalt und neue religiöse Strömungen als Herausforderung an das Christentum*, Gütersloh: Gütersloher Verlagshaus.

Griffiths, Paul (1994), *On Being Buddha. The Classical Doctrine of Buddhahood*, Albany, NY: SUNY Press.

Grosnick, W. H. (transl) (1995), 'The Tathāgatagarbha Sūtra', in D. S. Lopez (ed.), *Buddhism in Practice*, Princeton: Princeton University Press, pp. 92–106.

Grünschloß, Andreas (1999), *Der eigene und der fremde Glaube*, Studien zur interreligiösen Fremdwahrnehmung in Islam, Hinduismus, Buddhismus und Christentum, Tübingen, Mohr Siebeck.

Gundert, W. (1929), *Die japanische Literatur*, Wildpark-Potsdam: Akademische Verlagsgesellschaft Athenaion M.B.H.

Hackbarth-Johnson, Christian (2008), 'Henri Le Saux / Swami Abhishiktānanda', in R. Bernhardt and P. Schmidt-Leukel (eds), *Multiple religiöse Identität*, Zürich: Theologischer Verlag Zürich, pp. 35–58.

Haight, Roger (1992), 'The Case for Spirit Christology', *Theological Studies* 53: 257–87.

Haight, Roger (1999), *Jesus: Symbol of God*, Maryknoll, NY: Orbis.

Haight, Roger (2005), 'Pluralist Christology as Orthodox', in P. Knitter (ed.), *The Myth of Religious Superiority: Multifaith Explorations of Religious Pluralism*, Maryknoll, NY: Orbis, pp. 151–61.

Harrison, Paul (1992), 'Is the Dharma-kāya the Real "Phantom Body" of the Buddha?', *Journal of the International Association of Buddhist Studies* 15: 44–94.

Harvey, Peter (2004), *The Selfless Mind: Personality, Consciousness and Nirvāṇa in Early Buddhism*, reprinted, London and New York: RoutledgeCurzon.

Hedges, Paul (2008), 'Particularities: Tradition-specific, Post-modern Perspectives', in P. Hedges and A. Race (eds), *Christian Approaches to Other Faiths*, London: SCM Press, pp. 112–35.

Heelas, Paul (1978), 'Some Problems with Religious Studies', *Religion* 8: 1–14.

Heelas, Paul (1996), *The New Age Movement: The Celebration of the Self and the Sacralization of Modernity*, Oxford: Blackwell.

Heelas, Paul and Woodhead, Linda (2005), *The Spiritual Revolution: Why Religion is Giving Way to Spirituality*, Oxford: Blackwell.

Hick, John (1977), 'Jesus and the World Religions', in John Hick (ed.), *The Myth of God Incarnate*, Philadelphia, Westminster Press, pp. 167–85.

Hick, John (1985), *Problems of Religious Pluralism*, Basingstoke: Macmillan.

Hick, John (1988), *God and the Universe of Faiths*, Basingstoke: Macmillan (1st edition, 1973).

Hick, John (1988b), 'Hick's Response to Critiques', in S. Davis (ed.), *Encountering Jesus: A debate on Christology*, Atlanta: John Knox Press.

Hick, John (1989), *An Interpretation of Religion: Human Responses to the Transcendent*, Basingstoke: Macmillan.

Hick, John (1990), *Death and Eternal Life* (first published 1976), Basingstoke: Macmillan.

Hick, John (1991), 'Reply (to G. Loughlin)', in H. Hewitt (ed.), *Problems in the Philosophy of Religion*, Critical Studies in the Work of John Hick, Basingstoke: Macmillan, pp. 206–09.

Hick, John (1991b), 'Reply (to J. Lipner and J. Prabhu)', in H. Hewitt (ed.), *Problems in the Philosophy of Religion*, Critical Studies in the Work of John Hick, Basingstoke: Macmillan, pp. 242–3.

Hick, John (1993), *The Metaphor of God Incarnate*, London: SCM Press.

Hick, John (2005), *The Metaphor of God Incarnate*, 2nd and enlarged edition, London: SCM Press.

Hick, John and Askari, Hasan (eds) (1985), *The Experience of Religious Diversity*, Aldershot: Gower.

Hintersteiner, Norbert (2001), *Traditionen überschreiten: Angloamerikanische Beiträge zur interkulturellen Traditionshermeneutik*, with a foreword by Robert J. Schreiter, Wien: Universitätsverlag.

Höhensteiger, Petrus (1998), 'Einführung in Leben und Werk von Lynn de Silva' in Lynn A. De Silva, *Mit Buddha und Christus auf dem Weg*, Freiburg i.Br.: Herder, pp. 7–33.

Hookham, S. K. (1991), *The Buddha Within*, Albany, NY: SUNY Press.

Hübner, R. (1996), ''Εἰς Θεὸς Ἰησυς Χριστός Zum christlichen Gottesglauben im 2. Jahrhundert – ein Versuch', *Münchener Theologische Zeitschrift* 47: 325–44.

Hume, David (1983), *Dialogues Concerning Natural Religion*, edited by Richard Popkin, Indianapolis and Cambridge: Hackett Publishing (first published in 1779).

Ireland, John D. (transl.) (1997), *The Udāna: Inspired Utterances of the Buddha & The Itivuttaka. The Buddha's Sayings*, Kandy: Buddhist Publication Society.

Juergensmeyer, Mark (2003), *Terror in the Mind of God: The Global rise of Religious Violence*, 3rd edition, revised and updated, Berkeley: University of California Press.

Kalisch, Muhammad (2007), 'A Muslim View of Judaism', in L. Ridgeon and P. Schmidt-Leukel (eds), *Islam and Inter-Faith Relations: The Gerald Weisfeld Lectures 2006*, London: SCM Press, pp. 67–83.

Kasimow, Harold, Keenan, John P. and Keenan, Linda Klepinger (eds) (2003), *Beside Still Waters: Jews, Christians, and the Way of the Buddha*, Boston: Wisdom Publications.

Keel, Hee-Sung (1995), *Understanding Shinran: A Dialogical Approach*, Berkeley, CA: Asian Humanities Press.

Keenan, John P. (transl.) (1992), *The Summary of the Great Vehicle by Bodhisattva Asaṅga* (BDK English Tripitaka 46-III), Berkeley: Numata Center for Buddhist Translation and Research.

Kelly, J. N. D. (1977), *Early Christian Doctrines*, 5th revised edition, London: Adam & Charles Black.

Kern, H. (transl.) (1963), *Saddharma-Puṇḍarīka or The Lotus of the True Law* (SBE XXI, 1884), reprinted, New York: Dover Publications.

King, Sally B. (1991), *Buddha Nature*, Albany, NY: SUNY Press.

King, Sally B. (2003), 'The Mommy and the Yogi', in H. Kasimow et al. (eds), *Beside Still Waters: Jews, Christians, and the Way of the Buddha*, Boston: Wisdom Publications, pp. 157–70.

Klaes, Norbert (2004), 'Peace and Multireligious Co-operation: The World Conference of Religions for Peace (WCRP)', in P. Schmidt-Leukel (ed.), *War and Peace in World Religions*, London: SCM Press, pp. 199–224.

Kleine, Christoph (2006), 'Evil Monks with Good Intentions? Remarks on Buddhist Monastic Violence and its Doctrinal Background', in M. Zimmermann (ed.), *Buddhism and Violence*, Lumbini, Nepal: Lumbini International Research Institute, pp. 65–98.

Knitter, Paul (1985), *No Other Name? A Critical Survey of Christian Attitudes Toward the World Religions*, Maryknoll, NY: Orbis.

Knitter, Paul (1997), 'Five Theses on the Uniqueness of Jesus', in L. Swidler and P. Mojzes (eds), *The Uniqueness of Jesus: A Dialogue with Paul F. Knitter*, Maryknoll, NY: Orbis, pp. 3–16.

Knitter, Paul (2002), *Introducing Theologies of Religions*, Maryknoll, NY: Orbis.

Knitter, Paul (ed.) (2005), *The Myth of Religious Superiority: Multifaith Explorations of Religious Pluralism*, Maryknoll, NY: Orbis.

Kraemer, Hendrik (1938), *The Christian Message in a Non-Christian World*, London: Edinburgh House Press.

Kraemer, Hendrik (1958), *Religion and the Christian Faith*, London: Lutterworth Press (1st published, 1956).

Küng, Hans (1997), *A Global Ethic for Global Politics and Economics*, London: SCM Press.

Küng, Hans and Kuschel, Karl-Josef (ed.) (1998), *A Global Ethic: The Declaration of the Parliament of the World's Religions*, London: SCM Press.

Lampe, Geoffrey (1977), *God As Spirit*, Oxford: Clarendon Press.

Le Saux, Henri (1998), *Ascent to the Depth of the Heart: The Spiritual Diary (1948–73) of Swami Abhishiktananda (Dom H. Le Saux)*, a selection, edited with introduction and notes by Raimon Panikkar, English translation by David Fleming and James Stuart, Delhi: ISPCK.

Lefebure, L. (1998), 'Cardinal Ratzinger's Comments on Buddhism', *Buddhist–Christian Studies* 18: 221–3.

Leopold, Anita M. and Jensen, Jeppe S. (eds) (2004), *Syncretism in Religion: A Reader*, London: Equinox.

Light, Timothy (2004), 'Orthosyncretism: An Account of Melding in Religion', in Anita M. Leopold and Jeppe S. Jensen (eds), *Syncretism in Religion: A Reader*, London: Equinox, pp. 325–47.

Lindbeck, George (1984), *The Nature of Doctrine: Religion and Theology in a Postliberal Age*, Philadelphia: The Westminster Press.

Lyon, David (1993), 'A Bit of a Circus: Motes on Postmodernity and New Age', *Religion* 23: 117–26.

Maalouf, Amin (2000), *On Identity*, London: The Harvill Press (also published as *In the Name of Identity*).

Makransky, John (1997), *Buddhahood Embodied: Sources of Controversy in India and Tibet*, Albany, NY: SUNY Press.

Makransky, John (2003), 'Buddhist Perspectives on Truth in Other Religions: Past and Present', *Theological Studies* 64: 334–61.

Makransky, John (2005), 'Response to Perry Schmidt-Leukel', in P. Schmidt-Leukel (ed.), *Buddhism and Christianity in Dialogue: The Gerald Weisfeld Lectures 2004*, London: SCM Press, pp. 207–11.

Macquarrie, John (1995), *The Mediators: Nine Stars in the Human Sky*, London: SCM Press.

Maroney, Eric (2006), *Religious Syncretism*, London: SCM Press.

May, John D'Arcy (2000), *After Pluralism: Towards an Interreligious Ethic*, Münster, LIT-Verlag.

May, John D'Arcy (ed.) (2007), *Converging Ways? Conversion and Belonging in Buddhism and Christianity*, St Ottilien: EOS.

Merton, Thomas (1973), *The Asian Journal of Thomas Merton*, New York: New Directions Publishing.

Merton, Thomas (1999), *The Other Side of the Mountain the End of the Journey* (The Journals of Thomas Merton, Vol. 7), edited by Patrick Hart, San Francisco: HarperCollins.

Miksch, Jürgen (2007), *Evangelisch aus fundamentalem Grund: Wie sich die EKD gegen den Islam profiliert*, Frankfurt a.M.: Verlag Otto Lembeck.

Milbank, John (1990), 'The End of Dialogue', in G. D'Costa (ed.), *Christian Uniqueness Reconsidered: The Myth of a Pluralistic Theology of Religions*, Maryknoll, NY: Orbis, pp. 174–91.

Mischo, Johannes (1992), 'Empirische Reinkarnationsforschung aus sozialpsychologischer und parapsychologischer Sicht', in Hermann Kochanek (ed.), *Reinkarnation oder Auferstehung*, Freiburg i.Br.: Herder, pp. 159–80.

Moore, R. I. (1983), 'Heresy as Disease', in W. Lourdaux and D. Verhelst (eds), *The Concept of Heresy in the Middle Ages (11th–13th c.)*, Leuven: University Press, pp. 1–11.

Mulder, Dirk (1989), 'Dialogue and Syncretism: Some Concluding Observations', in J. Gort, H. Vroom, R. Fernhout and A. Wessels (eds), *Dialogue and Syncretism: An Interdisciplinary Approach*, Grand Rapids: Eerdmans/Amsterdam: Rodopi, pp. 203–11.

Nagao, Gadjin (1991), *Madhyāmika and Yogācāra: A Study of Mahāyāna Philosophies*, Albany, NY: SUNY Press.

Nagel, T. (1987), *What Does It All Mean?*, Oxford: Oxford University Press.

Ñāṇamoli and Bodhi (transl.) (2001), *The Middle Length Discourses of the Buddha: A Translation of the Majjhima Nikāya by Bhikkhu Ñāṇamoli and Bhikkhu Bodhi*, Boston: Wisdom Publications, 2nd edition.

Niewiadomski, J. (1996), 'Begegnung von Religionen im weltzivilisatorischen Kontext', in R. Schwager (ed.), *Christus allein? Der Streit um die pluralistische Religionstheologie*, Freiburg i.Br.: Herder, pp. 83–94.

Nishitani, Keiji (1983), *Religion and Nothingness*, Berkeley: University of California Press.

Ogden, Shubert (1992), *Is There Only One True Religion or Are There Many?*, Dallas: Southern Methodist University Press.

Ohlig, Karl-Heinz (1999), *Ein Gott in drei Personen? Vom Vater Jesu zum 'Mysterium' der Trinität*, Mainz: Matthias Grünewald Verlag.

Ott, Elisabeth (1977), *Thomas Merton – Grenzgänger zwischen Christentum und Buddhismus*, Würzburg: Echter Verlag.

Palihawadana, Mahinda (1978), 'Is There a Theravada Buddhist Idea of Grace?', in D. G. Dawe and J. B. Carman (eds), *Christian Faith in a Religiously Plural World*, Maryknoll, NY: Orbis, pp. 181–95.

Pandit, Moti Lal (1993), *Being as Becoming: Studies in Early Buddhism*, New Delhi: Intercultural Publications.

Panikkar, Raimundo (1978), *The Intrareligious Dialogue*, New York: Paulist Press.

Pannenberg, Wolfhart (1994), *Systematic Theology*, Vol. 2, Grand Rapids: Eerdmans.

Parrinder, Geoffrey (1997), *Avatar and Incarnation*, Oxford: Oneworld.

Phan, Peter (2004), *Being Religious Interreligiously: Asian Perspectives on Interfaith Dialogue*, Maryknoll, NY: Orbis.

Pieris, Aloysius (1982), *Rev. Dr. Lynn A. De Silva*. Supplement to *Dialogue* (New Series) 9.

Pieris, Aloysius (1988), *Love Meets Wisdom. A Christian Experience of Buddhism*, Maryknoll, NY: Orbis.

Pinnock, C. H. (1997), *A Wideness in God's Mercy: The Finality of Jesus Christ in a World of Religions*, Eugene, OR: Wipf and Stock Publishers.

Pye, Michael (1978), *Skilful Means: A Concept in Mahayana Buddhism*, London: Duckworth.

Pye, Michael (2004), 'Syncretism and Ambiguity', in Anita M. Leopold and Jeppe S. Jensen (eds), *Syncretism in Religion: A Reader*, London: Equinox, pp. 59–67.

Race, Alan (2001), *Interfaith Encounter: The Twin Tracks of Theology and Dialogue*, London: SCM Press.

Radhakrishnan, S. and Moore, C. (eds) (1989), *A Sourcebook in Indian Philosophy*, Princeton: Princeton University Press.

Rahner, Karl (1966), 'Frömmigkeit früher und heute', in *Schriften zur Theologie* VII, Zürich-Einsiedeln-Köln: Benziger, pp. 11–31.

Rahner, Karl (1967), 'Kirche, Kirchen und Religionen', in *Schriften zur Theologie* VIII, Zürich-Einsiedeln-Köln: Benziger, pp. 355–73.

Rahner, Karl (1978), *Foundations of Christian Faith*, London: Darton, Longman and Todd.

Rahula, Walpola (1994), *What the Buddha Taught*, 2nd enlarged edition, New York: Grove Press.

Ratzinger, J. Kardinal (1996), *Salz der Erde*, Stuttgart: Deutsche Verlagsanstalt.

Religionsmonitor (2008), edited by the Bertelsmann Stiftung, Gütersloh: Gütersloher Verlagshaus.

Rescher, Nicholas (1993), *Pluralism: Against the Demand for Consensus*, Oxford: Clarendon Press.

Rhys Davids, T. W. (transl.) (1963), *The Questions of King Milinda*, Part I and II (SBE 35 and 36, 1890–1894), reprint: New York, Dover Publications.

Ruegg, David Seyfort (1969), *La Théorie du Tathāgatagarbha et du Gotra*, Paris: École Française d'Extrême Orient.

Ruegg, David Seyfort (1989), *Buddha-Nature, Mind and the Problem of Gradualism in a Comparative Perspective*, London: SOAS.

Ruether, Rosemary (1974), *Faith and Fratricide: The Theological Roots of Anti-Semitism*, New York: Seabury Press.

Rudolph, Kurt (2004), 'Syncretism: From Theological Invective to a Concept in the Study of Religion', in Anita M. Leopold and Jeppe S. Jensen (eds), *Syncretism in Religion: A Reader*, London: Equinox, pp. 68–85.

Saroglou, Vassilis (2006), 'Religious Bricolage as a Psychological Reality: Limits, Structures and Dynamics', *Social Compass* 53(1): 109–15.

Scanlon, T. M. (1996), 'The Difficulty of Tolerance', in David Heyd (ed.), *Toleration: An Elusive Virtue*, Princeton: Princeton University Press, pp. 226–39.

Schmidt-Leukel, Perry (1992), *'Den Löwen brüllen hören': Zur Hermeneutik eines christlichen Verständnisses der buddhistischen Heilsbotschaft*, Paderborn: Ferdinand Schöningh.

Schmidt-Leukel, Perry (1997), *Theologie der Religionen: Probleme, Optionen, Argumente*, Neuried: Ars Una.

Schmidt-Leukel, Perry (1998), 'Gautama und Amida-Buddha. Das Buddha-Bild bei Shinran Shonin', in P. Schmidt-Leukel (ed.), *Wer ist Buddha? Eine Gestalt und ihre Bedeutung für die Menschheit*, München: Eugen Diederichs Verlag, pp. 119–39, 252–9.

Schmidt-Leukel, Perry (2000), 'Ist das Christentum notwendig intolerant?', in Rainer Forst (ed.), *Toleranz: Philosophische Grundlagen und gesellschaftliche Praxis einer umstrittenen Tugend*, Frankfurt and New York: Campus, pp. 177–213.

Schmidt-Leukel, Perry (ed.) (2001), *Buddhist Perceptions of Jesus*, St Ottilien: EOS-Verlag.

Schmidt-Leukel, Perry (2002), 'Beyond Tolerance: Towards a New Step in Inter Religious Relationships', *Scottish Journal of Theology* 55: 379–91.

Schmidt-Leukel, Perry (ed.) (2004), *War and Peace in World Religions*, London: SCM Press.

Schmidt-Leukel, Perry (2004b), 'War and Peace in Buddhism', in P. Schmidt-Leukel (ed.), *War and Peace in World Religions*, London: SCM Press, pp. 33–56.

Schmidt-Leukel, Perry (2005), *Gott ohne Grenzen: Eine christliche und pluralistische Theologie der Religionen*, Gütersloh: Gütersloher Verlagshaus.

Schmidt-Leukel, Perry (2005b), 'Inkommensurabilität oder Komplementarität? Zu den Kriterien wechselseitiger Beurteilung von Christentum und Buddhismus', in R. Bernhardt and P. Schmidt-Leukel (eds), *Kriterien interreligiöser Urteilsbildung*, Zürich: Theologischer Verlag Zürich, pp. 211–31.

Schmidt-Leukel, Perry (2005c), 'Exclusivism, Inclusivism, Pluralism: The Tripolar Typology – Clarified and Reaffirmed', in Paul F. Knitter (ed.), *The Myth of Religious Superiority: Multifaith Explorations of Religious Pluralism*, Maryknoll, NY: Orbis, pp. 13–27.

Schmidt-Leukel, Perry (2005d), 'The Unbridgeable Gulf? Towards a Buddhist–Christian Theology of Creation', in P. Schmidt-Leukel (ed.), *Buddhism, Christianity and the Question of Creation: Karmic of Divine?*, Aldershot: Ashgate, pp. 109–78.

Schmidt-Leukel, Perry (2006), *Understanding Buddhism*, Edinburgh: Dunedin Academic Press.

Schmidt-Leukel, Perry (2007), '"Light and Darkness" or "Looking Through a Dim Mirror"? A Reply to Paul Williams from a Christian Perspective', in J. D'Arcy May (ed.), *Converging Ways? Conversion and Belonging in Buddhism and Christianity*, St Ottilien: EOS-Verlag, pp. 67–88.

Schmidt-Leukel, Perry (ed.) (2008), *Buddhist Attitudes to Other Religions*, St Ottilien: EOS-Verlag.

Schmidt-Leukel, Perry (2008b), 'Pluralisms', in P. Hedges and A. Race (eds), *Christian Approaches to Other Faiths*, London: SCM Press, pp. 85–110.

Schmidt-Leukel, Perry and Ridgeon, Lloyd (eds) (2007), *Islam and Inter-Faith Relations*, London: SCM Press.

Schmithausen, Lambert (2000), 'Gleichmut und Mitgefühl. Zu Spiritualität und Heilsziel des älteren Buddhismus', in A. Bsteh (ed.), *Der Buddhismus als Anfrage an christliche Theologie und Philosophie*, Mödling: Verlag St Gabriel, pp. 119–36.

Schmithausen, Lambert (2003), 'Einige besondere Aspekte der "Bodhisattva-Ethik" in Indien und ihre Hintergründe', in *Hōrin: Vergleichende Studien zur japanischen Kultur* 10: 21–46.

Schnell, Tatjana (2008), 'Religiosität und Identität', in R. Bernhardt and P. Schmidt-Leukel (eds), *Multiple religiöse Identität*, Zürich: Theologischer Verlag Zürich, pp. 163–83.

Schorsch, Christof (1990), 'Der Drang nach Ganzheit: New Age als synkretistisches Phänomen', in W. Greive and R. Niemann (eds), *Neu glauben? Religionsvielfalt und neue religiöse Strömungen als Heraus-forderung an das Christentum*, Gütersloh: Gütersloher Verlagshaus, pp. 135–45.

Schreiter, Robert (1986), *Constructing Local Theologies*, Maryknoll, NY: Orbis (1st edition, 1985).

Schreiter, Robert (1998), *The New Catholicity: Theology between the Global and the Local*, Maryknoll, NY: Orbis (1st edition, 1997).

Senauke, Hozan Alan (2005), 'Response to Kenneth Fernando', in P. Schmidt-Leukel (ed.), *Buddhism and Christianity in Dialogue: The Gerald Weisfeld Lectures 2004*, London: SCM Press, pp. 253–7.

Sharma, A. and Dugan, K. (eds) (1999), *A Dome of Many Colors: Studies in Religious Pluralism, Identity, and Unity*, Harrisburg: Trinity Press International.

Shinran, Gutoku Shaku (1973), *The Kyōgyōshinshō*, translated by D. T. Suzuki, edited by The Eastern Buddhist Society, Kyoto: Shinshū Ōtaniha.

Shinran (1997), *The Collected Works of Shinran*, Volume I, Kyoto: Jōdo Shinshū Hongwanji-ha.

Siller, H. P. (ed.) (1991), *Suchbewegungen: Synkretismus – kulturelle Identität und kirchliches Bekenntnis*, Darmstadt: Wissenschaftliche Buchgesellschaft.

Smart, Ninian (1993), *Buddhism and Christianity: Rivals and Allies*, Basingstoke: Macmillan.

Smart, Ninian and Konstantine, Steven (1991), *Christian Systematic Theology in a World Context*, London: Harper & Collins.

Smith, Wilfred Cantwell (1975), 'Conflicting Truth-Claims: A Rejoinder', in J. Hick (ed.), *Truth and Dialogue: The Relationship between World Religions*, London: Sheldon Press, pp. 156–62.

Smith, Wilfred Cantwell (1976), *Religious Diversity*, edited by W. G. Oxtoby, New York: Harper & Row.

Smith, Wilfred Cantwell (1987), 'Idolatry: In Comparative Perspective', in J. Hick and P. Knitter (eds), *The Myth of Christian Uniqueness: Toward a Pluralistic Theology of Religions*, Maryknoll, NY: Orbis, pp. 53–68.

Smith, Wilfred Cantwell (1989), *Towards a World Theology: Faith and the Comparative History of Religion*, Maryknoll, NY: Orbis (1st edition, 1981).

Smith, Wilfred Cantwell (1997), *Modern Culture from a Comparative Perspective*, edited by J. Burbidge, Albany, NY: SUNY Press.

Sparn, Walter (1996), '"Religionsmengerei?" Überlegungen zu einem theologischen Synkretismusbegriff', in V. Drehsen and W. Sparn (eds) (1996), *Im Schmelztiegel der Religionen: Konturen des modernen Synkretismus*, Gütersloh: Gütersloher Verlagshaus, pp. 255–84.

Stosch, Klaus von (2002), 'Komparative Theologie – ein Ausweg aus dem Grunddilemma jeder Theologie der Religionen?', *Zeitschrift für Katholische Theologie* 124: 294–311.

Sutcliffe, Steven (2000), '"Wandering Stars": Seekers and Gurus in the Modern World', in S. Sutcliffe and M. Bowman (eds), *Beyond New Age: Exploring Alternative Spirituality*, Edinburgh: Edinburgh University Press 2000, pp. 17–36.

Suzuki, Daisetz T. (1973), *Zen and Japanese Culture*, Princeton: Princeton University Press.

Swatos, William and Christiano, Kevin (1999), 'Secularization Theory: The Course of a Concept', *Sociology of Religion* 60(3): 209–28.

Swidler, Leonard (1987), 'Interreligious and Interideological Dialogue: The Matrix for All Systematic Reflection Today', in L. Swidler (ed.), *Toward a Universal Theology of Religion*, Maryknoll, NY: Orbis, pp. 5–50.

Tacey, David (2004), *The Spirituality Revolution: The emergence of contemporary spirituality*, London and New York: Routledge.

Tachard, Guy (1985), *A Relation of the Voyage to Siam* (reprint; first published in 1688), Bangkok: White Orchid Press.

Takasaki, Jikido (1966), *A Study on the Ratnagotravibhāga (Uttaratantra) Being a Treatise on the Tathāgatagarbha Theory of Mahāyāna Buddhism* (Serie Orientale Roma 33), Rome: Istituto Italiano per il Medio ed Estremo Oriente.

Tauscher, Helmut (1998), 'Die Buddha-Wirklichkeit in den späteren Formen des mahāyānistischen Buddhismus', in P. Schmidt-Leukel (ed.), *Wer ist Buddha? Eine Gestalt und ihre Bedeutung für die Menschheit*, München: Eugen Diederichs Verlag, pp. 93–118, 247–51.

Taylor, Charles (2003), *Varieties of Religion Today: William James Revisited*, Cambridge, MA: Harvard University Press.

Thomas, M. M. (1985), 'The Absoluteness of Jesus Christ and Christ-centred Syncretism', *The Ecumenical Review* 37: 387–97.

Thomas, M. M. (2002), 'Syncretism', in N. Lossky et al. (eds), *Dictionary of the Ecumenical Movement*, 2nd edition, Geneva: WCC Publications, pp. 1085–8.

Vatsayana Mallanaga (2002), *Kamasutra*, a new, complete English translation of the Sanskrit text by Wendy Doninger and Sudhir Kakar, Oxford: Oxford University Press.

Veer, Peter van der (1994), 'Syncretism, Multiculturalism and the Discourse of Tolerance', in Charles Stewart and Rosalind Shaw (eds), *Syncretism/Anti-Syncretism: The Politics of Religious Synthesis*, London and New York: Routledge, pp. 196–211.

Vermes, Geza (1981), *The Gospel of Jesus the Jew: The Riddell Memorial Lectures*, University of Newcastle upon Tyne.

Vermes, Geza (1993), *The Religion of Jesus the Jew*, London: SCM Press.

Vermes, Geza (2001), *The Changing Faces of Jesus*, London: Penguin.
Vetter, Tilman (ed. and transl.) (1984), *Der Buddha und seine Lehre in Dharmakīrti's Pramānavārttika*, Wien: Arbeitskreis für tibetische und buddhistische Studien, Universität Wien.
Visser't Hooft, Willem A. (1963), *No Other Name: The Choice between Syncretism and Christian Universalism*, London: SCM Press.
Vivekananda (1994), *The Complete Works of Vivekananda. Mayavati Memorial Edition*, Vol. 3, 6th reprinting, Delhi: Advaita Ashrama (1st edition, 1989).
Vroom, Hendrik (1989), 'Syncretism and Dialogue: A Philosophical Analysis', in J. Gort, H. Vroom, R. Fernhout and A. Wessels (eds), *Dialogue and Syncretism: An Interdisciplinary Approach*, Grand Rapids: Eerdmans/Amsterdam: Rodopi, pp. 26–35.
Wagner, Falk (1996), 'Möglichkeiten und Grenzen des Synkretismus-begriffs für die Religionstheologie', in V. Drehsen and W. Sparn (eds) (1996), *Im Schmelztiegel der Religionen: Konturen des modernen Synkretismus*, Gütersloh: Gütersloher Verlagshaus, pp. 72–117.
Ward, Keith (1987), *Images of Eternity: Concepts of God in Five Religious Traditions*, London: Darton, Longman and Todd.
Ward, Keith (1991), *A Vision to Pursue: Beyond the Crisis in Christianity*, London: SCM Press.
Ward, Keith (1994), *Religion and Revelation: A Theology of Revelation in the World's Religions*, Oxford: Oxford University Press.
Ward, Keith (1996), *Religion and Creation*, Oxford: Oxford University Press.
Ward, Keith (1998), *Religion and Human Nature*, Oxford: Oxford University Press.
Ward, Keith (2000), *Religion and Community*, Oxford: Oxford University Press.
Weber, Max (1988), *Gesammelte Aufsätze zur Religionssoziologie* II, edited by Marianne Weber, Tübingen: UTB.
Wiebe, Donald (1981), *Religion and Truth: Towards an Alternative Paradigm for the Study of Religion*, The Hague: De Gruyter.
Williams, Bernard (1996), 'Toleration: An Impossible Virtue?', in David Heyd (ed.), *Toleration. An Elusive Virtue*, Princeton: Princeton University Press, pp. 18–27.
Williams, Paul (1989), *Mahāyāna Buddhism: The Doctrinal Foundations*, London and New York: Routledge.
Williams, Paul (2002), *The Unexpected Way: On Converting from Buddhism to Catholicism*, Edinburgh: T&T Clark.
Williams, Paul (2007), 'Buddhism, God, Aquinas and Morality: An Only Partially Repentant Reply to Perry Schmidt-Leukel and José Cabezón', in J. D'Arcy May (ed.), *Converging Ways? Conversion and Belonging in Buddhism and Christianity*, St Ottilien: EOS-Verlag, pp. 117–54.

Yagi, S. (1990), 'A Bridge from Buddhist to Christian Thinking: The "Front-Structure"', in S. Yagi and L. Swidler, *A Bridge to Buddhist–Christian Dialogue*, New York: Paulist Press, pp. 73–152.

Young, Frances (1983), *From Nicaea to Chalcedon*, London: SCM Press.

INDEX